THE HORSE IN AMERICA

THE HORSE IN AMERICA

by ROBERT WEST HOWARD

P 3

Follett Publishing Company
Chicago, New York

p 3

43887

Library of Congress Catalog Card Number: 65-25769
Manufactured in the United States of America
First Printing

Design by Gordon Martin
FOLLETT PUBLISHING COMPANY
1010 West Washington Boulevard
Chicago, Illinois 60607

To the memory of

EDWARD NORRIS WENTWORTH

and

CHARLES LYMAN ANSON

Their influence is perpetuated
not only in their books but
through the innate curiosity
and warmth that made them
superb teachers and
beloved friends.

CONTENTS

ILLUSTRATIONS

THE HORSE IN AMERICA

I am Buffalo Bill's horse. I have spent my life under his saddle. . . . My mother was all American —no alkali-spider about her, I can tell you; she was of the best blood of Kentucky, the bluest Bluegrass aristocracy, very proud and acrimonious—or maybe it is ceremonious. . . . My father was a bronco. Nothing as to lineage—that is, nothing as to recent lineage—but plenty good enough when you go a good way back. When Professor Marsh was out here hunting bones for the chapel of Yale University, he found skeletons of horses no bigger than a fox, bedded in the rocks, and he said they were ancestors of my father. My mother heard him say it; and he said those skeletons were two million years old, which astonished her and made her Kentucky pretensions look small and pretty antiphonal, not to say oblique. . . . Professor Marsh said those skeletons were fossils. So that makes me part bluegrass and part fossil; if there is any older or better stock, you will have to look for it among the Four Hundred.

—Samuel L. Clemens, "A Horse's Tale"

LARAMIE TRIUMPH

CHAPTER ONE

THE LARAMIE PLAIN is the field of a vast natural amphitheater in eastern Wyoming. The Shirley, Laramie, Freezeout and Medicine Bow mountains are its bleachers and grandstand. Prevailing west winds preside over seasonal shifts of the deciduous backdrop from April chartreuse to August dun, October scarlet and January white. Across it all, the sun, moon and clouds manipulate coloramas of emerald, fawn, thunder gray, mist blue and argent, blending them into dawn gold, sunrise cerise, and dusk purples cascading down the grandstand walls.

Throughout the plain, from Tie Siding on the east to the proud ruins of Fort Fred Steele on the west, are tawny bluffs, rush-fringed lakes, dim trails, century-old wheel ruts, silvery fence posts, railroad tracks and highways. All these are memorials to events that were critically important to the growth of modern America.

This is the triumph place of the horse. All of the memorials are geologic or technologic monuments to his fifty-five million years on the high-plains of our Continental Divide. They reveal his development through primordial epochs, his adaptations during the transition from tropic jungle to temperate grassland, and his contributions to the rise of civilization on this continent since A.D. 1521.

The memorial in the Cooper Lake badlands, twenty-seven miles west of the city of Laramie, is a deposit of fossil bones imbedded in rock strata formed during the Eocene epoch. Fifty miles north-

1

west, up the valley of the Little Medicine River, petrified trunks of tropical and subtropical trees testify to the environment in which the Equidae thrived during the first twenty-five or thirty million years of their evolution.

In the Geology Museum on the University of Wyoming's campus in Laramie are fossil bones, teeth and skulls discovered in the strata of Pleistocene and Recent deposits. These finds lead us to the conclusion that horses grazed on the floor of this amphitheatre as late as 9000 B.C., and hence were contemporaries of the early red man.

And everywhere across Laramie Plain are memorials to the critical contributions made by the horse to our pioneer era and the Machine Age. Saddleback Hills! Bridger Pass! Wild Horse Mountain! Battle Springs! Stampede Meadow! Bluegrass Wells! Medicine Hat! These colorful place names, and others, hint at the nature of the recent epic.

Some of the trails that arc down the Shirleys and Laramies were made by the hoofs of Indian war ponies between 1750 and 1868.

Fire-blackened stones in a cottonwood grove beside the North Platte may have been left from a campfire built during the 1820s by St. Louis fur traders en route, with a pony-train load of trade goods, to a Mountain Man rendezvous on the Green River.

Weathered fence posts in pastures outside Medicine Bow are memorials—at least for the history buff—to the horses and horsemen enhanced by Owen Wister when he made the village the locale of his cowboy classic *The Virginian*.[1]

The asphalt and concrete strips of the Lincoln Highway (U.S. 30) follow the route of the wagon roads that were pioneered between 1862 and 1868 by Wells-Fargo stagecoaches, U.S. cavalry patrols, wagon trains, circuit-riding preachers, country doctors, railroad surveyors and geologic explorers. (The words *horsepower, turnpike, hitch, tandem, trailer* and *station wagon,* of course, are etymologic memorials everywhere in America of the influence of the horse on our way of life.)

The epochal geologic and climatic changes evident in the Laramie

Plain amphitheater forced the horse to evolve toward the forms vital to civilization. Since these changes also created the Shirley Mountains–Laramie Plain–Red Desert topography that proved to be the most logical route across the Rocky Mountains for our first transcontinental railway, it seems that pre-history fixed the Laramie Plain as the triumph place for both the evolutionary and the recent achievements of the horse.

The Lincoln Highway and the Union Pacific Railroad both skirt a shore of Cooper Lake. Imbedded in adjacent cliffs are skeletons of the primitive animal called *Eohippus*. He was "no bigger than a fox," and just as speedy. His descendants paced out the route of the Lincoln Highway, and hauled the dirt, rock, fifty-pound iron rails, and hemlock ties that first linked America "from sea to shining sea."

Both the topography and the life forms of North America began to include currently familiar shapes during the millions of years of the Paleocene and Eocene epochs.[2] Earthquakes and volcanoes spewed the Rockies into a rock and dirt wall that may have reached elevations of more than six miles above sea level. Seas advanced over most of the Midwest, the Southeast and California. The climate of Nebraska, Wyoming and Montana warmed to year-round tropical languor. Families of palm trees, ferns, orchids and huge mushrooms flourished. Giant types of cats, dogs and rats evolved. The reptiles assumed the current shapes of crocodiles, lizards and snakes.

The jungle homeland of these creatures sheltered, and fed, the ancestor of the horse. He stood fifteen inches high at the shoulders, and had slender legs, an arched back and a long tail. His head was shaped like an elongated egg, set on a thick neck at an oblique angle. The lips were heavy, topped by deep-set nostrils, large eyes, and small erect ears jutting out of a sparse mane. On the swampy land surface, he had developed large, multi-toed feet. His forefeet had four toes; his rear feet had three. Each toe ended in a tiny oval hoof of horn. His short, low-crowned teeth were adapted to feeding on palm leaves, vine shoots and similar succulent foliage. When fleeing an enemy he instinctively broke into a gallop, in the midst of which all four of his feet were off the ground.[3]

This gentle creature was unknown to mankind until the 1830s when English naturalists discovered teeth and skulls of what seemed to be a type of prehistoric rodent in Suffolk and along the coast of Kent. A generation later the remains were classified by British scientists as fossils of a direct ancestor of the horse. This ancestor was given the name of *Hyracotherium,* Greek for "the beast like the coney, or rabbit."[4]

Fossil remains of the same type of horse ancestor were discovered in Nebraska and on the southern Wyoming high-plains in 1867–68 during the excavations for the Union Pacific Railroad. Others have been found in Colorado and New Mexico. American scientists named the animal *Eohippus,* meaning, in Greek, "the dawn horse."

Positive identification of *Hyracotherium* and *Eohippus* as the same genus did not come until the 1880s. By then, the American name, *Eohippus,* was established, and it has since been popularized by writers and cartoonists. But the brief priority of the British discoveries and identification perpetuates *Hyracotherium,* or "like a rabbit," as the official scientific name of the horse ancestor.

Modern methods of identification indicate that the Cooper Lake and other Rocky Mountain fossil beds are as old as, or older than, the *Eohippus-Hyracotherium* remains found in Europe and Asia. This, plus the disappearance of horse ancestors from Europe and Asia during the Oligocene epoch, justifies the assumption that the Laramie Plain was a "Garden of Eden" for horse evolution.

Development of the horse family before *Eohippus* is still uncertain. The common ancestor of all hooved animals is presumed to have been a creature belonging to a group called Condylarth. It looked like a pig-snouted hyena with a cat-like tail and five-toed feet. It probably ate both flesh and foliage. Condylarths vanished during the late Eocene; *Eohippus* continued.

Camels and giant hogs evolved in our West during Oligocene

times. Violent volcanic action throughout the Rockies helped maintain the tropical climate.

The family Equidae that descended from *Eohippus* grew larger and the number of front toes changed from four to three. Early in the Oligocene, most paleontologists believe, the Equidae abandoned Europe, Asia and Africa. The reasons for their flight, or extinction, are unknown. Then, for several millions of years, North America, and particularly the high-plains of Nebraska, Wyoming and New Mexico, became earth's principal habitat for the horse ancestors.

Volcanic action and earthquakes during the late Oligocene or early Miocene created an isthmus between present Alaska and Siberia. Tropical plants began to grow along the new coves. Herds of the Anchitherium sub-family of Equidae browsed northwest up the coves, ventured on across Asia's mainland, and eventually repopulated Europe with the pre-horse.

During the same millenniums the climate of the Rockies cooled to an approximation of our modern North Temperate Zone seasons. The palm trees and tropical forests died. Types of coarse grasses appeared on the high-plains.[5] The family of Equidae had multiplied in the tropical environment through thousands of generations. Their teeth, jaws and intestines were adapted to a diet of plant fronds and tendrils that did not require much chewing or grinding. Their feet had the multi-toed grip required for running across soft ground. But as the jungle vanished, and the ground dried, and coarse grasses began to appear, the Equidae were faced with physical adaptation, migration or extinction.

During the millenniums of the middle and late Miocene, one sub-family of Equidae succeeded in adjusting to a grass diet. This necessitated radical changes in the shape, composition and growth mechanism of the teeth, in the muscles, shape and chewing motions of the jaws, and in the metabolism and composition of the digestive organs.

The front teeth, now called the incisors, began to lengthen and develop the ridges and crests needed for successful grass cropping.

But grass has a high percentage of silica in its composition. Silica plus the grit adhering to the grass leaves quickly wore the enamel off the tooth surfaces. Heavier layers of enamel developed. So did an amazing trait called "hypsodonty," which produces long hard crowns that extend deep into the jaw socket. Then, as grazing literally files down the teeth, these enamel reserves grow down from the socket to maintain the essential grinding (i.e. milling) formation.[6]

Simultaneous changes took place, but at a rate so slow that we cannot truly comprehend them,[7] in the grinding teeth, the shape of the lips, the jaws, the forelegs, and the three-toed hoofs. The genus of Equidae that succeeded in the physical transformation from browser to grazer is called *Merychippus*. Paleontologists are satisfied that *Merychippus,* by the end of the Miocene, had achieved most of the physical characteristics of a modern horse. In 15,000,000 B.C. he was growing to the adult size of a Shetland pony, with deep jaws, a long head, a broad neck, and chunky legs adapted to the galloping run that would make him Man's favorite —and speediest—transport for fifty centuries. His skin may have had protective color striping like the zebra's. The changes that resulted in *Merychippus* occurred on the high-plains of the American West.

Then, during the Pliocene epoch's 110,000 centuries, a gap appears in paleontologic records. Dr. Paul McGrew, professor of paleontology at the University of Wyoming, believes that some form of natural catastrophe wiped out the ancestors of the true horse in North America. "The fossil records we have been able to develop show a sequence almost to the true horse, *Equus caballus,*" he explained. "By the earliest Pleistocene, approximately two million years ago, zebras were abundant, but there were no true horses in North America.

"We know that large and steady migrations of other species of grazing animals migrated between Eurasia and North America during the Pliocene. This knowledge, plus the absence of fossils of *Equus caballus'* immediate ancestors, leads to wonderment about a type of virus or plague that made North America untenable for this particular type of Equidae. There could have been some form of blight similar to the disease that killed off the American chestnut tree only a generation ago. Or there might have been an insect plague, such as the tse-tse fly infections of livestock in Africa or the ticks that spread hoof-and-mouth disease. Any explanation is, of course, sheer guesswork. All we know is that true-horse ancestors from the earliest Pleistocene have not been discovered in North America. Possible ancestors have been discovered in Eurasia. This suggests that the horse ancestor, *Equus caballus,* evolved there at the end of the Pliocene."[8]

Whatever did happen during the Pliocene, *Equus caballus* was at the ancient high-plains homeplace by the middle Pleistocene (1,000,000 B.C.). He possessed all of the basic characteristics of the modern horse: high-crowned and intricately ridged teeth; the single toe, or hoof, with a tough horn coating; the long neck; a stubby mane and pluming tail.

Glaciers were gouging the basins for the Great Lakes. Most of our mountains were already in their contemporary contours. The zebra's ancestors had migrated over the Alaska-Siberia bridge toward Africa. The camels were grazing in that direction, too. The big woolly elephants called mammoths and the saber-toothed tigers hunted south from the Arctic across Wyoming, Nebraska, Kansas and Oklahoma.

Then volcanic debris and runoff sediment from the glaciers filled in the strait that separated North and South America. Both *Equus caballus* and other types of Equidae began the migration across the new Panama Isthmus to the jungles and pampas of Colombia, Brazil and Argentina.

By the middle Pleistocene, about the time Man was learning how to build a fire and cook some of his food, millions of horses lived in North and South America. A variety of breeds evolved, particularly in the Andes and the lowland jungles of the Amazon. Some developed short stout legs for mountain climbing; some adapted teeth and jaws back toward the *Eohippus* practice of dieting on

jungle plants. There seems to have been constant migration between North America and Asia.

Paleontologists are certain that the horse was one of the most
numerous of the animals in South America and western North
America when the earliest red-man migrations reached the New
World about 25,000 B.C.[9]

During a fossil dig in the Wyoming desert Dr. McGrew and his
associates discovered the skeleton of a butchered mammoth. Its
skull had been fractured, probably by stones. The long bones had
been broken up for extraction of the marrow. Apparently the
mammoth had mired in a bog, and then been killed by Indians.
Nearby the paleontologists found fragments of horse bones and
teeth. Carbon-dating tests indicated that the mammoth and the
horse had both died about 9000 B.C.[10]

This discovery narrows the time span surrounding the second
puzzling disappearance of the horse from the New World. Again no
cause has been proved. But the horse did vanish from both North
and South America soon after 9000 B.C. This may have been due to
a reappearance of the plague that seems to have banished the true-
horse line at the end of the Pliocene epoch. No evidence has been
discovered to substantiate the theory that the horse was hunted to
extinction by the pre-Columbian red man. Most paleontologists
and archaeologists agree that the disappearance occurred between
9000 and 6000 B.C. and that the horse remained absent through
succeeding centuries. The disease or flight back to Asia was obviously limited to the Equidae family, although the mammoth disappeared about the same time. Bison, deer, antelope and other
grazing animals survived and continued to multiply.

Then another natural catastrophe destroyed the Alaska-Siberia
bridge, creating the present-day Bering Strait. Thus ended the
routine migrations by land animals between Eurasia and the
Americas. The belief prevails that the Bering Strait appeared between 6000 and 5000 B.C. Perhaps it was part of the legendary
Deluge, related in the Gulgamesh Epic of Ur, in the Bible and in

the Koran. Both the Koran and the Bible state that Noah's Ark landed on, or near, Mount Ararat, near the present borders of Turkey and Iran and the U.S.S.R. west of the Caspian Sea. Paleontologic and archaeologic evidence testifies that the domestication of *Equus caballus* began in this region before 3000 B.C.

THE MOUNT-UP

CHAPTER TWO

THE PRIMORDIAL TOPSOIL deposited on the eastern slope of our Continental Divide, from western Canada to Mexico, is predominantly *chernozem* and *chestnut-brown*. The mineral content of these two types, plus their location between the 30th and 50th latitudes of the North Temperate Zone, made them eminently suitable for the growth of grasses. Here *Merychippus* adapted from browser to grazer during the Miocene, and *Equus caballus* flourished during the Pleistocene and Recent ages.

Only one other belt of chernozem and chestnut-brown soil evolved in Earth's North Temperate Zone. It runs due east-west from Mongolia across the Soviet Union to the foothills of the Balkans at the western end of the Black Sea. Peninsulas from the main mass extend south into China, and between the Black and Caspian basins to the Caucasus Mountains barrier that dominated the north horizons of Ur, Nippur and Kish. An extension of these topsoil types covers much of Spain and the Algeria-Tunisia coast of the Mediterranean. The entire belt lies in the same North Temperate Zone latitudes that the high-plain strip in the Rockies occupies.

It would have been natural for the grazing horses to migrate to the Eurasian grasslands belt during the late Pliocene. Here, probably, *Equus caballus* evolved. Thus, after the mysterious extinction of *Equus caballus* in North and South America eight to ten thousand years ago, and the destruction of the Alaska-Siberia isth-

10

mus, the Eurasian grassland became the principal range of the wild horse.

Three subspecies of *Equus caballus* appear to have developed in sectors of this strip by 4000 B.C. The tarpan, occupying the region of the Black and Caspian seas, rarely stood more than four feet high at the shoulders, and had a large head with a moderately long, thick neck. His sleek body hair was colored mouse-gray, blending into fawn or dusty white across his belly and into a broad black or brown stripe above his backbone. Both his mane and tail were short, bushy and usually black.

A second distinct subspecies, named the Przewalski, is believed to have evolved before domestication on the steppes of Turkmen, Mongolia or Manchuria. This horse was smaller and stubbier than the tarpan, and must have stood about forty inches high at the shoulders, with a maximum weight of five hundred pounds.[1] He had a large, almost O-shaped head jutting from a short neck. His over-all color was a pale yellow, blotched with grayish-brown. His hairy black legs were so short that his long black tail often swept the ground.

Scientists are still in disagreement about the existence of a third subspecies of *Equus caballus* before domestication. Some contend that the fossil bones of horses dating from the late Pleistocene show the wide shank (i.e. cannon) bones and six vertebrae joints in the loin that distinguish the Percheron, Clydesdale, Belgian and other drafters bred from the Great War Horse of Normandy. The name *Equus abeli* has been assigned this presumed form. Reconstruction drawings depict him as a giant—compared to the Przewalski—for he stood sixty to seventy inches high at the shoulders, and his legs, proportionately, were as long as the tarpan's. The drawings picture him as having a small intelligent head set on a long neck, and a mane resembling the plume helmet adornments worn by Homeric warriors. Finally, the artists depicted the beast's lower legs as having the curly hair "feathering" of the modern draft horse.[2]

Other paleontologists believe that the "Forest Horse" ancestor

of the Great War Horse was a product of selective breeding, probably in Scandinavia, between 2000 and 1000 B.C. The foundation
sires, they suspect, were tarpans who explored down the Danube
River valley during the Pleistocene and slowly adapted to life in
the forests and marshland of the North Sea's basin.

There is general agreement, however, that the tarpan was the
first domesticated horse, hence the mount of the Centaurs of early
Greece and the drafter that pulled the chariots that conquered
Ur and Egypt.

The finger of chestnut-brown grassland that curves around the
west shore of the Black Sea, and past the Danube River's mouth,
ends in the Balkan foothills of Bulgaria. Beyond are the mountains
of Thessaly and the headwaters of the Aegean Sea. Mount Olym-
pus and sister peaks in Thessaly are occasionally shrouded in fog.
Greek mythology described the Centaurs as the bawdy, roughneck
masters of Thessaly and alleged that they descended from a bucolic
mating between the king Ixion and the cloud goddess Nephele.

In the earliest Greek statues and friezes, the Centaur was represented as having the full body of a man, with, jutting from the
buttocks, the belly and hindquarters of a small horse. By 1000 B.C.
artists were drawing the Centaur as a creature with the full torso
of a horse but also with the upper torso of a bearded man. Either
of these depictions would agree with the impressions gained by
shepherds of 3000 B.C. who had never seen, or heard of, a horse.
The saddle was not invented until 500 B.C.; stirrups were unknown
until A.D. 600 or 700.[3] The barbarian horsemen who began to ter-
rorize Greece and the Euphrates Valley soon after 3000 B.C. must
have ridden bareback or, at best, with animal skins strapped across
the horse's back. And they probably rode jockey-style, crouched
against the mount's neck. Thus they could easily have been accepted as supernatural creatures, half-*Equus* and half-human.

The Greek myths also ascribe folk habits to the Centaur that
are remarkably like those our novelists and script-writers gave the
Mountain Men, cowboys, "bad men," and other frontier types of
the 1780–1880 West. The early Centaurs of Greece whooped into
town, bullied homesteaders, seduced the most attractive wives and

daughters, and demonstrated an awesome capacity for wine and stronger spirits. In time, though, they "simmered down" and became as courtly and philosophical as Owen Wister's Virginian.

In the Greek myths the Centaur Chiron taught horsemanship and battle skills to Hercules and Achilles. Centaurs advised Jason on the route and equipment of the Argonauts in their quest for the Golden Fleece. (Again, archaeologic research provides both an explanation of the Golden Fleece and a clue to the homeland of the Centaurs! The sheepskin antedates the gold miner's placer-pan. Gold deposits along the shores of the Black Sea were originally mined by sluicing soil and pebbles over sheepskins spread on the ground. The gold particles adhered to the oily wool on the pelts, and could be reclaimed by combing or burning. Hence, archaeologists deduce, the Argonauts voyaged up the Aegean Sea past the site of present Istanbul to reach the Black Sea gold fields that were then being worked by tribes who had already succeeded in domesticating the horse. So the Golden Fleece may have been merely the world's original placer-pan![4])

Engravings of horse figures on bone implements and vases discovered at Susa, in the Caucasus foothills 150 miles from Ur and near Baghdad, are accepted as evidence that the domesticated horse was known in the Euphrates and Tigris valleys soon after 3000 B.C.[5] The warmer climate of the Mediterranean Basin could have been an initial reason for migrations across the Caucasus and Balkans by the broncbuster Centaurs. Then they learned about the wealth of the Sumerian cities and the Cretan trade colonies along the Aegean shore. They realized, too, that their horses could outmaneuver the teams of onagers and heifers that pulled the local war-chariots.

The horseback invasions down the Aegean shore before 1800 B.C. must have established the Mycenaeans, thus "setting the stage" for the conquests of Crete and Troy. At least once, in 2180 B.C., these barbarians ravaged the Tigris and Euphrates civilization. Two significant inventions are associated with this Centaur age: the bridle and the two-wheeled chariot.

Frederick Zeuner and other scholars of the era agree that the onagers and oxen used as drafters in pre-horse Ur were outfitted with metal nose-rings, similar to the nose-rings now used on dairy bulls.[6] It is presumed that the single guide-rein of the charioteers was looped through this nose-ring. The chariots used in early Ur rode on four small semi-solid wheels. This "rig," and the stubbornness and leisurely pace of the donkey family, substantiates the conclusion that any battle charge by Ur's chariots could achieve no greater speed than ten miles an hour. Furthermore, these chariots were topheavy, hence incapable of "tight" turns or other rapid maneuvers.

In contrast, the Indian raiders—riding bareback—who attacked wagon trains on the high-plains of our West achieved speeds up to forty miles an hour. Even conceding that the tarpan mounts of the Centaurs were smaller than the Indians' ponies, it seems certain that the Centaurs in a battle charge could go faster than twenty-five miles an hour, and easily rout the warriors of Ur and their slower chariots.

The descendants of the Centaurs must have improved the design of the chariot. Concrete evidence that they invented both the bridle and the two-wheeled chariot comes from the conquest of Egypt by the Hyksos between 1720 and 1710 B.C. The Hyksos, too, were a people from the Eurasian grasslands. Their agile two-wheeled chariots, powered by bridled teams of horses, gave them a series of victories over the donkey- and ox-powered chariots of the Egyptians, and established the Shepherd Kings (i.e. the Fifteenth to the Eighteenth dynasties) as rulers of Egypt, Palestine and Syria.

The Hyksos' conquest established the bridle and bit as the superior control tools of the equestrian, and the two-wheeled chariot as the best battle machine. It may also have inaugurated a folk habit that is as thoughtlessly rampant today as it was in early Greece. The battle superiority of horse power over donkey power somewhere somehow influenced, or spawned, the conviction that the horseman was both the physical and intellectual superior of a donkey (or mule) driver or rider. This fetish pushed the donkey and mule down the social scale to become beasts of burden, or the mounts of farmers, peddlers and social inferiors. Eventually the words *ass, mule* and *donkey* became similes for *buttocks, stupidity,* and *obstinacy.* This persistent folkway may be an etymologic inheritance from the horse-and-chariot victories of the Centaurs and the Hyksos.

The overthrow of the Hyksos before 1300 B.C. indicates how quickly the Egyptians adopted horse power and its corps of wranglers, drivers, harnessmakers, wainwrights, and grooms. The conquest of Crete by the Mycenaeans in 1425 B.C. and the Trojan War of 1194–1184 B.C. are classic examples of the spread of the Centaurs' descendants across the Mediterranean Basin.

No detailed description of the grassland home of the Centaurs was recorded until 450 B.C. when Herodotus journeyed to the country of the Scythians, north of the Black Sea. He found an economy based on horses and horsemanship. Wealth was determined by ownership of horses. Mare's milk was an important part of the diet, and the favorite liquors were brewed from it.

The saddles of Scythian warriors were upholstered in carpet and etched with symbols and figures traced in gold leaf. The horses wore leather breastplates and leather headdresses that protected their throats, muzzles and ears. Some of the headdresses were decorated with stuffed owls or ravens, the skull of a goat, or a similar clan or shaman symbol.

A year after the elaborate funeral of a Scythian king, Herodotus wrote, "Another ceremony takes place. They take fifty of the king's remaining servants, strangle and gut them, stuff the bodies with chaff, and sew them up again. . . . Fifty of the finest horses are then subjected to the same treatment. The next step is to cut a number of wheels in half and to fix them in pairs, rim down, to stakes driven into the ground—two stakes to each half-wheel. Then stout poles are driven lengthwise through the horses from tail to neck, and by means of these the horses are mounted on the wheels, in such a way that the front pairs support the shoulders and the rear pairs the belly between the thighs. All four legs are left dangling clear of the ground. Each horse is bitted and bridled, the bridle being led forward and pegged down. The bodies of the men are dealt with in a similar way; straight poles are driven up through the neck, parallel with the spine, and the lower protruding ends fitted into sockets in the stakes which run through the horses; thus each horse is provided with one of the young servants to ride him."[7]

Investigation of tombs throughout the five-thousand-mile width of the chernozem and chestnut-brown grasslands has revealed a similar horse-based culture among its pre-history peoples. The custom of burying a chieftain with his attendants, concubines and horses reached China before 2000 B.C. Excavation of a king's tomb of the Yin period, near Anyang—350 miles south of the Gobi Desert in Honan—revealed the skeletons of horses, probably the remnants of the royal cart, and bronze horse bits buried beside the king. Nearby graves held the remains of 152 men and women, all of whom had been beheaded. Other excavations in the vicinity of Anyang exposed a "horse-and-chariot cemetery, with hundreds of horses buried in special graves," suggesting that the Chinese regarded their horses as "comrades rather than slaves."[8] These horses were of the Przewalski subspecies.

A type of cavalry was invented by China's war lords about 1000 B.C. when they organized troops of skilled bowmen who, during a battle charge, guided their horses with their knees while they loosed their arrows at the enemy. This technique was also used by the hordes of Hun and Mongol horsemen who pillaged Europe, the Near East and most of Asia between A.D. 400 and 1500. As a form of cavalry, the mounted Chinese bowman antedates by at least five hundred years the heavy cavalry of Darius the Great and his son, Xerxes. The Persian "invention" of cavalry lancers and swordsmen may have been an adaptation of the Chinese method. Both, of course, derived from the bareback Centaur raiders. (Carleton S. Coon provides evidence of skillful horse breeding in ancient Persia.[9] The Nisean breed developed on the grasslands of present Iran became so famous by 200 B.C., he says, that the Chinese sent emissaries thirty-five hundred miles across the grasslands and mountains to purchase stallions and mares.)

Evidence of the progress of horse culture down the Danube Valley to central and northern Europe is not as clear as the evidence of the tarpan's conquest of Greece, Ur and Egypt, and the acceptance of the Przewalski by the Chinese. Two basic types of *Equus caballus* appeared in the Alpine and Scandinavian forests between 2000 and 1000 B.C. One was a small, wiry horse whose later services with the early Britons, Irish and Scotch earned him the family name of Celtic pony. The second was the big-boned, tall Forest Horse. Both of these types would play as important roles in American civilization as the Arabian and Barb interbreds of the tarpan and the Przewalski on the shores of the Mediterranean.

The Celtic pony is the acknowledged ancestor of the Shetland, Icelandic, Connemora, Dartmoor, Welsh and most other pony breeds popular today. He was also the principal foundation stock for the horses who carried the Irish cowboys from, at least, A.D. 1000, then were bred into the beloved Hobbies of A.D. 1300 and imported to Virginia in 1620; these are considered one of the foundation sires for New England's first domestic breed, the Narragansett Pacer.

The Forest Horse was used as a mount and drafter in Sweden before 1000 B.C. The Germanic tribes valued him both as a war steed and as a source of meat. The invasions of western Europe by Etruscans and Carthaginians certainly introduced Mediterranean blood-lines to the breed. Crossbreeding with Przewalski blood-lines occurred, too, during the Hun and Mongol invasions that swept as far south as Italy and, for a time, ruled most of Europe north of France. These blood changes, plus selective breeding and the superior farming methods developed along the North Sea Lowlands, changed the Forest Horse into the Great War Horse of the Middle Ages and eventually the mighty drafter of our 1865–1930 Machine Age.

Another essential invention may have come down from the Centaurs. Primitive man did not have our linear system of measurement. But the width of an adult male hand, from the base of the thumb across the palm, is approximately four inches. Long before there were "inches," horsemen measured the height of their animals in "hands." Thus the tarpan mounts of the Centaurs, measuring about forty-eight inches from ground to top of shoulder, were twelve hands high. The aboriginal Przewalskis of Yin Dynasty China were about 10 hands high or forty inches from ground to top of shoulder. The Lowland farmers, through patient cross-breeding, a regulated grain-and-grass diet, and wintertime shelters, built the Forest Horse up to a sixty-inch height, or fifteen hands, by the time the Moors conquered Spain and, in A.D. 732, rode their fawn-colored horses northward across the Pyrenees into the land of the Franks.

The system of determining the height of a horse by hand width became a symbol of understanding between every race and nation. Still today only the rankest amateur will identify the height of a horse in linear feet; a horse five feet high is fifteen hands, and one five feet three inches high is fifteen hands and three inches.

By November 1491, when the armies of Aragon and Castile finally conquered Granada and ended Moorish rule in Spain, intense interbreeding had produced three regional horse types that would have critical influence on the development of America's civilization.

On the uplands of Spain evolved the fiery desert-type horse called the Andalusian.

Across the Pyrenees, the Great War Horse shared the knight's defeat by musket and cannon power, and was being used to haul farm tools, freight wagons and coaches.

In Ireland, the export market for Hobbies, cow ponies and saddle ponies for children remained brisk.

Eleven months after the Moors' surrender, Christopher Columbus discovered (or rediscovered) North America. On his second voyage in 1493 he landed Andalusian horses in the West Indies. In 1521 Ponce de León landed horses from Cuba or Puerto Rico on the Gulf Coast of Florida. In 1541 French explorers landed Norman horses in Canada. In 1585 Sir Walter Raleigh sent horses, presumably Irish, to his colony at Roanoke. Thus *Equus* returned to his native land.

RETURN OF THE NATIVES

CHAPTER THREE

THE HORSES WHO ENDED the six- to eight-thousand-year exile of *Equus caballus* from the New World were peddlers' nags and cart drafters.

In the fall of 1493, Queen Isabella sent a company of twenty lancers, riding purebred Barbs, down to Cadiz to go along as cavalry guards in the colonies Columbus would establish in "the Indies." But the lancers sold the purebreds to dealers along the way. They showed up in Cadiz riding "sorry hacks"[1] and presumably spent the profits on tavern brawls and bawds. Considering the audacity of Columbus in deciding to transport cattle and horses across three thousand miles of open sea might lead one to conclude that the lancers' sale of the purebred Barbs was actually an act of mercy.

There is no record in human history of a previous effort to transport herds of large animals across so broad and perilous a body of water. The biblical account of Noah's Ark alleges a trip of forty days; Columbus' colonizing expedition sailed on September 25, 1493, and the animals were not landed on Haiti until January 1494 —a time lapse of more than one hundred days. Shipments of horses across the Mediterranean during the Crusades involved voyages of fifteen hundred miles from Venice to the coast of the Holy Land.

19

But the vessels were never more than two hundred miles from land, and rest stops were usually made en route.

None of Columbus' ships was more than a hundred feet long. The animals had to be crowded into pens on the open deck. The stallions were segregated from the mares, and from each other. Exercise was impossible. Forage, grain and drinking water were severely rationed. A storm, a plague of distemper, panic, infection from rat bites—any of a dozen hazards could kill a majority of the animals.

A final peril confronted the horses who survived the voyage. The Venetians had improved Roman ship design and developed broad-bottomed transports for the delivery of livestock to the Crusaders. These vessels were called *huissiers* because of a door (i.e. *huis*) built into the stern that enabled loading and unloading via a ramp. Each *huissier* could comfortably carry forty horses.[2] But *huissiers* were not considered seaworthy enough for Columbus' voyages. So the horses brought to America by Columbus must have been lifted aboard on wooden platforms, or via leather belly-bands, attached to ropes and pulleys. This method could not be used for the unloading off Haiti (i.e. Hispaniola). The beach and tides were so treacherous that the expedition anchored a half mile offshore. There were no lighters. The animals were simply pushed overboard although the waters were normally infested by sharks.

Another shipment of horses arrived one summer's day in 1521, at a scallop-shell and coquina beach somewhere between the sites of Venice and Placida on Florida's Gulf Coast. The evening before, Juan Ponce de León had ordered his caravels to anchor offshore. Old and battle-weary, he was gambling his fortune and a waning reputation on a venture to establish a colony on the "island" of Florida, which he had discovered eight years before. More than two hundred adventurers from Cuba and Puerto Rico were with him. So were fifty horses, as many cattle and more than a hundred hogs, all crammed into pens on the decks.

All that day, and all the next day, crewmen pushed and kicked the livestock into the plunge overboard and the frantic swim toward shore. An Indian arrow ended the dream when it pierced Ponce de León's throat, and the colonists panicked, and fled to the ships.

This "jump and swim for it" method of coming ashore prevailed for most of the livestock brought to America before 1750.

The loss of horses during transatlantic crossings in the Colonial era is estimated at a minimum of 25 per cent, and may have been closer to 50 per cent. A report about a shipment of cattle from Virginia to Massachusetts in 1630 states that "two hundred Cattell were so tossed and bruised, three score and ten died." Governor John Winthrop's *Journal* for the same year records:

"July 1: The Mayflower and the Whale arrived safe in Charlton harbor. Their passengers were all in health, but most of their cattle dead (whereof a mare and a horse of mine). Some stone horses [i.e. stallions] came over in good plight. . . .

Oct. 29: The Handmaid arrived at Plimouth having been twelve weeks at sea, and spent all her masts and of twenty-eight cows she lost ten."[3]

The vast Atlantic Ocean north and south of the Equator, between 30 degrees north and 30 degrees south latitude, was notorious among Spanish and Portuguese seamen for its fickle winds. Tradition—but not recorded fact—relates that in these latitudes hundreds of horses died of thirst and ship-madness as the vessels carrying them to New World colonies were becalmed. The Spanish called the region "The Mare's Gulf," a term that English and American mariners translated to "The Horse Latitudes."

Superstitions and medical beliefs that were deadlier than the panthers, wolves and snakes of the West Indies jungle followed Columbus' pioneer herd ashore. Europe's blacksmiths had assumed the role of horse-doctors. (They favored the title "farrier," an ancient Gallic word that means "worker in iron.") They accepted the precept that bloodletting was an essential first step in combating most human ailments, so prescribed "bleeding" as the routine spring tonic for prized racers and "gentlemen's mounts."[4]

The most popular remedies advocated by the smith-farriers of England were collected by Gervase Markham and published in London during 1610 under the title of *Markham's Maister-Peece*. The book became the favorite reference for horse cures in colonial America and was pirated by at least one of our farrier-author teams as late as 1797.[5] Markham, too, ruled that whenever a horse showed signs of sickness, "let blood instantly, and for the three following mornings, the horse being fasting."

In 1751 the fashionable *Gentleman's Magazine* of England published the following under the headline, "Receipts for Horses":[6]

A medicine for the epidemic distemper among horses, and also for horned cattle supposing the disorder inflammatory.

Take of salt prunells, two ounces; of the whitest chalk and bone armoniac, of each one ounce; of camphire, two drams; of emetic tartar, four scruples; of blue vitriol, two scruples; let the whole be rubbed in a mortar to a fine powder, and divided into four doses; with one of which, mixed with a proper quantity of warm water, let the suffering animal be drenched every night and morning, be kept warm; and drink and food be given as symptoms may indicate.

A remedy for a cold or cough in a horse.

Take a quart of ale or strong beer, warm it, and put thereto a quarter of a pound of treacle or molasses, and a quarter of a pint of distilled aniseed water; stir it well together and give it to the horse at night, after his ordinary food; the next morning give him a pail of warm water with a handful of oatmeal in it, and a mash of malt with a handful or two of beans; and let this be repeated till the horse be cured. It will cure an ox or cow.

An "infallible cure" for intestinal worms prescribed: A quart of new milk sweetened with honey, followed by black soap dissolved in white wine, followed by a two-hour fasting. If the worms persisted, "Take the soft downy hairs which grow in the ears of an horse . . . mix them well with half a gallon of sweet oats, and give them to the horse. There is nothing that will kill worms more certainly." In the most "extream cases," this author continued, prepare a liquor containing "about four or five lumps of the white dung of a hen, and three pints of good ashes, and much chimney soot [which] will perfectly cleanse his stomach, kill the worms and cause him to rope at the mouth abundantly."[7]

Belief in witches and devils had already generated the European's conviction that it was good luck to find a horseshoe, and that the shoe should be nailed above a door with the prong ends up so that the "good luck can't run out." The "sacred Cross" design of the panels in the doors of early New England homes was as intentional insurance against witches and evil spirits as the "hex" symbols the German farmers of Pennsylvania put on the walls and doorways of their bank-barns.

Similiar beliefs must have caused as much distress and fatal illness among colonists' horses as the nauseating remedies of the smith-farriers. A few of the beliefs popular in the Spanish, French, Dutch, Swedish and English settlements along the Atlantic seaboard edicted:

To prevent sickness in livestock, make three crosses on the door sill of the stable.

To cure distemper, feed the horse a hornet's nest.

To cure sweeny, tie a live toad to the withers of the afflicted horse.

Be sure the stable has many cobwebs.

Keep a goat running with horses and cattle.

Rub bacon fat on the object that causes a wound, and the wound will heal in a few days.

If a horse will not eat, smear his teeth with onion, or cook a half ounce of asafetida in a pint of wine and give it to him.

If a horse cannot urinate, take a seemly number of child-lice and put them in the horse's genitals.

To stop bleeding, take grass which grows on a grave, pulverize it and put it on the wound.[8]

Despite the perils, horses multiplied as rapidly in the West Indies and along our mainland coast as *Equus caballus* did on the Pleistocene's high-plains. By 1630 herds were established in Florida, Virginia, Pennsylvania, New Jersey, New York, Massachusetts, Canada, New Mexico, and, possibly, in Mississippi or western Tennessee.

Ponce de León's landing of fifty horses in 1521 was followed in 1528 by the Pánfilo de Narváez expedition, with eighty horses. Lucas Vásquez de Ayllón, five hundred colonists and eighty-nine horses landed in the vicinity of Pawley's Island, north of Georgetown, South Carolina, in 1526. Hernando de Soto brought his task force of five hundred and fifty men and more than three hundred horses ashore at Charlotte Harbor or Tampa Bay in 1539. Jacques Cartier landed twenty horses at the site of Quebec in 1541. Thus, over a twenty-one year period, *Equus caballus* was reintroduced along a two-thousand-mile expanse of seaboard that was rich in grasslands and sweet water and located in those equus-favored latitudes of the North Temperate Zone.

De Soto's brutal search for "cities of gold"[9] continued across our Southeast to the Mississippi Valley, then penetrated Arkansas. When De Soto died, three hundred and twenty of the survivors reached Mexico via Texas, after abandoning their horses somewhere in the Mississippi Valley.

The De Soto cavalcade all but met the explorers led out of Mexico by Francisco Coronado, equally intent on plundering the "golden cities of Cibola." These two expeditions, between 1539 and 1542, demonstrated the horse and the deadly potentials of the horseman to most of the Indian tribes between Georgia and southern California and north to the Kansas and Nebraska high-plains.

The total number of horses landed in United States and Canadian territory between 1521 and 1542 could not have exceeded six hundred. The Spanish believed that a *caballero* should display his virility and horsemanship by riding only stallions; hence not many mares were in the Narváez, De Soto and Coronado remudas.

But Ponce de León, Vásquez de Ayllón and Jacques Cartier

came to found colonies, and their herds were intended for breeding, as well as for cavalry and explorations. This fact suggests that there must have been 150 or more mares and stallions in Florida, North Carolina and the St. Lawrence Valley when the colonization efforts were abandoned. In the retreat of the Narváez expedition a few more stallions and mares could have been released in Florida, just as in the flight of De Soto's bullies toward Mexico horses were abandoned on the grassland of the Mississippi delta.

Historians have concluded, since 1920, that all these herds must have been killed and eaten by Indians, wolves or wildcats. This does not credit the Indian tribes with much ingenuity, or the abandoned horses with any instinct for survival and multiplication. Yet the breed-up of the Chickasaw horse in the Mississippi delta before 1725 and the independence of the horses of Chincoteague, Sable Island and pioneer Canada testify to both Indian ingenuity and horse initiative.

The evidence of the initiative appeared first. When in 1598 the French established a colony on Sable Island, a desolate sand shoal in the North Atlantic one hundred miles east of Nova Scotia, they landed horses. They left them on the island when they abandoned it in 1603. Sable is twenty-five miles long and never more than a mile wide. Its contour offers little refuge from storms and the long winters. The grasslands are sparse. Nevertheless, the abandoned horses perpetuated themselves for three hundred and thirty-three years! In 1936 more than one hundred ponies in the Sable Island herd were rounded up and shipped to the mainland.[10]

Similar evidence of horse independence persists on Chincoteague Island, off the Virginia shore of the Delmarva Peninsula. Its "wild ponies" were still being publicized in the mid-1960s. Chincoteague's herd free-bred from horses marooned on the island at least two hundred years ago. Henry A. Wise, onetime governor of Virginia and a Confederate officer during the Civil War, reminisced during the 1880s that: "There has been, since long before the Revolution, on the islands along the seaboard of Maryland and Virginia, a race of very small, compact, hardy horses, usually called beach-horses. They run wild throughout the year, and are never fed. When the snow covers the ground for a few days in winter, they dig through it in search of food. They are very diminutive, but many of them are of perfect symmetry and extraordinary powers of action and endurance."[11]

Most of the horses introduced to the Atlantic Seaboard before 1700 were forced to become semi-feral. Neither the French in Canada, the British in New England, New York, Maryland and Virginia, nor the Spanish in Florida built barns for livestock shelter or provided their animals with regular diets of grain and cured forage. A system for the "inclosure" of stallions and the selective breeding of mares had been introduced to England during the reigns of Henry VII and Henry VIII. Similar practices had long been routine among the agricultural pioneers of Normandy and the North Sea Lowlands. But the perils of wresting a livelihood from the land were so great that early New World colonists fell back on the practice of common-pasture, free breeding and semi-feral survival for their livestock.

The observant Baron de Lahontan was in Canada and the "western wilderness" during the 1680s. "The way of traveling in the winter, whether in town or country," he wrote from Quebec on May 14, 1684, "is that of sledges drawn by horses, who are so insensible of the cold that I have seen fifty or sixty of 'm in *January* and *February* stand in the snow up to their breast, in the midst of a wood, without ever offering to go near their owner's house. In the wintertime they travel from Quebec to Montreal upon the ice, the river then being frozen over; and upon that occasion these sledges will run you fifteen leagues [i.e. forty-eight miles] a day. Others have their sledges drawn by two mastiff dogs, but then they are longer on the way."[12]

Proof that not all of the aborigines of our Southeast slaughtered and ate every stray and feral horse they captured is offered in the still-mysterious appearance of the Chickasaw horse. "South Carolina and Georgia had one notable breed of horses more highly prized than any other," James Westfall Thompson reported. "These were the Chickasaw horses, named after the first mounted Indians with whom the whites of the English colonies came in contact. The Chickasaws were fully aware of the value of the breed and carefully guarded it from admixture. They even tried to prevent the sale of their horses to the whites, and most of the horses in South Carolina and Georgia were stolen and smuggled out of the Indian country. The horses were small, seldom being over 13½ hands high, but active and beautiful. . . ."[13]

James Adair, a South Carolina trader and Indian agent, lived among the Chickasaw, Choctaw and Cherokee tribes in the Great Smokies and west to the Mississippi Valley between 1725 and 1765. In 1775 he published his *History of the American Indians*. In describing the Chickasaw, Choctaw and Cherokee, he wrote that "almost every one hath horses, from two to a dozen, which makes a considerable number through their various nations. The Cheerake had a prodigious number of excellent horses. . . . They are skilful jockies and nice in their choice. . . . The horses are commonly of a good size, well made, hard hoofed, handsome, strong, and fit for the saddle or draught; but a person runs too great a risk to buy any to take them out of the country, because every spring season most of them make for their native range."[14]

Further testimony occurs in Dr. David Ramsay's *History of South Carolina*. "Before the year 1754," Dr. Ramsey wrote in 1808–9, "the best horses for the draft or saddle in Carolina were called the Chickasaw breed. These were originally introduced by the Spaniards into Florida and in the course of time had astonishingly increased. Great numbers ranged wild in and near the Apalache old field. Many of them were caught and tamed by the indians [sic] and sold to the traders. They made use of them for pack horses to bring their peltry to market and afterwards sold them in the low country. These horses in general were handsome, active and hardy, but small; seldom exceeding thirteen and a half hands in height. The mares in particular, when crossed with English blooded horses, produced colts of great beauty, strength and swiftness."[15]

Neither James Adair's 1775 narrative nor Dr. Ramsay's 1809 *History* attempts to describe the spread of horsemanship among the Chickasaw, Choctaw and Cherokee Indians. Obviously, the equestrian skills were already developed and the Chickasaw horse was an established breed when James Adair began trading with these nations in 1725. This indicates that both the equestrian learning and the breed-up began before 1700, at the latest. The probability exists, thus, that the parent stock of the Chickasaw horse were either feral descendants of horses who survived the Ponce de León, Narváez, De Soto or Vásquez de Ayllón herds of 1521–42, *or* were strays from Florida, Virginia and Maryland herds of 1625–50, *or* both. The absence of both feral and Indian horses west of the Mississippi before the 1680s all but precludes the West as a primary source of the parent stock. From the testimony of Adair, Ramsay, Bartram and others, plus the remarkable research of Thompson, the Chickasaw horse emerges as the first domestic breed evolved in America. Its origins may never be determined.

Juan de Oñate introduced horse domestication to our trans-Mississippi West on April 20, 1598, when his *conducta* of eighty-three wagons and seven thousand horses, donkeys, cattle and sheep crossed the Rio Grande into present Texas near the site of El Paso. Ten days later, Governor Oñate took formal possession of the region as the Colony of New Mexico. So the meadows between Santa Fe and Albuquerque became the first permanent home, of record, for horse domestication within the present boundaries of the United States.

Mexican traditions developed from the feats of Hernando Cortes' cavalry troop during the 1520–30 conquest of Mexico. The horse was regarded as one of the conquistadore's most valuable possessions, excelled only by his guns. In New Mexico, too, Indians were denied the right to own horses; the penalty for stealing a horse was death by hanging.

Nine years and two weeks after Juan de Oñate took ceremonial possession of New Mexico, three ships sent out by the London Company began landing 144 settlers on a swampy island in Virginia's James River. The fort and encircling huts erected during the next months was named Jamestown.

During 1613 Hendrick Christianson and Adriaen Block opened a trading post on the island at the mouth of Henry Hudson's River of the North. Settlers from Holland and Sweden followed within a few years. By 1630 they were importing Holland's breed of Great War Horses and Sweden's hybridizations of Celtic ponies, Barbs and Mongolians to farms and villages developing between Schenectady on the north and the site of Chester, Pennsylvania, on the south.[16]

The Pilgrim settlement at Plymouth, started on Christmas Day, 1620, and the first log cabins of the Puritans built on the shore of Salem harbor during the fall of 1628 established horse domestication in New England.

The Cavalier tradition was as firmly rooted among the English as the *caballero* tradition was among the Spanish. The colonies in New England and Virginia formally forbade ownership of horses by Indians.

But the Hollanders and Swedes must have been more lenient. During the summer and early fall of 1687, Baron de Lahontan served with the expedition of fifteen hundred militiamen that Governor Denonville of New France led against Iroquois strongholds on the south shore of Lake Ontario. Through late June and early July, the Baron reported, the soldiers burned the "Hutts of Bark" and "spoiled the corn" of Seneca villages between present Victor and Honeoye Falls, east and south of the city of Rochester, New York. "In all these villages," the Baron recalled, "we found plenty of horses, black cattel, fowl and hogs."[17]

Thus, less than sixty years after the first Dutch and Swedish importations of horses to their Hudson Valley and New Jersey colonies, the Iroquois had learned horse domestication and had acquired "plenty" of stallions and mares. The villages Baron de Lahontan helped plunder were only sixty miles east of Niagara Falls. That winter Iroquois war parties not only besieged the French and their Huron allies at the new "Fort of Pales with four bastions" guarding the portage around Niagara Falls, but raided west as far as the Indiana prairies and the Ohio Valley.

Thus a mystery develops about the heritage of the horses who enabled the mount-up of the Western red men and their development into superb horsemen. Historians have assumed that the pinto, Cayuse, Appaloosa, Painted ponies, and other horse types and breeds developed on the high-plains before 1850 were all descendants of Andalusian, Barb and Arabian horses strayed and stolen from Mexico and New Mexico.

But Baron de Lahontan's statement that the Iroquois of upstate New York had "plenty of horses" by 1687 is as provocative as James Adair's testimony that aborigines in the lower Mississippi Valley bred up the Chickasaw horse before 1725.

Were Chickasaws, Dutch Great Horses, Normans and Irish Hobbies also parent stocks of the herds on whom the trans-Mississippi red men developed their fearsome skills?

If horses from the East *did* join the Andalusians, Arabians and Barbs out of New Mexico and Old Mexico, the breed-up of the Appaloosa, pinto, Cayuse and Painted pony would be easier to comprehend!

THE PURITAN COWBOYS

CHAPTER FOUR

THE ONLY HORSE of record in Plymouth Colony by 1632 was a mare used as a saddler by Governor Bradford.[1] The fleet that brought the first Puritans to the site of Salem in 1628 carried 110 cattle, but only thirteen horses. More than sixteen thousand "dissenters" migrated to Salem, Boston and the other settlements of Massachusetts Bay Colony during the next decade. But there seem to have been only about two hundred horses in New England by 1640. That year a mare bought "at shipside" cost from thirty-four to forty pounds sterling; an adult ox or milch cow cost only twelve to twenty pounds sterling.

Most of the Puritans came from England's farms and villages. The feudal environment had conditioned them to the conviction that horses "belong to the gentry." Cattle, sheep and pigs seemed far more useful to these yeomen, franklins and villagers. Pork and bacon were the common man's everyday meats. The tradition of Christmas roast beef grew from the essential practice of aging the coarse, tough meat from old oxen and milch cows. (Butchering usually took place about Martinmas, on November 11. Then the beef joints were hung in a shed for five or six weeks until putrefaction tenderized them.[2]) The milch cow provided milk, butter and cheese. Cows and oxen could be yoked to plows, carts or mill-sweeps. Cowhide, cowhorns, tallow, glue, gelatin, felt, sausages, intestines were all essential products of "the kine" in the medieval English home. Sheep and swine similarly yielded meat and a

31

variety of by-products deemed necessary to the women's home economy and the men's plow-and-pasture economy.

But the horse had little value after its death. Heritage had firmly fixed an English bias against using horseflesh for human food.[3] The market for horsehide leathers had not yet developed. (Cordovan, the durable and superior leather made from horsehides, was a product of the Moors in Spain and named for their former capital city, Cordova.)

The severity of the New England winters and the need for pack horses caused a breed-up of horses soon after 1640. Horses were speedier than oxen, both as pack animals and as saddlers, on the narrow forest trails. The New England winters were much more severe than old England's, and horses were better than oxen for transportation through snowdrifts or along the glassy natural highways of frozen waterways.

Pack trains of horses carried the supplies and household effects of the Puritans who founded Hartford, Springfield and other pioneer communities in the Connecticut River valley. Shaggy horses, hitched to canoe-shaped sleds, paced the farmers and fishermen of Cape Ann, Cambridge and the South Shore to "Sabbath meetings." When the weather was clear and the ice firm, horse sleds could haul passengers or freight forty-five to fifty miles along a riverway in ten hours.

In 1653, the court of Massachusetts Bay Colony reduced the value of a "sounde horse" to sixteen pounds sterling, then, in 1668, lowered it to five pounds sterling. During 1650, Secretary von Teinhoven of the Dutch West India Company advised prospective immigrants to Nieuw Amsterdam that it was unnecessary to undergo the expense and trouble of bringing horses across the Atlantic because "they can be got at reasonable expense from the English who have plenty of them."[4]

A variety of evidence indicates that importation of both horses and skilled horsemen from Ireland between 1640 and 1660 not only furnished the animals and skills for the Puritans' conversion to horsemanship, but introduced the cowboy to America and began the breed-up that led to the important "jockey ship" trade and the Narragansett Pacer. The brutalities of the Puritan armies in Ireland during 1649, the Puritan victories over the Scotch in 1648 and 1650, and the shipment of Scotch and Irish prisoners of war to New England as indentured servants add to the credibility of the theory.

Ireland became a center for beef and dairy production before the Norman conquest. Her warriors and cattlemen were ardent horsemen. The minstrels who composed *The Triads* before A.D. 900 chanted that "Three glories of a gathering are: a beautiful wife, a good horse and a swift hound." By A.D. 1000 there were minstrel songs about "the cowboy."[5] The beloved rocking horse of the children's playroom shares its name with a breed of Irish pacers who had a gait "as comfortable as a rocking chair on the hob." The fireplace hob was the most restful place in the home. The gentle horses, called Hobbies, were popular in London before 1350; and children of squires, merchants, clergymen and other horse-owning "gentry" proudly claimed the same name for their rocking horses.

Deane Phillips, author of *Horse Raising in Colonial New England,* believed that Irish Hobbies imported to New England may have been the progenitors of the Narragansett Pacer. "The Irish Hobbies' . . . natural pacing gait made them especially desirable in any place where travel was of necessity on horseback," he theorized. "It is not at all improbable, therefore, that some of them found their way to New England, where they would have been especially serviceable. There seems to be no direct evidence to this effect, but any comparison of such fragmentary descriptions of the two as are available discloses a rather striking similarity between these Irish Hobbies and the famous Narragansett Pacers which were later developed in Rhode Island."[6]

Further reference to Hobbies and indentured Irish and Scotch cowboys can be found in the career of Major Daniel Gookin. James Westfall Thompson reported that "In a resolution adopted by the directors of the Virginia Company on July 7, 1620, it was proposed to ship 200 head of cattle, 400 goats, 80 asses and 20 mares. . . .

Daniel Gookin, later destined to become one of Cromwell's right-hand men in Ireland, as well as famous both in Virginia and Massachusetts, was the contractor. The cattle he brought out were obtained in Ireland. . . . This transaction seems to have been the beginning of an important trade in cattle between Ireland and Virginia."[7]

Forty years later, Daniel Gookin—with the rank of major—lived in Cambridge, Massachusetts. There he had two secret house guests during the fall and winter of 1660–61: Edward Whalley and William Goffe, both members of the High Court of Justice that imposed the death sentence on Charles I.[8] The general amnesty declared by Charles II at the Restoration did not include the surviving members of this Court.

By February 1661, the King's agents had traced the pair to Boston. Major Gookin arranged for a new hideout with the Reverend John Davenport in New Haven and helped smuggle them down-country. (The Puritans' "underground" was so successful that Whalley and Goffe spent the last fifteen or twenty years of their lives as house guests in Connecticut Valley communities.)

Daniel Gookin's residence in both Virginia and Massachusetts, his familiarity with Ireland and his position as a contractor for Irish livestock all suggest the importation of Hobbies and indentured "cowboys" to Massachusetts Bay Colony. The absence of records about these imports may be due to the bonfires of "incriminating evidence" that occurred in many Puritan homes when the agents of Charles II landed at Boston in 1661.

Five springtimes before Whalley and Goffe were spirited into the Gookin home, John Pynchon and a trail crew drove a herd of stall-fattened Devon and Durham cattle over the Old Bay Path from Springfield to Boston Common. This was the first long drive on record of a herd of fat-cattle to a city market anywhere in the present extent of the United States. Since the cowboy was, is, and will be a professional herdsman and a drover of beef cattle, the Pynchon trail-drive and the preliminary stall-feeding on the meadows south of Springfield were the official birth ritual of the American cowboy.[9]

The important role of horses in the feed-out, roundup, sorting and on the drive itself is obvious. The type of horse used has never been identified. But evidence indicates that the West Indies' "boucaneers," a giant Negro from Jamaica named Peter Swink, an indentured Scotch blacksmith named John Stewart, and an Irishman named John Daley were directly involved. The necessary horsemanship, Daniel Gookin's career, and John Pynchon's reputation for trying out new ideas sustain the "hunch" that the horses used were Hobbies.

John Pynchon was born near Springfield, Yorkshire, in central England during 1626. His family was moderately prosperous and owned farmland "in fee simple." His father, William, studied at Oxford University and was a student of theology as well as a shrewd businessman. William Pynchon's Puritan convictions persuaded him to join the migration to Massachusetts Bay Colony in 1630. He was one of the founders of the village of Roxbury and, in 1632, was appointed treasurer of Massachusetts Bay Colony. Then "the West" lured him. In 1635, when John was nine years old, William secured permission to develop a settlement in the Connecticut River valley, twenty-five miles north of the Reverend Thomas Hooker's new community of Hart's Ford.

A dozen families joined his venture. The site Pynchon selected was on a glacial lake-bed, fed by several brooks. Its prairie-flat grassland was hedged by hardwood and white-pine forests. A falls in the river a few miles south meant that a boat-wharf would have to be built there.[10] South of the falls the Connecticut's channel was deep enough for seaworthy vessels all the way to its estuary on Long Island Sound.

Pynchon's purchase of the Scottish war prisoner John Stewart, who became the resident blacksmith "in indenture" for the new village, is a matter of record. The Irishman John Daley may have been purchased, too, and others whose records have been lost. Whatever, the new community was named Springfield, after the Pynchons' ancestral village in Yorkshire. It was soon a center for fur trading with the Indians, and for pig, cattle, sheep and horse production on the rich riverside pastures.

By 1645, Pynchon was growing wealthy from the beaver, mink and otter pelt trade he developed with the Mohawk and Mohican Indians in eastern New York. At least once, the Dutch formally complained to London about Pynchon's commercial invasion of their territory and the high prices his agents were offering for pelts. Then, during 1646 or 1647, a crisis in other English colonies centered Pynchon's interest on Springfield's livestock.

The climax of the Civil War between Oliver Cromwell's Roundheads and Charles I's Cavaliers delayed shipment of supplies to Newfoundland, Barbados, Bermuda and Jamaica. The governors of these colonies appealed to Massachusetts and Virginia for foodstuffs and plantation supplies. The response was prompt; Governor Winthrop noted in his *Journal* for 1648 that "Now the country doth send great store of biscott, flour, peas, beef, pork, butter and other provisions to the supply of Barbados, Newfoundland and other places."

Some of this "beef, pork, butter and other provisions" was trundled across the new wharf William Pynchon had built south of the Connecticut River falls. Most of his meat shipments went to Bermuda, Jamaica and Barbados. He must have produced quality products; his repeat orders were so numerous that he built New England's—and America's—first commercial meat-packing plant.

During the 1640s, some of the freebooter bands in the West Indies still used the profession-name *boucanier* or "boucaneer." The French word for "smokehouse" is *boucan*. The boucaneers were groups of vagrants and renegade galley slaves who butchered wild cattle and smoke-cured the beef into long leather strips called "charqui" or "jerky." They peddled this product, plus the cured hides, to trading ships in exchange for clothing, wine, dried beans, rum, saleratus, cognac and other essential items. The sales trip out to a ship also afforded an excellent opportunity to inspect the vessel and decide whether it was worth pirating. (Later, of course, the spelling of "boucaneer" was corrupted to "buccaneer"!)

Some of the boucaneers were Flemish, Norman and Dutch who had grown up on the farms along the English Channel and North

Sea. Their fathers had scoffed at the British yeoman's conviction that "a cow kept indoors will stop giving milk and then sicken and die." These were the Lowlanders who invented the grain stripper in A.D. 100 and the stirrup before A.D. 732 and the horse-collar before A.D. 1000. They housed livestock in barns and routinely fattened pregnant mares and cows. Livestock intended for sale in the village markets was fattened, too, by feeding them liberal rations of dried clover, lucerne-grass (i.e. alfalfa), turnips, oats and barley.

Some of the boucaneers adopted this feed-out technique for the West Indies cattle. They substituted Indian maize and the pulpy wastes from sugar-cane mills for the root crops and small grains their fathers and uncles used.

Peter Swink, the robust Negro who became one of the Pynchons' most trustworthy retainers—*and* a friend—came from Jamaica to Springfield between 1648 and 1650. Perhaps he, or one of the meat-ship captains, brought in the tale about the boucaneers' feed lots. William Pynchon saw their potential for the springtime markets at Boston and Salem.

Spring was the traditional "starving time." By then, the fall's harvest of root crops, grain and fruit was consumed, or had spoiled. Through February, March and April, people lived on scant rations. The livestock became scrawny bags-of-bone. The prospect of driving maize-fattened cattle—and perhaps pigs, too—into Boston and Salem markets during the spring starving time was dazzling.

But a vicious book-burning delayed the experiment for several years and prevented William Pynchon from becoming America's first trail boss. Pynchon's concern for morality had caused him to write out his convictions in a work entitled *The Meritorious Price of Our Redemption.*

The book was distributed in Boston during the spring of 1652. Puritan ministers denounced it as "ungodly." Copies were formally burned, by order of the General Court, on Boston Common; its sale was banned in Massachusetts and Connecticut. The General Court ordered William Pynchon to resign as Judge of the Springfield Court.

That summer William bequeathed most of his Massachusetts

properties to John and returned to England. John, then twenty-six
years old, decided to carry out the stall-fattening operation, but
was so involved in details of the family's fur-trading and meat-
packing operations that he did not start the process until the fall
of 1654.

A law passed by the General Court during 1647 gives another
clue to the increasing importance of the horse and horsemanship
in New England. It required that every horse and cow in Massachusetts must be doubly branded: first with the symbol of the
township in which it was commoned, and secondly with the registered brand mark of its owner. The Devon and Durham cattle prev-
alent in New England during this period were not docile. They
lived on the commons the year around. Each bull belligerently
bullied (precisely what the word means) his family of cows and
calves. Herding and branding the animals on foot would have been
dangerous, as only trained horses and deft riders could bunch and
sort a herd of spooky Devons and Durhams. And it took as much
skill to throw and hold a heifer beside a branding fire in a Connecticut Valley pasture in the 1640s and 50s as it did to "spraddle" a
longhorn heifer in Texas two hundred years later. Similar tussles
were necessary when calves were captured and subjected to the
operation that turned them into oxen or "steers."

The stallion, too, bossed his group of mares and colts, and fought
intruders to the death. It took a horseman to catch a horse for the
branding or for the castration operation that changed a stallion to
a gelding.

The "sorting" routine that precedes a branding or the journey
toward the butcher shop must have been used on the pastureland
south of Springfield during the fall of 1654. John Pynchon and his
cowboys selected cattle for the feed-out experiment, segregated
them from the bulls, and herded them off to a fenced enclosure.
Since Pynchon's career reveals that he was careful about details,
it seems probable that he ordered a pole-and-plank shed built at
the center of the pen to provide shelter for the cattle during the
winter's blizzards and "cold snaps." Wheat straw and cornstalks

strewn across the floor of the shed would have served as bedding and as a diet supplement. With this system, every day or two for five or six months the cowboys brought dried corn-on-the-cob, cured hay, vegetable scraps from the Springfield kitchens, the malt-hops-barley residues from a family's homebrew, pulp from the cider mill and similar protein feeds to the enclosure.

By February the boucaneers' technique was proved. The cattle left to forage at the haystacks across Springfield's common were rail-thin and as wild as hawks. But Pynchon's stall-fed cattle were plump, gentle, and friendly.

So one spring morning in 1655 the crew assembled for the hundred-mile drive across the Bay Path to Boston Common. No artists or writers were present to record "the rig" or the cowboy costumes. However descriptions are extant of the costumes worn by the Texans who inaugurated the Chisholm Trail drives across Oklahoma and Kansas during 1865–66. The Texans wore the shabby army jackets and pants they rode home in after the Confederate States collapsed. These garments, plus sun-bleached derbies, forage caps, calico shirts and five-button vests, were the first cowboy costumes in the West. The first Puritan cowboys must also have dressed in old work clothes. Jackets and vests stitched from moose-hide or deerskin were common garments for winter wear among the Puritans. So were flat-topped caps made from beaver felt or fur. Homespun shirts, buckskin breeches and leather boots shiny with bear grease would have been logical attire for a wilderness journey that would take two or three weeks. Heavy dark wool greatcapes were favored as outer garments during the mid-seventeenth century. These could also serve as blankets, so would have been strapped on behind the saddles.

Any wheeled vehicles used on the Pynchon drive would have been two-wheeled carts drawn by ox teams or donkeys. (The chuck wagon and hoodlum wagon, both essentials of our 1865–1910 trail drives across the West, were nineteenth-century American inventions, based on Mexican ranch skills.) The rocky country-side between Springfield and Boston plus the narrowness of the

Bay Path suggest that supplies for the drive were carried by a string of pack ponies.

Records of the daily progress of the drive and of any attempts at theft by Agawams, Nipmucks, Nonotucks and other Indian tribes along the route have never been discovered. A translation of the account books and records that John Pynchon kept—in a system of shorthand he invented—may one day provide more detail about this pioneer trail drive. It is known that most of the fat-cattle reached Boston and that they yielded Pynchon a handsome profit. (Further evidence of the equestrian skills of John Pynchon and his herdsmen occurred during King Phillip's War in 1675–76 when Pynchon won more laurels as a major in command of troops from the upper Connecticut Valley. Then the companies of Springfield cavalry fought valiantly. Josiah Turnbull, Constable Thomas Miller and other horseback messengers made daredevil rides along the valley that were as heroic and dangerous as any Pony Express man's exploit 185 years later.)

The winter feed-out and spring trail drive was not the only incentive for Yankee horsemanship introduced from the West Indies by the 1647–48 supply ships. Crewmen spread the rumor that an excellent market for both saddle and work horses existed on British, Dutch and French plantations in the West Indies and Central America. Horses, as well as oxen, were used to power the brass and iron rollers that crushed the juice from sugar cane. The death rate of these animals was appalling; any plug-ugly freebred on the commons could be used on these millsweeps. Prime prices were also being offered, especially in Barbados and Jamaica, for lively pacers who would carry the plantation overseers on inspection trips.[11]

The first record of a shipment of Massachusetts horses to the West Indies appears in John Winthrop's *Journal* for 1648.[12] In 1649, the General Court forbade further exportation of mares, and levied a tax of sixpence on each gelding shipped out of the colony. This does not appear to have slowed the trade since, Deane Phillips reported, "in 1673, Captain Gorges was instructed by the Assembly of Barbados to insist to the English Parliament on the dependence of the island on New England for boards, timber, pipe staves and horses, to the end that no act might be passed which would interfere with the trade."[13]

By 1700 the horse trade was so important that sailing ships were being designed with built-in deck pens to hold 150 to 200 horses. These vessels took the Scotch nickname of "jockey" (i.e. "small Jack"). Fore and aft rigged, they averaged two round trips a year between New England and Bermuda, Jamaica, Barbados or Surinam. Other schooner-type traders often carried a deckload of twenty to forty horses on the run south. For seventy-five years, until the outbreak of our Revolution imposed a British blockade on New England's ports, horse loadings and "jockey ships" were commonplace in the harbors of Salem, Boston, Providence, New London and New Haven.

This export trade caused stud farms to be established throughout Rhode Island, Connecticut and the Connecticut River valley. The broad pastures of salt hay and the prevalence of springs and brooks on the south shore of Narragansett Bay, south of Providence, assured the development of the area as the premier center for horse breeding.

"The first suggestion of horse-raising in Narragansett," Alice Morse Earle concluded, "was without doubt given by Captain John Hull of 'Pine Tree Shilling' fame, who was one of the original purchasers of the Petaquamscut Tract, or Narragansett, from the Narragansett Indians. He wrote in April, 1677: 'I have often thought if we, the partners of Point Judith Neck, did fence with a good stone wall at the north end thereof, that no kind of horses or cattle might get thereon, and also what other parts thereof westerly were needful, and procure a very good breed of large and fair mares and horses, and that no mongrel breed might come among them, we might have a very choice breed for coach-horses, some for the saddle, and some for the draught; and in a few years might draw off considerable numbers, and ship them for Barbados, Nevis, or such parts of the Indies where they would vend. We might have a vessel

made for that service accommodated on purpose to carry off horses
to advantage.' "[14]

Captain Hull's plan, or one remarkably like it, was adopted. Point
Judith, the peninsula that juts into Rhode Island Sound from the
southeast shore of Narragansett Bay, became the first center for
controlled breeding of horses in America. The colts produced there
were beginning to earn a reputation in 1711 when Rip Van Dam, a
merchant living in New York City's "Southe Ward," wrote a friend
in Philadelphia about a horse he had recently purchased from
Rhode Island. "He always plays and acts and will never stand still,"
Van Dam alleged. "He will take a glass of wine, beer or cyder, and
probably would drink a dram on a cold morning."[15]

The Reverend James MacSparran, pastor of a Narragansett
church between 1721 and 1759, reminisced that he had seen some
of the local horses "pace a mile in a little more than two minutes
and a good deal less than three" and that he had ridden several of
them "fifty; nay, sixty miles a day even here in New England where
roads are rough, stony and uneven."[16]

The breed of Narragansett Pacers developed on Point Judith
and neighboring stud farms was never, it appears, clearly described
by contemporary writers or sketched by artists. The best descriptions available were written by James Fenimore Cooper and Robert
Livingston, in 1826 and 1830. But by that time the breed was vanish-
ing. "They have handsome foreheads, the head clean, the neck
long, the arms and legs thin and tapered," Livingston reported in
the first American edition of the *Edinburgh Encyclopedia*. "The
hindquarters are narrow and the hocks a little crooked, which is
here called sickle hocked, which turns the hind feet out a little.
Their color is generally, though not always, bright sorrel. They are
very spirited and carry both head and tail high. But what is most
remarkable is that they amble with more speed than most horses
trot, so that it is difficult to put some of them upon a gallop. Not-
withstanding this facility of ambling, where the ground requires it,
as when the roads are rough and stony, they have a fine easy single
footed trot. These circumstances, together with their being very

sure footed, render them the finest saddle horses in the world; they neither fatigue themselves or the rider."[17]

James Fenimore Cooper praised the Narragansett Pacer in his *Last of the Mohicans*. "Horses of this race were, and are still," he said in a footnote, "in much request as saddle horses, on account of their hardiness, and the ease of their movements. As they were also sure of foot, the Narragansetts were greatly sought for by females who were obliged to travel over the roots and holes in the 'New Countries.' "[18]

The founding sires and dams of the breed have never been identified. It became fashionable among horsemen during the nineteenth century to claim a mount's descent from "the fiery Andalusian." So the story grew that a stallion imported "from Andalusia, Spain, by Deputy Governor Robinson"[19] was the breed's foundation sire. But Deane Phillips deduced, in his excellent study, that Irish Hobbies were the founding sires and/or dams.

There is also the strong possibility of Canadian heritage. Some of the horses observed by travelers in Quebec and Nova Scotia before 1700 were described as "natural pacers" and "about fourteen hands high." Soldiers and sailors from Rhode Island helped to capture Port Royal, Nova Scotia, during Queen Anne's War; Nova Scotia was ceded to Great Britain in 1713. Canadian pacers who were freebred descendants of Norman and Lowland horses may have been among the booty brought to Rhode Island.

The continuing demand for saddlers and mill horses in the West Indies similarly influenced the development of stud farms up the Connecticut River valley and south along Long Island Sound as far as New Haven.

"As the West Indies trade increased from year to year," Frances M. Caulkins reported in her *History of New London*, "the raising of horses became very profitable and many farmers entered into it largely. Lands being unenclosed, it was easy to run such horses off to a port where the mark of the owner was not known, or the mark itself could be altered. A bold rover in the woods might entrap half a dozen horses with ease and, shooing them off through Indian

paths by night, reach some port in a neighboring colony; and before
the owner could get hold of them, they were far off upon the ocean,
out of reach of proof. Many persons otherwise respectable entered
into this practice or connived in it. Men who would scorn to pocket
sixpence that belonged to another seemed to think it no crime to
throw a noose over the head of a horse running loose and to nullify
the signet of the owner or engraft on it the mark that designated
their own property."[20]

These references to brand altering, "noose" throwing, and furtive
backcountry trail drives by night attest to a New England introduction of practices that became "Wild West" traditions two centuries later. The horse thief became a criminal of grave concern
to Yankee lawmakers and police officers. Massachusetts Bay
Colony ordered a toll book established in each township, where
descriptions of every local horse must be posted. Horse owners
were assigned horse-license numbers. Any sale of a horse made
without toll-book listing of the seller's and buyer's license numbers
was illegal. In 1701 the government office of Horse Inspector was
created at every seaport. The Horse Inspector recorded the license
number, description and destination of each horse loaded on a ship,
plus the name of the animal's alleged owner and his place of residence. The fine ruled for any violation of this law was ten pounds
sterling per horse.

Thus, between 1640 and 1710, the Puritan cast off his feudal conviction that "the horse is a gentleman's mount" and, in the new
guise of "shrewd Yankee," introduced the cowboy, the commercial
trail drive, the jockey ship, and the woes of horse thievery to
American folklore. The possessions of a moderately prosperous
Connecticut farmer during the 1750s included "four negro servants, 50 head of cattle, 800 sheep and 30 to 40 horses."[21] Still in
1774 New England's jockey ships delivered an average of four
thousand horses a year to the West Indies.

POPE'S PLOT

CHAPTER FIVE

ABOUT A.D. 1215, when the English barons bullied King John into signing the Magna Charta, thousands of slim steely-eyed Indians hitched dogs to sledges and began a migration south from the Mackenzie River basin near the Arctic Circle. A century and a half later, about the time that Edward III began to use cannon in English battles against the French knights, the Indian migrants lived in caves along the western shore of Utah's Great Salt Lake. Archaeologists identify the migrants as members of the great Athabascan family and conclude that they were the last major group of red men to explore south from the sub-Arctic. But the folk name they carried into history as the first and most relentless of the West's red horsemen was "Brutal Enemy," or, as the Zuni phrased it, *Apachu*.[1]

The Apachu—the Spanish and Americans spelled it *Apache*— existed by plundering. Their priests instructed youngsters in the details of ambushes that must take place precisely at dawn. Five-and six-year-old boys learned how to steal through grass and over earth embankments so quietly that not even a dog or coyote would sound a warning. Teen-agers learned to garrot sentries silently, to stab sleeping warriors, to collect the women prisoners and the plunder, then to vanish into the dawn mists without having spoken a word. The schedule that the priests and chiefs devised for these raids allowed fifteen minutes from the attack on the sentries to the time the captives were carrying the plunder back toward the dog teams waiting behind a nearby hillock.

Columbus landed the deckload of "sorry hacks" on Haiti while groups of Apache were crossing present day Wyoming, Nebraska and Kansas and heading southwest across Oklahoma toward the Arkansas River's headwaters. Like every pre-horse group that ventured across the high-plains, the Apache depended on dog-power to transport their goods. The need for a wheel did not occur to a red man, probably because of his lack of domesticated animals. His only summertime conveyance was the travois. This vehicle consisted of two long sticks with an oblong of reed or rawhide webbing woven between them. It looked like a toy stretcher that had shrunk at the upper end. The narrow ends of the poles could be attached to a dog's shoulders by thongs; the wide lower ends were dragged along the ground. Supplies were carried on the central webbing and strapped in place. During winter travel, the dogs hauled sledges and the men and women walked on snowshoes.

The mysterious abandonment of Sapawe Pueblo in the upper Rio Grande Valley may identify the approximate time of the Apache's arrival in the Sangre de Cristo Mountains, overlooking the site of Santa Fe. Archaeologic research at the twenty-six-acre site of Sapawe indicates that the pueblo was hastily abandoned about A.D. 1500 and that "most of the possessions" were left in the homes.[2] Raids by the Apache periodically devastated the Zuni, Tehua and other northern pueblo tribes generations before Juan de Oñate's expedition founded New Mexico.

The few Spanish priests who survived missions into the New Mexican mountains before 1650 reported that the Apache homes were so skillfully designed that they blended into the landscape from a distance of one hundred feet. The Apache called his dwelling a *qogan* (now spelled *hogan*). Basically, the hogan is the semi-spherical "igloo" home of the Arctic. During the migration down the Rockies and across the high-plains, the tribes learned to build the igloo semisphere with log side walls, a brush or pole ceiling and a sod roof. Hogans constructed into the side of a hill or in a shadowed gorge provided almost perfect camouflage. The temporary brush and grass shelters the Apache built during their summer-long hunting expeditions were just as cleverly blended into the land contour and vegetation.

The religion evolved by Apache teacher-priests prescribed physical and mental harmony with the forces of primitive Nature. Usen, their god of the Universe, was both male and female and had no fixed habitation. His intermediaries included the sun, lightning, snakes and birds. Formal religious dances and ritualistic appeals to Usen and his intermediaries were held at night inside sacred enclosures built from newly-cut bushes.[3]

Convictions about the superiority of Usen over the Christians' "God and Mary" resisted the missionary efforts of the Spanish, until the Apache learned that the friars would pay handsomely— in trade goods—for supplies of piñon nuts, beaver pelts and blankets. The most valuable blankets needed for the friars' cart-trade to Mexico were woven from wool. Their methods of sheep husbandry, hand looming and dying had been taught to many of the pueblo women. Apache raids on San Juan, Taos and other pueblos yielded herds of sheep and women captives. Then some of the Apache settled into the life of shepherds; by 1650 their dog-trains were travoising bales of blankets as well as sun-dried strips of bison and antelope meats, beaver pelts, and rawhide sacks of piñon nuts down to the fall trade fairs at the northern pueblos. These shepherds also began to grow maize, chili peppers and pumpkins near their canyon villages. The Spanish named these groups *Apachu les navaju,* meaning "The Apache of the cultivated canyons." In time, the *Apachu* prefix was dropped. The mountain shepherd-farmers took the American name, *Navaho.*

The Apache-Navaho were the first Indians west of the Mississippi and north of Mexico to own horses.[4] A few horses and mules may have been stolen before 1680. But the bulk of testimony, both from contemporary records and from modern research, indicates that Popé, shaman-priest of the San Juan pueblo, was indirectly responsible for the birth of the red horseman.

As an orator and organizer, Popé should rank with Pontiac, Tecumseh, Sitting Bull and other great Indian leaders. All through the 1670s, Popé cajoled, harangued and threatened every pueblo and plains and mountain tribe within 250 miles of Santa Fe to join in a massacre of New Mexico's whites. No description of his physical appearance exists. He is reputed to have been a master of mob psychology as well as a wily diplomat. The legend persists that his principal counselor was a Negro slave who escaped from Santa Fe about 1670 and took refuge with the Apache. The ex-slave coached Popé in every furtive move of the campaign and shrewdly fostered the belief that his magic plus the Indian gods would assure victory over "the Christians' God and Mary."

The Apache and Navaho joined the plotters. Every ranch and mission owned a herd of horses. Estimates of the Spanish population in New Mexico in 1680 vary from thirty-five hundred to five thousand. There were at least three thousand horses and possibly six thousand, plus donkeys and mules.

The Apache technique of plundering suggests that groups of Apache-Navaho youngsters loitering on the pueblo and Santa Fe market places would have been a commonplace sight during the summers of 1678 and 1679. They had been assigned to memorize every detail of Spanish horsemanship, and every item of armor and harness displayed on the cavalry patrols. The promptness with which the Apache-Navaho produced troops of horseback warriors between 1681 and 1685 suggests this kind of pre-planning. (Moreover, their first horsemen wore suits of leather armor that faithfully reproduced the metal helmets, vests and leg guards worn by Spanish cavalrymen.[5])

Popé and his confederates agreed on dawn, August 13, 1680, for the opening of the massacre. Fear of Popé's magic was so great that no hint of the plot reached Santa Fe until August 9. Then Popé, quickly learning that two of his messengers had been captured and were probably being tortured into confessions, sent out runners with orders for the slaughter to begin at dawn on the tenth.

Indian servants stole into the ranchers' bedrooms, and garroted and stabbed. Priests were murdered at their sunrise prayers. Herdsmen ganged up on the white foremen and clubbed them to death.

Governor Otermin and 1,020 survivors abandoned Santa Fe on August 21 and marched off toward the White Sands Desert and El Paso. Otermin's report to Mexico City admitted that "more than three hundred eighty" Spanish had been slain during the August 10 massacre and subsequent battles with Popé's warriors. Some students of New Mexico history believe that the dead outnumbered the living and that more than two thousand whites were killed.[6]

The Apache-Navaho plundered the abandoned studs and corrals.[7] Then they encouraged fueds among the Popé allies and thus succeeded in looting pueblo after pueblo. Even Ute Indians from the Colorado highlands obtained horses and booty in New Mexico before 1683.

Robert Cavelier de La Salle, who was shipwrecked on the Texas coast in 1685, explored up the Trinity River valley that summer and visited a village of the Cenis Indians. He found the lodges littered with plunder from New Mexico. "These treasures, as well as their numerous horses, were obtained by the Cenis from their neighbors and allies, the Comanches," Francis Parkman writes in his biography of La Salle.[8] ". . . A party of these wild horsemen was in the village. . . . They invited the French to join them on a raid into New Mexico."

Parkman erred in identifying the Cenis' "wild horsemen" visitors as "Comanches." He did the research for his biography during the 1850s. Then the Indians called "Padoucas" on early Spanish maps were still being identified as "Comanches." But subsequent research has established that the Padoucas were actually the Apache horsemen who terrorized the southern high-plains until 1710–20.

Nevertheless, the meeting between Indian horsemen, laden with New Mexican plunder, and Robert Cavelier de La Salle in the Texas bush in 1685 ilustrates the speed with which the red horsemen progressed into the high-plains after the Popé Revolt. It also serves to focus the Hapsburg-Bourbon enmity between the French and the Spanish, and the influence this enmity had in expanding horseback warfare across the West before 1715.

While Popé plotted the Rio Grande revolt, La Salle rode the first sailing ship (the *Griffin*) down the Great Lakes and established the first French fort in Illinois.[9] During 1682 La Salle explored the Mississippi to its mouth, then claimed the entire region for France. He named it "Louisiana" in honor of Louis XIV. This proclamation intensified the struggle between the royal families of Bourbon and Hapsburg.

Spain based her claim to the Mississippi Valley on De Soto's discovery of the river in 1541. The 1682 proclamation by La Salle, followed by his 1684–85 expedition to colonize Louisiana, occurred during critical years for the Spanish monarchy. Spain had been ruled by the Germanic House of Hapsburg since 1516. But Charles II, a cripple, failed to produce an heir. His closest relatives included a son of Louis XIV of France and the future Emperor Charles VI of Austria-Hungary. Political maneuvers by France and Austria-Hungary to win the Spanish succession for their claimants threatened Europe with a major war.

Charles II lived until 1700. The Hapsburg-Bourbon enmity grew. The Viceroys of Mexico were Hapsburg appointees. So were the governors and military commanders of New Mexico. Thus, between 1681 and 1692, the refugee government of New Mexico at El Paso was not only charged with the task of reconquering the upper Rio Grande Valley but was also responsible for learning about, and frustrating, French trade on the high-plains.

Popé and his Negro counselor were dead when General Diego de Vargas and two hundred soldiers reoccupied Santa Fe in 1692. The old soldier listened impatiently while Indian elders recited details about inter-pueblo feuds during the twelve years, and the cavalry raids by Apache, Navaho and Ute that ravaged eight pueblos.[10] But he gave full attention, and began to bark questions to the interpreters, when the elders reported that a few pieces of French clothing had shown up at the Taos trade fair the fall before. Groups of Apache and Navaho, and occasionally some Ute, still came to the fall trade fairs. Now they rode in, guarded by horsemen armed with guns and clothed from leggings to helmets in stiff suits of bullhide armor. Instead of the dog travois, they led mules and donkeys loaded with the familiar trade goods, plus choice battle plunder. The French coats and vests, the elders insisted, were among battle loot offered for sale by Apache in 1691; the pueblo traders refused to buy them.

During the fall of 1694, a cavalcade of Navaho led in a score of children they claimed to have captured after a battle with "the people-who-wear-their-hair-like-horns" (i.e. the Pawnee). This tribe, the Navaho alleged, lived along the Platte River in Nebraska and boasted of friendship with "bearded white men." The white men, they insisted, must have equipped the Pawnee with guns and horses because, during the summer of 1693, Pawnee horsemen with guns had killed many Navaho horsemen in a high-plains battle. Thus, in 1694, the Navaho gained revenge by massacring a Pawnee village; the children were the only survivors.

During 1695, Apache reported the destruction of one of their villages by eastern plains Indians and the French. In 1697, Navaho traders told of the French and Pawnee killing "hundreds" of Navaho during the summer bison hunt.[11] In 1699 or 1700, trading expeditions of Ute from Colorado showed up at the Taos pueblo trade fair with a party of their allies, the Comanche. Their stories at the fair indicated that the Comanche then occupied territory in Wyoming.[12] During the next decade, the Comanche, armed with French guns and riding horses, launched relentless warfare against both the Apache and Navaho.

Doubtlessly some of the stories told by Apache and Navaho traders were exaggerations or outright lies, devised in the hope of procuring more guns. But the reports of La Salle and other French explorers in the West testify to the existence of Indian horsemen in eastern Texas and Arkansas before 1690, and agree that the Pawnee and Ute had troops of horsemen before 1700 and that the Comanche were horsemen before 1710.

This spread of horses and horsemanship from New Mexico to eastern Texas, Nebraska and Wyoming in thirty years raises questions about the activities of the French *coureurs de bois*. Were they

trading horses as well as guns to the Pawnee, the Ute, the Comanche
and other tribes? Did the Pawnee ride Chickasaw horses and/or
Norman free-breds in their 1693–1700 battles with the Navaho?

The *coureurs de bois* were independent traders who, quite consistently, defied the rules of the New France officials at Quebec.
Pierre Moreau, an infamous *coureur de bois* nicknamed "La Tau-
pine," was trading out of Indian villages in Illinois before 1675.[13]
Several of the survivors of La Salle's last expedition, including two
of the group who assassinated him, "went native" with tribes on
the eastern high-plains; Parkman reports that one of them, an ex-
buccaneer named Heins, joined an Indian war party that obtained
"48 scalps" and "some horses."[14] Scores of French and half-breed
freebooters traded out of Detroit, Vincennes, Kaskaskia and other
French trading posts. Robert Leslie Jones states in "The Old
French-Canadian Horse"[15] that "New France furnished the horses
taken to the western settlements at Detroit and in the Illinois country." By 1759, the horse herds at Detroit were large enough to outfit "a large party of French and Indians not less than 700" sent
down Lake Erie to besiege Fort Pitt.[16]

It would have been a highly profitable undertaking for *coureurs
de bois* to deliver horses to the Pawnee and other tribes on the
central high-plains between 1685 and 1692. Horses *were* available!
The Chickasaw horse was in pasture in Mississippi and western
Tennessee; French traders were in the Chickasaw-Choctaw country before 1700. By 1670, planters in Virginia and Maryland were
grumbling about the nuisance of "wild horses" invading their corn-
fields and enticing their brood-mares. Baron de Lahontan reported
in 1687 that the Seneca tribe of the Iroquois had "plenty of horses"
in their villages fifty to seventy miles east of Niagara Falls. And,
although hazardous, it would have been possible to raft horses up
the Ottawa River from Montreal, then take them across the favorite
portage to North Bay and Lake Huron.[17]

However the Pawnee and other tribes of the Nebraska, Kansas
and Arkansas valleys obtained their horses, they did obtain guns
from the French—and they learned about slave trading from them.

1. The triumph place of the horse, the Laramie Plain, as seen looking west toward the Snowie Range. *Courtesy of the University of Wyoming.*

2. The restoration above, by Charles R. Knight, shows the first horse, fox-sized *Eohippus* (*Hyracotherium*); the one below, by the illustrators of the American Museum, shows *Merychippus,* the first grazer. *Courtesy of the American Museum of Natural History.*

3. Albrecht Dürer's "The White Horse," done in 1505, has become the classic illustration of the Great War Horse of feudalism. The Percheron, Clydesdale, Shire and other draft-horse breeds all descended from Great War Horse strains. *Courtesy of Culver Pictures, Inc.*

4. Frederic Remington, a New Yorker who became one of the most famous illustrators of the Wild West, displayed cynicism about the legends of the conquistadors' "purebred stallions and mares" in this drawing of a bony, "fisheyed" nag. *Courtesy of the Bettmann Archive, Inc.*

5. This drawing of the stallion Louis XIV sent to Quebec in 1665 appears in the *Codex Canadiensis*. Either the animal was an Appaloosa or the artist was familiar with the "spotted horse" family from which the Appaloosa breed developed. *Courtesy of the Public Archives of Canada.*

6. The horses of "New Holland in America" also bore the spectacular black and white markings of the Appaloosa, in the estimation of the artist assigned to illustrate the 1670 to 1680 section of the *Codex Canadiensis*. *Courtesy of the Public Archives of Canada.*

7. Black horses, harnessed in single tandem, pulled two-wheeled carts through the streets of Quebec in 1700. *Courtesy of the Public Archives of Canada.*

8. Oxen and mules first squealed the carreta into the United States in 1598 when Juan de Oñate colonized New Mexico. *Courtesy of the Smithsonian Institution.*

9. William Pynchon, founder of Springfield, Massachusetts, and America's first commercial meat-packer, shares with his son, John, a place as organizer of the first recorded commercial cattle drive in the colonies. Our cowboy legend grew from this. *Courtesy of the Essex Institute, Salem, Massachusetts.*

10. Ireland's gentle Hobby Horse, a seventeenth-century favorite, inspired this toy and gave it its name. This hobby horse, in Boston's Old State House, was imported from England in 1752 for the children of Lieutenant Governor Samuel Phillips. *Photo by Barney Burstein, courtesy of the Bostonian Society.*

11. Boston celebrated Massachusetts' ratification of the U.S. Constitution by parading city and state officials through the city in a boat-shaped wagon drawn, with appropriate symbolism, by a matched team of thirteen gray horses. This diorama shows the vehicle passing the Old State House. *Photo by Barney Burstein, courtesy of the Bostonian Society.*

12. Quarter-milers and semi-wild Chickasaws pulled these 1790 "hot rods" along the roads the Crackers' trail-drives created in the South. *Courtesy of the Library of Congess.*

13. The Apache, superb horsemen, used donkeys as well as mustangs and stolen horses on their deadly raids against ranchers. This drawing by P. Frenzeny, entitled "An Apache Raid," was first published in *Leslie's Illustrated Weekly*, June 19, 1886. *Courtesy of the Joslyn Art Museum, Omaha, Nebraska.*

14. The "waggones" used by "noble ladies" of the fourteenth and fifteenth centuries A.D. in Great Britain hinted the shape the Conestoga and its American contemporaries would take during the eighteenth century. The team of "dapple grays" have the bulk of the Great Horse, hence were "cold blood" ancestors of the Percheron, Clydesdale and other modern draft horses. *Courtesy of the National Archives.*

15. The Conestoga wagon and its six-horse hitch were invented by the Pennsylvania Amish during the 1730s. This "rig" is the larger Pitt-wagon type used to pioneer freight traffic across the Alleghenies between 1790 and 1840. *Courtesy of the Bureau of Public Roads.*

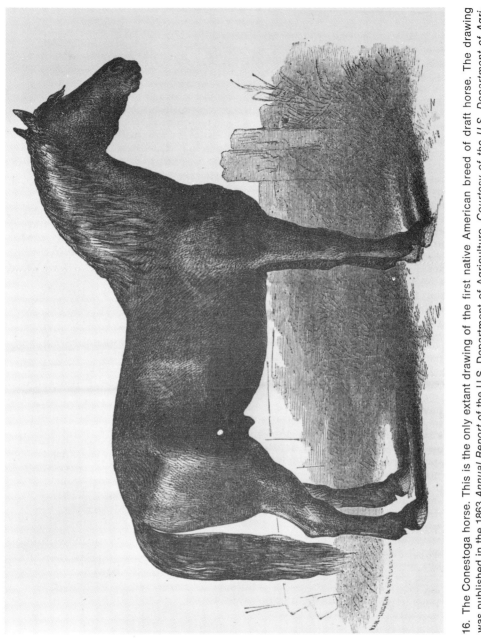

16. The Conestoga horse. This is the only extant drawing of the first native American breed of draft horse. The drawing was published in the 1863 *Annual Report of the U.S. Department of Agriculture. Courtesy of the U.S. Department of Agriculture.*

17. A turnpike inn during the mid-nineteenth century. *Courtesy of the Library of Congress.*

18. Painted-ponies really were painted with petroglyph symbols by some Indian tribes. This drawing, after a sketch by Karl Bodmer, captures the first meeting between Prince Maxmilian of Wied, Bodmer and a chief of the Minatarre outside a fort on the Yellowstone in 1833. *Courtesy of the Joslyn Art Museum, Omaha, Nebraska, from the Northern Natural Gas Company of Omaha Collection.*

19. Graceful, high-stepping Canadians powered traffic over the frozen St. Lawrence past the Falls of Montmorenci in this 1781 painting by James Peachey. *Courtesy of the Public Archives of Canada.*

20. The donkey served as commendably as a shepherd's mount as it did as a pack animal. *Courtesy of the Western History Research Center, University of Wyoming.*

21. Jog-a-bye, baby! Indian babies, like this tiny Navajo, took their airings on pony or mule back. *Courtesy of the Western History Research Center, University of Wyoming.*

22. Donkey and mule power became commonplaces in the American Way as the nineteenth century began. *Courtesy of the Library of Congress.*

23. A mule team powers the spring plow-up on an Alabama farm. *Courtesy of the U.S. Department of Agriculture.*

Oliver La Farge, writing about the Pueblo peoples, commented, "It is a question whether the slave-taking pattern that existed to some extent in the Southwest was not introduced by the Christians."[18] George E. Hyde boldly concluded that "The French officials, while pretending that there was no trade in Indian slaves, were worried about the possible loss of that trade. . . . Bourgmont was given authority in Paris to stop the trade in Padouca slaves and even to confiscate the goods of traders engaged in the slave trade. The traders and officials in Louisiana were infuriated and attempted to sabotage Bourgmont's expedition."[19]

The Council of the Indies in Madrid ruled in 1695 that the Royal Treasury would reimburse New Mexico's government for all funds spent to ransom any prisoner, Indian or white, brought to the pueblos by the Apache, Navaho or any other "gentile" tribe. (The ransomed prisoners were thereupon sold, in indenture, to a rancher, or sent in chain-gangs to work in the Cordillera mines.)

Soon after 1700, the French had economic need for slaves in the Mississippi Valley. Slaves were needed for construction work and farming at Detroit, Kaskaskia, Vincennes, and after 1718 at New Orleans.

There was an inexhaustible market for slaves, too, in the West Indies. Also, slaves could be traded off to the Chickasaw, Choctaw, and other Southeast tribes who could trade them on east, tribe by tribe, for eventual purchase by the Virginians and the Carolinians.

In addition, lead mining got under way near Galena, Illinois, and in southeast Missouri. In 1719, Phillipe Francois Renault left France for "upper Louisiana and Illinois, bringing with him 200 artificers and miners, tools and provisions and even a supply of bricks for a smelting furnace."[20] He began lead-mining operations in the creek valleys west of St. Genevieve, Missouri, and by 1725 was shipping fifteen hundred pounds of refined lead a day downriver to New Orleans.

These slave markets led the French to make agreements with the Pawnee and Kansa, and later with the Ute and Comanche, to buy captives. The Spanish "ransoms" at Santa Fe encouraged the

Apache-Navaho to bring in more captives. Thus the Christians' cash markets in New Mexico and the Mississippi Valley quickened warfare and horsemanship across the high-plains.

So, between 1680 and 1715, Popé's plot of insurrection launched horsemanship among the Indians of the West, and the Hapsburg-Bourbon struggle encouraged it toward the fury that the Americans would inherit after 1803.

QUARTER-MILER AND CRACKER

CHAPTER SIX

THE "SIX HORSES AND A MARE" from Plymouth, England, landed at Jamestown during the summer of 1610 were eaten by the colonists in the late winter starving-time. A herd of seventeen stallions and mares from England arrived during 1611. During 1614, Captain Samuel Argall presented the Virginians with a deckload of Norman, or Breton, horses that had been taken in the sack of Port Royal and Acadia (i.e. Nova Scotia).

The get of these English and French breeds in the swampy James River pastures were not sufficient for the colony's farm and saddle needs. The severe laws imposed by Governor Thomas Dale included the ruling that "No man shall dare to kill or destroy any bull, cow, calfe, mare horfe, colt, goate, swine, cocke, henne, chicken, dogge, turkie or any tame Cattel or Poultry of what Condition soever . . . without leave."[1]

On July 7, 1620, the directors of the Virginia Company, in London, resolved to send "20 mares" plus goats, cattle and "80 asses" to Jamestown. They commissioned Daniel Gookin to purchase and deliver them. Gookin purchased the horses and cattle in Ireland, and this "seems to have been the beginning of an important trade in cattle between Ireland and Virginia."[2] Thus it appears that English, French and Irish horses were inter-breeding on the James Valley range by 1621.

A system that would become as meaningful to cattlemen across the continent as John Pynchon's Springfield roundups and Bay Path trail drive developed during the 1630s along Chesapeake Bay and on the Delmarva Peninsula.³ The salt hay and marsh grass in these areas provided excellent pasture for livestock. Large areas of shore land were enclosed—by building the zigzag rail-and-post fences nicknamed "rattlesnake"—for use as common pasture. The pastures were called "cow-pens." Here, after branding, the livestock were left to breed and forage the year around. Patrol of these cow-pens seems to have been casual. "If fed at all in the Winter," Philip A. Bruce reported, "[the livestock] received only husks of the maize, with a few grains."⁴

Storms and rot soon created passageways through the cow-pen fences, and stallions led their mares and colts off to the woods. In 1670, tobacco planters near Williamsburg complained about invasions by "bands of wild horses." Similar complaints echoed along the Maryland frontier a few years later; in 1694, 1695, 1699 and 1712, the legislators of Maryland adopted laws "to prevent the great multitude of horses in this province." Finally, in 1715, the General Assembly at Anne Arundel Towne (i.e. Annapolis) ruled that "owners of horses, mares, colts and geldings shall keep them within enclosure" between May 1 and November 1, and that any "horse" (i.e. stallion) breaking out of enclosure could, after two notices had been served to the owner, be seized or shot "for trespass." All stallions over eighteen months of age, the act continued, must be continually "fenced or tethered"; breeding mares were not permitted to graze in the woods.⁵

The wild horse bands soon established themselves in the Blue Ridge foothills and on grassy inlets and islands along the Virginia and Carolina coast. They free-bred the ancestors of the Chincoteague ponies and the "tackies"⁶ on which Virginia and Carolina youngsters learned horsemanship throughout the Colonial era. The 1611, 1614 and 1620 importations indicate that these herds must have been crosses of English, French and Irish breeds. There is also reference, in the correspondence of seventeenth-century planters, to the use of Galloways as saddle horses. This indicates early importations of horses from southwestern Scotland. Before 1690, the feral herds were mating with Andalusian horses that either had descended from the sixteenth-century herds of the Spanish explorers and colonizers, or had escaped from St. Augustine and other pioneer settlements in Florida. Thus an all-Europe hybrid developed in the Appalachian highlands of western North Carolina, South Carolina and Georgia. The herds grew fat on the succulent wild pea-vines, buffalo grass and shrubs of the sheltered valleys. Stallions successfully fought off most of the attacks by wildcats and wolves. In the way of all feral horses, the mares produced shaggy swift offspring who grew only thirteen to thirteen and a half hands high and weighed six hundred to seven hundred pounds at maturity.

Meanwhile, tobacco prosperity was beginning to "make the mare go" on straightaway turf tracks in the Virginia low-country. Europe's hunger for tobacco brought wealth to some Virginia planters. The use of Indian slaves, Negro slaves and indentured servants hastened the development of a leisure class. By 1671, in England, Charles II had completed the new palace at Newmarket, was sponsoring a "Spring meet" of horse races on adjacent Newmarket Heath, and had sent agents to France, Italy and Spain to procure "the best of Barbary mares" for his stables.[7] Virginia's tobacco aristocracy accepted the Merry Monarch's dictum of "the new sportsmanship." They created fox-hunt clubs, then laid out race tracks that were exactly one fourth of a mile long from turf starting line to finish post. The first of these courses were in use before 1690 at Malvern Hills and Middle Plantation. The race fans called them quarter-paths.[8]

A straightaway race on a quarter-path called for horses with strong leg muscles and enough nervous alertness to make a "fast start." The purse and side bets collected for a single race by owners of winning quarter-pathers at Malvern Hills and Middle Plantation are reputed to have exceeded $40,000, in gold, hogsheads of cured tobacco, bolts of cloth and silver plate.

The quarter-path race became the most popular horse sport in the Colonial South. Planters' sons began enclosure breeding programs to develop horses with strong legs, a quick getaway, and endurance for a mad gallop over the quarter-path. These ponies, usually thirteen to fourteen hands high, took the name of Quarter-Pathers. A century later the name was clipped to Quarter Horse.

Otherwise, the planters, overseers and tradesmen of Virginia's low-country were so indifferent about the welfare of their horses that, in 1688, the Reverend John Clayton of Jamestown felt obliged to complain about it in a letter to the Royal Society. "There are good stor of Horses," he wrote, "though they are very negligent and careless about the breed. It is true there is a law that no Horse shall be kept stoned [uncastrated] under a certain size, but it is not put in Execution. Such as they are are of good stock, and as cheap or cheaper than in England, worth about five pounds apiece. They never shoe them nor stable them in general: some few Gentlemen may be something more curious but it is very rare: yet they ride pretty sharply, a Planter's Pace is a Proverb, which is a good sharp hard gallop."[9]

A French visitor in Virginia during 1686 expressed indignation at the treatment of horses. "All the care they take of them at the end of a journey," he wrote, "is to unsaddle, feed a little Indian corn and so, all covered with sweat, drive them out into the woods, where they eat what they can find, even though it is freezing."[10]

Nearly a century later, in 1784, travelers who were familiar with horse care and the development of sanitary stabling in Europe criticized the "great negligence" of horses that was apparent throughout eastern Virginia.[11]

The first importation of English "Bred" race horses, between 1730 and 1770, caused a few sportsmen to construct stables, assign slaves as grooms and stable hands, and experiment with growths of "lucerne hay" (i.e. alfalfa) and oats as diet supplements for their stallions and pregnant mares. But racing and race-horse breeding was considered a monopoly for, and by, "the genteel." During 1674, the court at York ruled that it was "contrary to Law for a Labourer to make a race, being a sport only for Gentlemen."[12] And an act passed by the Virginia Assembly during 1713 prohibited "landless men" from operating studs, and limited plantation overseers (i.e. foremen) to ownership of one horse each.

This class system, with the coincidental development of feral horse bands in the Blue Ridge and other sectors of the Appalachian Mountains, seems to have been one of the primary influences in developing the cow-pens into a unique frontier institution. As in New England, shiploads of Scotch and Irish were imported to Jamestown and auctioned off to planters and merchants as indentured servants. Many of them adventured to North Carolina and the "Great Valley" of the Shenandoah after they had worked out their terms of servitude. Others fled to these frontiers during the turmoil of Bacon's Rebellion in 1676. They were joined, soon after 1700, by young German and Swiss immigrants exploring south from the Conestoga-Lancaster-York frontier of Pennsylvania.

The haphazard livestock production of the Virginia tobacco planters and Carolina rice planters, these frontiersmen realized, could not supply the meat, leather and work animals needed in the low-country. Moreover, the plantations on the Bahamas and Bermuda were only a week's sail from Wilmington or Charleston, and they had similar needs.

So the plan for cow-pen communities was born. The first of these log-cabin, corral, and field-crop communities were built near the fall lines of the Savannah and Pee Dee rivers about 1710.

"Having selected a tract, where cane and pea-vine grass grew most luxuriantly," John H. Logan wrote about the cow-pens' inventors, "they erected in the midst of it temporary cabins, and spacious pens. These were used as enclosures in which to collect [the livestock] for the purpose of branding them. . . . At an earlier day, a cow-pen was quite an important institution. It was usually officered with a superintendent, and a corps of sub-agents, all active men, experienced woodsmen and unfailing shots at long or short sight with a rifle. For these a hamlet of cabins was erected, besides the large enclosures for the stock; all of which, with a considerable plat of cleared land in the vicinity for the cultivation of corn, made quite an opening in the woods."[13]

The technique used for stocking a cow-pen was similar to the one used by Texans 175 years later when they herded feral longhorns out of the chaparral for the trail drives to Kansas. A troop of horse-

men, armed with bullwhips and guns, encircled a feral horse or
cattle herd from downwind, then "worked" it toward the cow-pen
and a V-shaped fence that opened, at the point of the V, into a
stout high-walled corral.

The deft skills of sorting and branding followed the roundup.
"Once branded with the owner's mark," James Westfall Thompson
reported, "the cattle were let out again to forage in the woods.
From time to time salt was placed in the neighborhood of the cow-
pen in order to familiarize the stock with the place and accustom
them to having men around. . . . Wild horses were caught in the
same way, and some of the streams in upper South Carolina still
retain names, such as Horse Pen Fork, in reminiscence of this
custom."[14]

Successful operation of a cow-pen obviously depended on superior horsemanship, the use of horses that could "start off like jack-
rabbits" and "stop on a two-bit piece," plus casual skill in the use
of lariats, blacksnake whips, pegging-strings, slipknots and branding irons. Far too little is known about the daily routine, cropping
practices, sports, costumes and traditions at the cow-pens, although
they were an important factor of frontier life in Virginia, the Carolinas and Georgia until the 1770s, when they were relocated in
Tennessee and Kentucky. During the 1820s the development of
American colonies in Texas lured many of their "drivers" and
"bosses" there.

Gentleman travelers and explorers in the early South visited
cow-pen communities and wrote brief descriptions about them in
their diaries. "Set out from Mr. Galphin's to vifit the cowpens, accompanied by that Gentleman, and fome attendants, which are the
greateft curiosity this country affords," William Bartram jotted
into the September 18, 1767, entry of his *Obfervations in a Journey
Up the River Savannah in Georgia*. ". . . In the evening after having
traveled 25 miles thro' much poor piney barren ground, we arrived
at the firft cow pen, being a kind of houfe, or hut, near a good
fpring, in which four or five negroes, with one white man, generally live to look after a number of cattle of various kinds, that

occupy a range of country of fix or ten miles round; the chief employment of thefe herdfmen, as they may be called, is to tend the
calving of the cows, and the foaling of the mares, and to bring thofe
to the pen that ftand moft in need of affiftance and care; feveral of
the inhabitants have two or three of thefe cow pens, at ten miles
diftance from each other, and the cattle are kept in diftinct herds
and feed, both summer and winter, in their refpective walks. Thefe
herdfmen are very dextrous in catching and training the wildeft
horfes, and great profit is made to their mafters by the sale."

But the excitement generated by the French and Indian Wars
and the Revolution held the attention of most writers and authors
of the era. Also our lack of magazine and book publishers during
the cow-pens' heyday frustrated "on the scene" literary expressions such as the later creations of Charles Russell, Andy Adams,
Joseph McCoy and Theodore Roosevelt, which did so much to
validate the environment of the 1865-1900 cattlemen in the trans-
Mississippi West.

James Westfall Thompson compared the South's cow-pen communities to "Miles City and Ogalalla in the palmy days of the
western cow country."[15] Horse thieves and cattle thieves mingled
there with honest men. Some of the pens contained two thousand
cattle at a time, as many hogs and hundreds of horses. All of the
stock was branded with the cow-pen's insignia; colts were "altered" into geldings and bull calves into oxen. Lewis C. Gray consistently refers to the cow-pen crews as "cowboys," and contends
that the term was widely used in the Southern mountains before
1750.[16] The Spanish term *cimmarones* ("the wild ones") became a
routine cow-pen term for unbranded animals. There were quarter-
path races, shooting matches, trick-roping and whip-cracking demonstrations and most of the other cowboy "show-offs" that, between
1880 and 1910, developed into the West's cowboy exhibition and
rodeo. Thompson justly concluded that "the ranches and cowboys
of the nineteenth century were the counterpart of the cow-pens and
cow-drivers of the eighteenth century."[17]

One tool in which the cow-pen horsemen specialized was the

blacksnake whip. It had a hardwood handle, preferably cured hickory, about three feet long and two inches in circumference. A braid of leather ten to fifteen feet long was lashed to the tip of the handle by linen cord. At the opposite end of the braid, a sliver of soft rawhide or boot leather, five to six inches long, was woven on. This tip piece was the "popper."

A cow-pen horseman used his blacksnake whip in more ways than the "Old West" cowboy later used his six-shooter—and some of the uses were fatal. The secret was in the popper. When a horseman whirled the whip braid above his head, then flicked it straight out with a sudden jerk of his wrist, the popper moved so rapidly through an arc that it broke the sound barrier[18] and made a noise as loud as a rifle shot. Good whipmen could—and still can—behead a rattlesnake or a copperhead at ten to twelve feet, trip a charging bull, or turn the leaders of a herd of stampeding livestock. Snapping a cheroot or pipe out of a friend's lips, without touching his lips or nose, at "five paces" was a favorite show-off.

Before 1715, Charleston buyers were shipping horses, beef, leather and other by-products from the cow-pens to the West Indies. During 1722, Scotch-Irish and Germans built the first corrals and cow-pen cabins in the Georgia highlands. Horses, cattle and pigs reproduced so healthily in the upland pastures that cow-pen owners decided to experiment with trail drives to Salem and Wilmington, North Carolina. During the 1740s, drives were extended to Wake Courthouse and Warrenton, near the Virginia line. Through the 1750s and 1760s, drives of more than two thousand horses and cattle, guarded by whip-cracking horsemen, were normal midsummer traffic beside the cart ruts that connected Baltimore, New York, Philadelphia and Boston. These drives created the first through trails between the South and the North.

Hullooing and whip-cracking through Augusta, Camden, Elizabethtown, Wake Courthouse and Richmond, the drovers won a distinctive nickname from the townspeople. It banged from their whips' poppers whenever they "horsed it up a bit" during the rides along Main Street. Barmaids and tradesmen began to call them "Crackers."

The title outlived the cow-pen era. Dr. Johann David Schopf, a German physician stationed with the British troops in New York City, received permission in 1783 to make a tour of the new "American Confederation." In his book about the journey he writes: "The population in the back parts of South Carolina has for some time been considerably increasing through emigrations from the northern states. The most remote inhabitants, who in Pensylvania [sic] and Virginia are called 'Back-Wood-Men' are here denominated 'Crackers' . . . from the noise, it is said, which they make with their whips when they come to town with their teams."[19]

Thus between 1685 and 1725 two vital factors of American horsemanship evolved in the colonial South. The quarter-mile race of Virginia would follow the frontier to Kentucky, Illinois and Texas and eventually produce the great Quarter Horse. The cow-pen skills of the Cracker would cross the mountains to Tennessee and Kentucky, travel on to Texas, and, after a forty-year blending with the customs and costumes of Mexico's *vaquero*, would "head 'em north" up the Chisholm Trail.

THE CONESTOGANS

CHAPTER SEVEN

A NEW TYPE OF freight wagon, a new breed of horse, and the bank-barn all appeared in a creek valley on the frontier of Penn's Sylvania between 1700 and 1730. The wagon, with only moderate change in shape, became one of our most beloved symbols of initiative and pioneer daring. The horse, our first native drafter, created legends and folk sayings as he conquered the Allegheny barrier, then maintained our commerce to and from the "New West." The bank-barn became the control center for the family farm, hence for our system of diversified agriculture.

William Penn planned his colony, located between the vague boundaries of Maryland and New Jersey, as a haven for small landowners. Most of the first shiploads of settlers to Penn's Sylvania in the 1680s were farmers. They brought sacks of clover seed and grains in order to develop superior forage for their deckloads of horses, cattle and sheep. They welcomed instruction in local biology, weather patterns and soil peculiarities from the Swedes, Dutch and Finns who had been farming in the Delaware River valley since 1643. Within two years the new Pennsylvanians were marketing horses and sawed lumber in the Barbados. By 1690, their dairies and diversified farms were producing export surpluses of cheese, butter, beef and pork products.

The colony's farm rules were strict. All livestock had to be earmarked, or branded, before it was six months old; unless the mark was registered with the county clerk, the animals were "taken up as estray."[1] Both the croplands and the clovered pastureland were enclosed by stone or post-and-board fences. Horses and cattle that showed a tendency for "fence leaping" were chastened by leather hobble-thongs or long wooden neck-yokes. The Quaker farmers stored their harvests of hay and straw in neat stacks, then covered them with wood or thatch roofs, so that the stock could obtain both feed and shelter through the winter.

Convictions about agricultural self-sufficiency persuaded William Penn and his backers to recruit colonists from Germany, Switzerland and the North Sea Lowlands, where civil wars and religious persecution had created an age of terror and famine. The first group, including thirteen families of Mennonites from the deltaland of the Rhine River, landed at Philadelphia on October 6, 1683. They settled on a fifteen-thousand-acre tract six miles west and established the settlement of Germantown. Similar migrations from Bohemia, the Palatine, Alsace-Lorraine, and Switzerland continued for ninety years; in 1775 there were more than 100,000 "Pennsylvania Germans."[2]

These refugees were descendants of the farmers who invented grain-harvesting machines before A.D. 300, bred up the Great War Horse, and perfected the system of operating a farm program of varied crops and several species of domestic animals from a barn control center. Their system of agricultural production took the name of *diversified farming*. In contrast to the one-crop agriculture of the Virginia tobacco planters and the Carolina rice planters, diversified farming permitted greater self-sufficiency, better control of soil fertility, and superior animal husbandry—plus various social attributes that can be summarized as "democratic behavior."

The introduction of Europe's finest system of diversified farming to the Pennsylvania backcountry between 1683 and 1730 was one of the most meaningful events in our colonial history. Diversification became the favorite system for farmers north of the Potomac and Ohio river valleys. The one-crop system, abjectly dependent on slave labor, imported supplies and soil-plundering, continued to dominate the South. Our Civil War was, primarily, a struggle between the two farming techniques.

In 1709 Hans Herr and Martin Kendig paid William Penn's agents five hundred pounds for ten thousand acres on the north side of Pequa Creek in Lancaster County.[3] Hundreds of converts to the Amish-Mennonite faith trekked into this area during the next decades. Its hills and creek valleys were shadowed by oak, maple and other hardwood forests. Household effects had to be carried pack-a-back or roped on their cattle and horses. The appeal of the area for the Amish puzzled Penn's agents until the Amish explained that "hardwood forests grow this big only on land rich in limestone; the soil will produce fine crops."

As soon as he had cleared forest space for a first stumpland crop and a building site, a Lancaster County pioneer began stacking movable stones and "cobblers" at the site he had selected for his barn. Then he hewed his finest hardwood logs into beam timbers and boards, while his wife and children whittled cuttings from hemlock and white-pine trees into shingles.

"The German was sure to build a large, fine barn before he built any dwelling house for himself except a rude log cabin," James Westfall Thompson reported. "This German, or Swiss, 'bank' barn was—and still is—the [best] type of barn known. New England and Virginia created the plain 'shed' barn, a simple structure that was sometimes connected with the house by a woodshed or other outhouse. The Dutch barn in New York and northern New Jersey was an immense improvement upon this. It was a spacious structure with ample mows and stalls. The German bank-barn was like neither of these. Its basement was walled against a hill, and was used as a stable for horses, cattle, sheep and even hogs. The threshing floor was above the basement with mows on either hand; occasionally there were double decker floors. A driveway led up to the threshing floor on the second story, and thence around the barn. Through trapdoors in the floor, the corn or other feed could be dropped from the wagons directly into the stalls below. Finally, the Pennsylvania German farmer took the precaution of attaching ventilators made of chimney pots to his barn. This device survives today and has been universally imitated."[4]

The Germans called this type of barn a "Holzsteiner" because it was built from wood (*Holz*) and stone (*Stein*). Early barns on the Pennsylvania frontier were thatched with bundles of rye straw, tied to the roof laths with strips of bark or bands of twisted straw.[5]

Scores of these bank-barns rose in the stump-pocked fields of the Conestoga Creek valley, near the site of the city of Lancaster. They served as each farm's storage center, livestock shelter and animal nursery. The straw bedding and dung from the stall floors were piled outdoors for curing. During late winter, all of it was loaded on carts, hauled out to fields that had been selected for the spring grain plantings, and hand-spread. Blended with soil particles by the rains and plowing, this compost fertilized the soil.

But the barn stalls were more than a collection center for fertilizer. "They keep their horses and cattle as warm as possible in the winter," the astute Dr. Benjamin Rush said of the Pennsylvania German farmers of 1787, "by which means they save a great deal of their hay and grain; for these animals when cold eat much more than when they are in a more comfortable situation."[6]

Similar shrewdness produced a multitude of products in the farm kitchens. Cow milk was skimmed, churned, processed into salt and sweet butters and a half-dozen varieties of cheese and clabber. The whey remaining, mixed with food scraps, was noisily welcomed by the pigs. Also, whey mixed with bull blood and lard produced a commendable dark red paint. Other *Frau*-magic produced hickory-smoked hams, bacon and loins, aromatic links of braunschweiger, Lebanon bologna and "summer" sausage, blocks of headcheese, and pans of scrapple, an ambrosia conjured from bits of pork and corn meal.

This wealth of harvest and home processing needed a market for its surpluses. But no waterways connected the Conestoga settlements with Philadelphia, and the adjacent Susquehanna River had too many rapids and snags for round-trip freight traffic with Baltimore and the other trade centers on Chesapeake Bay. The logical solution was construction of a road across the sixty miles of forest, slate cliffs and swamp that separated Conestoga Creek valley from Philadelphia.

In 1718, the Provincial Council in session at Philadelphia re-

ceived "A Peticion of several of the Inhabitants of & near Conestogoe setting forth the Great necessity of a Road to be laid out
from Conestogoe to Thomas Moores and Brandywine."[7] The road
was not built until 1733. These two dates are the best clues extant
for approximating the first appearances of the Conestoga horse
and the Conestoga wagon.

The breeding, or selection, program that produced the first
Conestoga horse teams is as much of a mystery as the development
of the Chickasaw horse. The heritage of the Germanic pioneers of
"Conestogoe" urged them to seek stallions and mares comparable
to the Great War Horse. The Hollanders had imported drafters
from Flanders during the forty years of their rule at Nieuw
Netherlandes (i.e. New York); the first Quaker farmers in the
Delaware Valley herded some of them home across New Jersey.
The folk tale persists, too, that during the 1680s William Penn
shipped a deckload of Great War Horses into Philadelphia.

By 1710, Amish frontiersmen had discovered the plateau route
to Virginia's Shenandoah Valley and were building Holzsteiner
barns near the sites of Charles Town and Harper's Ferry. Some of
them developed cow-pens. They knew the problems of their Conestoga cousins and brothers, so gave them priority in bidding for
any big-barreled stallions or mares among the feral Florida-Vir-
ginia hybrids their Cracker crews herded in from the mountains.

The splendid drafters from the Conestoga barns and the wagons
they drew soon won praise from Philadelphians. A tavern named
"The Sign of the Conestogoe Wagon" began advertising in Ben
Franklin's *Pennsylvania Gazette* on February 5, 1750. "The
Oeconomy of the Germans," Lewis Evans reported in 1753, "has
taught us the method of bringing produce to market from the re-
motest part at a small expense. Every German farmer in our
Province almost has a Waggon of his own. . . . In the Spring and
Fall of the year, when it is here a vacation from farming, they load
their Waggon and furnish themselves with beasts and provender
for the Journey. The Waggon is their Bed, their Inn, their everything. Many of them will come 150 miles without spending one
shilling."[8]

The most thorough description of the Conestoga horse was, like the Livingston and Cooper descriptions of the Narragansett Pacer, a memoriam. It was written during 1863 by John Strohm, a scholarly farmer of New Providence, Pennsylvania. The United States Commissioner of Agriculture agreed to publish it in his *Agricultural Report* for that year.[9]

"I came to the conclusion," John Strohm wrote, "that the Conestoga Horse is not a distinct species or strain of that noble quadruped, but belongs to a class that has attained a great degree of efficiency for a particular purpose; and that the appellation by which this class is so widely known denotes superior excellence in the class of draft horses, although the individuals composing it may have sprung from a crossing or mixture of various breeds or families.

"This frugal people [i.e. the Amish]," he explained, "always having an eye to economy and utility, kept neither males nor females for the exclusive purpose of breedings. Sometimes a stud horse was absolved from labor during the last two months of spring and the first of the summer season; but at the expiration of that term, he was put to the harness again and compelled to do his share of the labor which the interest of his proprietor required. So with the mare; she was generally worked until within a few weeks of foaling. . . . In about a week after the mare was foaled, she was again put to the harness to perform her ordinary share of labor.

"The colt was permitted to run with its dam until about three months old; it was then weaned and turned to pasture, generally receiving a little oats once or twice a day for a month or longer. Judicious farmers advised the feeding of a small quantity of oats daily during the first winter. . . . The second winter they require no grain and, unless regularly and very sparingly fed, are considered better without it. At about two and a half years old they were usually 'bridle broken' and sometimes lightly worked for awhile in the autumn; but during the ensuing winter they were commonly suffered to run idle, being seldom regularly worked until fully three years old.

"Under this system of breeding, by selecting their best stock for the purpose, the [horses] of the Conestoga valley arrived at a degree of beauty and perfection seldom found in any other country, and much surpassing the original stock."

The Conestoga horses first won the attention of Philadelphians because of the dazzling hooded "Waggons" they drew. These wagon bodies were painted a bright "Prussian" blue; the wheels were scarlet; a white linen or hemp hood arced over the body. The average wagon was sixteen feet long and boat-shaped. The floor of the body tilted down toward the center from each end, in order to keep its freight from shifting on steep hills or in ruts. Because of ruts, rocks and stream fordings, the wheels were huge, with rims two and a half to three inches wide and an inch thick. The rear wheels, higher than the front ones, were five to five and a half feet tall.[10]

William Douglass, writing in 1749, estimated that seven thousand of the wagons were in use throughout Pennsylvania by that time.[11]

No effort to identify the wagon's inventor was ever recorded. The vehicle was similar to freight and produce wagons that teams of Great Horse drafters hauled along the Rhine Valley and over trans-Alpine and Lowlands roads during the Middle Ages. Presumably a Conestoga blacksmith fashioned the first ones from homeland memories, with a Mennonite preacher as his relentless coach and a group of bearded farmers as final inspectors. The mammoth wheels and the tilt of the floor were shrewd adaptations to overcome the natural hazards on "the road from Conestogoe."

A six-horse team became the standard "hitch" for a Conestoga wagon. The front horses, known as the "leads," were the lightest and liveliest. The middle horses were called the "swings." The "wheelhorses," largest and strongest of all, paced at the rear and provided most of the power on the hills. A single rein, called the "jerk line," was attached to the near lead-horse. A short tug of the rein turned the team to the right; a long pull turned it to the left. With these came the driver's shout of "Gee" for a right turn, "Haw" for a left turn, "Ho" for stop, and "Gee-up" for start.

An arch of four bells, identical in size and tone, hung above each horse's mane. The smallest soprano bells were on the "leads." Medium-sized tenor bells hung over the "swings." Large basso janglers formed the arch over each of the "wheelhorses." These, plus bearskin and red braid "foofaraw," made the Conestoga rig as spectacular as a circus wagon. (Our gaily-painted circus wagons, bedecked with pompoms and red trimming and led by a blaring steam calliope, did not appear until after the Civil War. The red-white-and-blue Conestoga wagon and its belled team, "half covered with heavy bear-skins, or decorated with gaudily fringed housings," may have been the prototype of the circus wagons. Phineas T. Barnum, the circus pioneer, was born in Bethel, Connecticut, in 1810, and grew up while Conestoga and Pitt wagons were still the wagon-wonder of the New World.)

When testy Major General Edward Braddock, during the spring of 1755, ordered fourteen hundred British regulars and seven hundred Colonials across the Alleghenies to capture the French forts at the headwaters of the Ohio River and at Niagara Falls, more than 150 Conestoga wagons carried the expedition's baggage. One of the wagonmen was Daniel Boone, a youngster from Reading, Pennsylvania. Boone obtained his first impressions of the West on this journey. Another wagonman was Daniel Morgan, the Jerseyman who later commanded the regiment of riflemen that played such a critical role at the Battle of Saratoga. The road that Lieutenant Colonel George Washington and his advance guard cut and graded through the Allegheny forests that spring and summer was our first wagon route across the Alleghenies. All of the wagons were abandoned after the French and Indian ambush at Monongahela crossing.

Throughout the American Revolution, red-white-and-blue Conestoga wagons and their teams hauled commissary and artillery supplies. But their glory days came after 1790 on the new turnpikes to Pittsburgh and the West. The size of the wagons was increased. Each carried between three and four tons. Then the "Pitt wagons," as they were nicknamed, traveled in trains of twenty to thirty vehicles. They covered fifteen to twenty miles a day and averaged a round trip a month between Philadelphia and Pittsburgh.[12] During 1817, Morris Birbeck reported from Pittsburgh that "About 12,000 waggons passed between Baltimore and Philadelphia and this place in the last year."

The musical jangle of the Conestoga wagon bells is reputed to be the origin of the pioneer American boast, "to be there with bells on." The nickname "stogie" for a cigar came from the Conestoga wagon drivers' practice of earning a little more "jingle stuff" by peddling long black "Kentucky burley" cigars along their routes.

An ancient English tune became a favorite for humming during the hauls through the mountains. Perhaps the wagonmen adopted it as a sort of Conestoga theme song because its cadence matched the hoofbeats of their horses, the gay jangle of the harness bells, and the echoes tinkling back from granite cliffs. Sometime between 1800 and 1840, probably during song-fests at taverns, forgotten wagonmen composed a dozen stanzas for the tune. So "On Top of Old Smoky" became an all-time "pop" for our folk singers. The hoofbeats and tinkling bells still echo when we sing,

> "It's a-rainin', it's a-hailin',
> The moon gives no light.
> Your horses can't travel
> This dark lonesome night."[13]

It was almost inevitable, then, that sometime between 1820 and 1830 an Ohio or western Pennsylvania wainwright would redesign the Conestoga wagon to a slimmer body for use as a family vehicle on trans-prairie migrations toward the "promised lands" of Indiana, Michigan and Illinois. Perhaps he was a newly converted Methodist and considered red wheels and a blue body to be "lustful and ungodly," or he may have worried about camouflage colors that would blend with prairie tones and provide a bit more protection against Indian attack. Anyway, he painted his prairie model of the Conestoga in dull browns and greens. That was the first prairie schooner.

Thus, between 1730 and 1830, Conestoga horses and Conestoga wagons pioneered transportation to and from the West, and became symbols of American opportunity and individual freedom. Did their red-white-and-blue panorama have subtle influence on the color design of our Stars and Stripes, too?

THE ROAD-MAKERS

CHAPTER EIGHT

EVEN IN PROGRESSIVE Pennsylvania, road construction lagged for decades after the introduction of the Conestogans' wagon-hitch. This was due, as Stevenson W. Fletcher diagnosed it, to "the policy of placing responsibility for building and maintaining roads solely on local governments. . . . Few streams were bridged; fords were difficult and often dangerous; ferries, which were privately owned, were few and crude. Rails were piled by the roadside for use in prying wagons out of the mud. . . . A teamster who was stalled in the mud might have to wade in and unhitch his team and spend the night by the side of the road until assistance came."[1]

The other colonies were even more isolated or, to coin a phrase, trail-confined. The best transportation was by boat. But all of the rivers ran west-to-east off the mountain ranges. This limited most inter-colony travel to an ocean voyage, a horseback journey, or walking. All were perilous.

Oxcarts created local tracks down to riversides. There farm crops and handicrafts could be transferred to a raft, an ark or a Durham boat. The spring thaws and late fall rains created floodwaters. Boats attempted to run downstream on these through the rapids, chutes and snags.

The trappers, hunters, Indian traders and frontiersmen used trains of shaggy horses, usually only thirteen hands high and hitched in tandem, to pack their goods in and out of the wilderness. A horse could carry one hundred and eighty to two hundred pounds on its pack saddle. Freight rates were exorbitant. In 1784 the pack-horse fee for delivering a ton of trade goods or household equipment from eastern Pennsylvania to the new village of Erie on Lake Erie was $249.[2]

"The acquisition of the indispensable articles of salt, iron, steel and castings presented great difficulties to the first settlers of the western country," Joseph Doddridge wrote in 1824. "Every family collected what peltry and fur they could obtain throughout the year for the purpose of sending them over the mountains for barter. In the fall of the year, after seeding time, every family formed an association with some of their neighbors for starting the little caravan. A master driver was selected from among them, who was to be assisted by one or more young men and sometimes a boy or two. The horses were fitted with pack-saddles, to the latter part of which was fastened a pair of hobbles made of hickory withes. A bell and collar ornamented their necks. The bags provided for the conveyance of the salt was filled [sic] with feed for the horses; on the journey a part of this feed was left at convenient stages on the way down to support the return of the caravan. Large wallets, well filled with bread, jerk, boiled ham and cheese furnished provisions. At night, after feeding, the horses were hobbled and the bells opened [i.e. unstuffed]."[3]

Planters, preachers and government officials rode over the pack-pony trails on Narragansetts, Chickasaws or Galloways. Most of their horses were between fourteen and fifteen hands high and weighed about one thousand pounds. Luggage was limited to the few items that could be forced into their saddlebags alongside food supplies and a reserve supply of lead, wadding and gunpowder for the musket or pistol. A horseback journey between New York and Boston in 1750 took twelve days, an average of seventeen miles a day. Travelers were such a rarity in some areas that the courts ordered innkeepers to notify the local constable whenever a person applied for lodging.

Except for the red-white-and-blue Conestogas on Philadelphia–Susquehanna Valley lanes, wagons were a rarity. During the spring of 1755, General Braddock sent agents into Virginia and Maryland to lease wagons for the baggage train of the expedition against Forts Duquesne and Niagara. They rode back to the army's camp on the Potomac with the news that only twenty-five wagons fit for the wilderness journey existed in all of Virginia and Maryland. In desperation, Braddock appealed to Benjamin Franklin, newly appointed Postmaster General for the Northern Colonies. Franklin hurriedly printed handbills, in which he personally guaranteed that "fair wages" would be paid, and sent them via Post Riders to be displayed at every church, store and blacksmith shop in the Conestoga country. Within two weeks, Braddock had 155 fully equipped Conestoga wagons at the camp.

A survey taken in 1761 indicated that only eighteen families in Pennsylvania owned carriages.[4] The sedan chair, carried on poles by four footmen (i.e. runners), was the only conveyance vaguely resembling a public transportation vehicle, and not more than twenty-five of them existed in the thirteen colonies.

Already famous as editor of the *Pennsylvania Gazette* and as the puckish author of *Poor Richard's Almanac*, Ben Franklin in 1754 received King George II's appointment as Postmaster General for the North. At the time he secured the wagons for the Braddock expedition, he was reorganizing the haphazard system for inter-colony mail deliveries. He recruited a corps of young horsemen to serve as Post Riders, and announced that it would maintain year-round deliveries between Philadelphia and Boston. The schedule, he promised, would average forty miles a day, requiring a week for the ride from the west bank of the Delaware to the south bank of the Charles.

The announcement seemed as impossible a boast to the Colonials as the Russell-Majors-Waddell promise of two hundred miles a day by Pony Express riders did to Californians in 1860. But, like the Pony Express, the Post Riders held to schedule.

Next, Franklin began a campaign to improve the inter-colony trails. The threat of French and Indian invasions in Pennsylvania, New Jersey, New York and New England during 1755–56 and the difficulties experienced in delivering supplies to the New York and St. Lawrence Valley campaigns against the French during 1756–59 sustained his arguments. Soon after word reached Philadelphia that the Treaty of Paris had been signed on February 10, 1763, and the French and Indian Wars were over, Franklin decided on a maneuver that would publicize the "better roads" campaign and —since postal fees were based on a mileage rate—simplify the Post Riders' bookkeeping.

During the summer of 1763, Franklin and his daughter, Sally, drove a gig, or perhaps a one-horse chaise, from New York City to Boston. The vehicle is reputed to have been equipped with a hardwood slat attached to one of the wheel-rims. Each time the wheel turned, the slat clacked against an iron peg projecting from the carriage body. Franklin had measured the circumference of the wheel and figured out the number of clacks per mile. He drove the horse. Sally counted the clacks, then shrilled "Ho!" at the end of each mile. At this signal Franklin stopped the horse, climbed down, and pulled a stake from the bundle beneath the seat. He scratched Roman numerals and capital letters on the stake, jammed it into the dirt at the roadside, and drove on.

Miles behind the carriage, a cart loaded with engraved slabs of stone creaked along the trail. When the cart reached one of the stakes, the teamster and his helper unloaded the proper slab, carried it over to the stake and dug a hole. Tamped upright in the hole, with its semispherical top eighteen inches above the ground, the stone displayed the same numerals and letters that Franklin had scratched on the stake. A typical one told travelers:

N.H.
XVI
M

It indicated that the stone stood "to the clack" sixteen miles from New Haven.

With the final stone set up, probably on Boston Common, America had its first set of highway markers. Franklin's installation of the labeled stone posts, plus his organization of the Post Riders, gave the New York–Boston throughway the name it still bears: the Boston Post Road.[5]

All along the way Franklin also harangued New York, Connecticut, Rhode Island and Massachusetts officials into agreement on a system of highway improvements and maintenance. Some towns began to permit farmers to work off annual taxes by removing stumps and cobbles from the right-of-way, or laying corduroys of logs across boggy sections, or building bridges over creeks. Other communities organized convicts and "public offenders" into chain-gangs for work on road construction. Although the result was a hazardous strip of quagmire, hub-deep ruts, and steep hills, it enabled the use of carriages, freight wagons and the first "publick conveyances" between New England and New York City.

The box wagons that began offering these "accommodations" were advertised as "coaches." The European coach of the 1760s was an enclosed private carriage. The vehicle was invented by, or for, the princelings and nobility of central Europe sometime between 1350 and 1400. It presumably appeared first in the village of Kocsi (i.e. Kitsee) in Hungary and took its name from the village. By 1600 it was being copied in England.[6] Each European coach seated four passengers, and had a driver's seat perched above the front wheels. The body of the vehicle was usually decorated with carvings of lions or griffins and the owner's coat of arms.

The first American coaches were springless box wagons. When they traveled over level countryside, the passengers could ride on wooden cross planks doweled between the sideboards of the box. But on uphill pulls, or across bogs, everybody walked—and often helped to push the coach.

Our first scheduled coach service seems to have been a weekly trip started by the Moravians of Bethlehem, Pennsylvania, in 1742 to deliver mail and travelers to and from Philadelphia. In 1756, a John Butler established a line between Philadelphia and New York that took three days for the hundred-mile journey and included six ferryboat rides. An "express coach" service between

Philadelphia and New York began biweekly service during the 1760s. It used four-horse teams, maintained a schedule of forty-eight hours through most of the year, and called its vehicles "The Flying Machines."

During the 1760s, too, initial efforts were made to surface the principal streets and market places of cities with cobblestone or brick paving. Benjamin Franklin preferred plank highways and promoted them; a few short stretches were laid along waterfronts and in the vicinity of iron furnaces and shipyards. These experiments, all manifestations of an oncoming horse-and-wagon age, influenced the blacksmith and wainwright professions.

Before 1750, few American horses were shod. Few blacksmiths knew how to trim hooves, hammer out the proper size and shape of horseshoes and fit them. But the new cobblestone and brick paving, plank roads and "corduroys" caused the same wear and splintering on the hooves of colonial drafters and saddlers that the stone "Vias" had inflicted on the Romans' mail-carrier mounts. So the regime of the blacksmith shop as the town center for horsemen developed during the decade preceding the Revolution.

Post roads and paving on city streets naturally encouraged the sale of horse-drawn vehicles. Scores of wainwright shops opened. These usually began as a sideline production at the blacksmith shops, then, as the Wagon Age clattered in, grew into separate industries that employed wheelwrights, turners, whitesmiths, harnessmakers, and similar parts specialists.

Little is known about the French-Canadian influences that caused "shays," "buggies" and "chariots" to become popular in New England after 1760. The Yankees called a two-wheeled cart with a high-backed seat a "shay"; the French word for "chair" is *chaise*. A one-seat carriage, with four wheels, was known as a "buggy"; the French word *bouger* means "to move about." Large carriages with two seats (an unmistakable status symbol of the aristocrat) took the Yankee name "chariot"; the French word *chariot* means "car."

The New Englanders had borne the brunt of wars with New

France and French-inspired Indian raids for 140 years. When they brought plunder home from the final conquest of the St. Lawrence valley in 1760, they may have borrowed the designs of Quebec and Montreal vehicles and their names, too.

There are records about the brisk trade in horses that developed between New England and Canada after 1760. Thousands of heavy draft horses from Kamouraska and other communities east of Quebec, plus trotters from Montreal and natural pacers from Nova Scotia, were purchased by New Englanders, who herded them from the Montreal and Quebec market places to studs and jockey-ship loading pens in Rhode Island and Connecticut. These trail drives took place during the winter months so that the herds could be driven over the ice. The principal trail used Lake Champlain through the Fort Ticonderoga narrows to the vicinity of Whitehall, New York. There the New York fork led over the divide to the Hudson Valley; the east fork was blazed through the Green Mountains to the Connecticut Valley and its cattle trails to Springfield, Hartford or Rhode Island. There is evidence that small herds of Narragansett Pacers were driven north from Rhode Island to the St. Lawrence Valley and sold to the new British army posts.

These horse drives had direct influences on the New England economy and at least one direct influence on our Revolution. One of the most prominent jockeys in the 1763–73 trade was Benedict Arnold, a native of Norwich, Connecticut. Masterful research of the Revolution's 1775–77 campaigns led Kenneth Roberts to the conclusion that Arnold's experiences during the 1763–73 jockey-drives provided Arnold with details of the "North Country" that contributed mightily to his campaign strategies during 1775 and 1776 at Quebec, Montreal and Valcour Island, and to the American victories at Stanwix and Saratoga.[7]

The influences of Canadian horse imports on the growing stagecoach, carriage and freight-wagon traffic in New England have never been adequately researched. Available testimony indicates that crossbreeds of Kamouraska drafters, Narragansett Pacers and Anglo-Irish hybrids were the teams preferred for powering the hundreds of stagecoach lines established in New England between

1783 and 1800. Draft horses used for industrial work profited from similar hybridization.[8] Crossbreeding with Canadian drafters prevailed as far south as New Jersey during the 1820s and 1830s. Canadian stallions are also believed to have been the foundation sires for a superior breed, or type, of drafter that became popular in Vermont and New Hampshire between 1790 and 1830. These impacts on American carriage, coach and freight horses of the Northeast between 1760 and 1830 could have been achieved, of course, by twenty or twenty-five stallions. At least ninety per cent of the Canadian horses trailed south by Benedict Arnold and the other 1763–73 jockeys were shipped on to the "horse killer" sugar plantations and mills in the West Indies.

A second significant hybridization of quarter-path racers, Galloways, cow-pen ferals and imported English "Breds" was under way in Virginia. The Stuart kings' fascination for horse-racing established it as a fashionable British institution. Three horses of Barb, Arab or crossed parentage proved unique superiority as English race-horse sires. They were named Darley Arabian, Byerly Turk and Godolphin Barb. Their colts, bred on both African and English mares, were such consistent winners that sportsmen began to regard them as a distinct breed. By 1720, the Darley, Byerly and Godolphin descendants were being praised, and promoted, as the English "Breds." The "Breds" performed best as gallopers, under saddle, in races around a circular track a mile long. Early match-races were four to twenty miles long, and run in one-mile "heats."

The first "Bred" imported to Virginia is reputed to have been a stallion named Bulle Rock. Little is known about the animal, or his get. Most saddle-race historians allege he was "got by the Darley Arabian: Byerly Turk: Lyster Turk out of a natural Arabian mare" about 1718 and, in 1730, was imported to a Hanover, Virginia, plantation owned by a Samuel Gist.[9] At least six more "Breds" were imported to Virginia before 1753, and a total of thirty-seven before 1775. Meanwhile, circular race tracks were built outside Williamsburg, Gloucester, Leeds and Fredericksburg.

"The influence of these importations was not merely to improve the race horse," Fairfax Harrison contended. "They were marvelous tonic also upon the general standard of the Virginia horse. From having been a spirited pony, he now became a respectable cavalry remount." This "hot blood" strain in the horses ridden by the Virginia Dragoons, under the command of "Light Horse Harry" Lee, during the Revolution was largely responsible "for its efficiency . . . at once the scourge and terror of the enemy," according to Harrison.[10]

Virginia "Breds" . . . Canadian drafters and saddlers . . . Narragansett Pacers . . . Conestogas . . . Chickasaws! All of them performed heroic services through the eight years of the Revolution. As the battles thundered from Bunker Hill to Saratoga to King's Mountain, then back to the final entrapment of Lord Cornwallis at Yorktown, the commissary wagons, artillery and cavalry they powered created new wagonways along the Atlantic Seaboard.

The capture of splendid English and Hessian saddle horses at Stanwix, Saratoga, Trenton and Yorktown . . . the popularization of Ben Franklin's Post Road markers . . . blacksmith inventions of new types of horseshoes . . . wainwright inventions of iron rims for wagon wheels and leather springs for coaches . . . all heralded a horse-and-wagon age in full gallop alongside the political revolution.

The Wagon Age shaped quickly after Yorktown. On April 16, 1789, General George Washington left Mount Vernon in a white coach that was to carry him 250 miles to the presidential inauguration ceremony in New York City. The coach was a radical new vehicle. Its body was egg-shaped and had glass windows leaded into the doors on each side. Padded leather cushions and back-rests were suspended across the interior. This "cab" hung three feet above the ground on a leather cradle anchored on the axles of the tall rear wheels and small front wheels. The driver and footman rode outside on a padded seat built five feet above the front wheels. A four-horse team of matched gray trotters, each about fifteen hands high, was hitched to the single drawing-pole. At a dozen "refreshment and speech-making" stops along the route, relay teams of gray horses awaited their proud hours in the journey.

Washington's seven-day trip was a triumph for the new Wagon Age as well as for the new United States of America. Hundreds of planters, merchants and army officers drove gigs, chariots, shays and buggies down to the Post Roads, so that their families could join in the waving and bowing as Washington's coach cantered by. Philadelphia and New York experienced the worst traffic jams in their histories as hundreds of horse-drawn vehicles converged on the route of "General Washington's equipage."

That same summer, a hitch of Conestoga horses drew John Hayden's red-white-and-blue freight wagon across the Alleghenies from Hagerstown, Maryland, to Brownsville, Pennsylvania. The trip inaugurated freight deliveries to new Pittsburgh and the Ohio headwaters.

Virginia was already building a "waggon route" over the Blue Ridge from Alexandria to the Shenandoah's "Great Valley." Powder-gangs blasted roadbeds for two other trans-Allegheny routes across Pennsylvania. Hundreds of six-horse Pitt wagons were being built at the fifteen to twenty wainwright factories in Lancaster and other communities along Conestoga Creek.

Then, in 1792, the Pennsylvania Legislature authorized the Philadelphia & Lancaster Turnpike Company to sell $465,000 worth of stock. The money would finance, the permission stipulated, construction of a road of "artificial beds of stone and gravel" between the two cities. The stock was oversubscribed within two weeks. The Lancaster Turnpike, twenty-five feet wide, with adjacent strips of "summer road" (i.e. unpaved dirt track), each ten feet wide, opened in 1794; the construction costs averaged $7,500 a mile. Tollkeepers collected fees at each ten-mile post. The tolls varied from "one-sixteenth of a dollar for every horse" drawing a Conestoga wagon, to "¼ Dollar" for a four-wheel carriage drawn by two horses.[11]

The Lancaster Turnpike earned profits for almost fifty years, and triggered turnpike construction throughout New England and the Middle Atlantic states.

THE HIGH-PLAINS REVOLUTION

CHAPTER NINE

THERE WERE TWO American Revolutions. The one that created the United States of America centered in an Atlantic coastal-plain area of approximately 300,000 square miles. The one that created the Indian horsemen established a new way of life in an area totaling approximately 3,000,000 square miles. The high-plains culture developed between 1750 and 1800 dominated the growth of civilization in 75 per cent of the present United States during the nineteenth century.

Again, topography and climate influenced the pattern of history's course. When Cro-Magnon man began to experiment with the cultivation of food and fiber crops, he learned that a consistent supply of water was essential to the growth, and annual harvests, of trees, plants and grasses. By the time the ancestors of the red man migrated to North America, crop growers knew that most grains, vegetables and fruits require a minimum of twenty inches of rainfall—or its equivalent—each year.

This knowledge, plus the lack of large domesticated animals, prevented the development of red-man communities away from river valleys or lake shores on our high-plains. West of the 100th Meridian—which runs through central North Dakota and central Texas—the average annual rainfall drops from between twenty and forty inches a year to between ten and twenty inches a year. This amount of moisture denied the pre-Columbian red man a normal expectation of the maize, squash, bean and fruit crops on

84

which his sedentary agriculture depended. Consequently, the few human inhabitants on our high-plains before 1750 lived near dependable water supplies in the Missouri, Platte, Arkansas, Red and other river valleys.

The Sioux, Blackfoot, Cheyenne, Kiowa, Nez Percé, Shoshone and other tribes who became extraordinary horseback warriors during the nineteenth century were still sedentary mountain or prairie-forest farmers in 1750. Their transformation into hunters and nomads on the high plains of the *Eohippus-Equus* evolution occurred after 1750 and was made possible by the arrival of the horse.[1]

Europe's wars and the relentless economic pressures exerted by white Colonials began this high-plains revolution. The dispersion of horses from Mexico and New Mexico—and possibly from western Tennessee, western New York, and the trading posts of New France—provided a means of escape from the guns, disease, slavery and greed introduced by, or because of, the white man.

The Treaty of Utrecht, and subsequent documents, ended the War of the Spanish Succession during 1714. These international agreements conceded that Louis XIV's grandson, Philip V, could perpetuate a Bourbon dynasty for Spain. But France was forced to cede Hudson's Bay and her sub-Arctic territories in North America to Great Britain. This assured a trading monopoly for "the Governor and Company of Adventurers Trading Into Hudson's Bay." It also assured speedy French exploration throughout the prairie and high-plains west of Lake Superior.

Between 1715 and 1740, French explorers, traders and priests crossed Minnesota, the Dakotas, Montana and Manitoba. They established missions and trading posts that spread knowledge of the white man, his guns, horses, enslavement practices, and lust as far west as the sites of Great Falls and Calgary. Similar civilization pressures were created during the same years by British trading posts and explorations across the Canadian sub-Arctic.

Also, between 1700 and 1711, a dauntless Jesuit missionary, Eusebio Francisco Kino, carried New Spain's frontier north and

west into Arizona and California. Father Kino was a native of the
Tyrol, and was farm conditioned.[2] His belief in the peaceful influences of animal husbandry caused him to import cattle, horses and
mules across the Sonora deserts to mission farms at San Xavier del
Bac and other Indian centers near the site of Tucson. He rejected
New Spain's convictions about Indians-on-horseback, and trained
the missions' converts in all the Tyrolean-Spanish skills he knew
about animal husbandry. The Jesuits who succeeded him perpetuated the training.

Between 1675 and 1700, Virginians and South Carolinians established trade relations with the Cherokees, Choctaws and Chickasaws in western Tennessee and Mississippi; before 1700, French
traders and *coureurs de bois* were buying furs, ginseng root, and
possibly horses from these tribes in exchange for guns, metal goods
and trinkets.[3] The Chickasaws soon succumbed to offers of "more
guns if you will bring in slaves," and began selling captives to
South Carolina traders. By 1725, gangs of Indian slaves were being
delivered to South Carolina. Both South Carolinians and the New
Orleans French shipped Indian slaves to the West Indies.[4] South
Carolinians were trading with Indians "from across the Mississippi" before 1700.[5]

Before 1700, too, New York's fearsome Iroquois had obtained
guns from the Dutch and British. They began relentless raids
against their traditional enemies, the twenty to thirty thousand
Hurons of eastern Michigan. The Iroquois were cannibals.[6] They
became slave traders, too.

These reactions to the white man's way of life swept west across
the prairies and forests like the shock waves of an atomic bomb.
The Chippewas obtained guns from either the Hudson Bay British
or the French traders in Illinois, and used them to attack their
ancient enemies, the Sioux. The Sioux began to migrate toward
Minnesota's western prairie. They encountered the Cheyennes and
drove this Algonkian tribe farther west. The Delawares, forced to
give up their Pennsylvania, New York and New Jersey homeland
to the whites, became dependents of the Iroquois, migrated to Ohio

and helped, with the refugee Shawnees, to introduce guns and horses to prairie-edge tribes of the central Great Lakes Basin and Ohio Valley. The Fox, driven from homelands near the west end of Lake Erie by the Iroquois-Huron struggle, fled to the Wisconsin forests, formed an alliance with the Sauks, and settled along the Iowa shore of the Mississippi.

The Sioux, Cheyennes, Arapahos, Kiowas and Blackfeet all began their migrations to the high-plains after 1750. Oliver La Farge reported that these tribes of "western farmers" used only dogs for transportation in 1725 and that in 1760 the eastern Sioux still performed most of their freighting and travel through the Minnesota forests by canoe.[7] But, before 1800, "they had abandoned the use of canoes and taken completely to horses." Most of the other red men who became the fierce horsemen of the northern high-plains during the nineteenth century made a similar transition from woodlands farmer to high-plains nomad hunter between 1750 and 1800.[8]

All of these tribes must have realized that great social and economic changes confronted them if they were to "make a living" on the high-plains. Descriptions of the trans-Missouri West by Zebulon Pike, Lewis and Clark, and other American explorers there between 1804 and 1815 caused geographers to label the entire high-plains area as "The Great American Desert." The Sioux, Cheyennes, Kiowas, Blackfeet and other woodland groups had practiced agriculture for thousands of years, hence realized their dependence on forests, annual crops and a constancy of moisture. They abandoned all of these livelihood-securities for a nomad-and-hunter pattern of life when the horse became available. Thus, between 1750 and 1800, the brush and timber huts of the forest homes, the adjacent maize, bean and squash gardens, the wild-rice harvests on Minnesota's ten thousand lakes, the utensils created from reeds and wood were abruptly exchanged for the tepee village, the horseback chase after bison and antelope, the horse-drawn travois, the endless struggle with other high-plains invaders. All of this constituted a revolution as violent, and as meaningful to the American future, as the battles and political

arguments under way between the Tories and Continentals on the
Atlantic Seaboard.

The supply-sources of the horses that enabled the mount-ups by
Sioux, Cheyenne, Blackfoot, Kiowa, Shoshone, Nez Percé and
Cayuse tribes remain a mystery. It is difficult to accept the prevail-
ing belief that all of the animals' came out of New Mexico and
Mexico, with the Apache-Navaho, Ute and Comanche of the south-
ern high-plains as the primary suppliers.

By 1806, herds of feral horses existed as far north as Colorado.
Captain Zebulon Montgomery Pike, a native of Trenton, New
Jersey, explored the Colorado plains that year and, on November
15, first sighted the mountain, "like a small blue cloud," that became his namesake, Pike's Peak. On November 1, Pike wrote in
his journal: "Upon using my glass to observe the adjacent territory, I observed on the prairie a herd of horses. Dr. Robinson and
Baroney accompanied me to go and view them: when within a
quarter of a mile they discovered us, and came immediately up
near us, making the earth tremble under them: this brought to
my recollection a charge of cavalry. They stopped and gave us an
opportunity to view them; among them were some very beautiful
bays, blacks and grays and indeed of all colors. We fired at a black
horse, with an idea of creasing him, but did not succeed; they
flourished around and returned again to see us, when we returned
to camp."[9]

Decades before the Pike and Lewis and Clark expeditions, the
high-plains newcomers had rediscovered the riding method that
the world's first cavalrymen, the Chinese bowmen, perfected about
1000 B.C. "They rode on a pelt cinched around the horse," Robert
M. Denhardt explained. "Their riding bridle was just a thong
looped around the lower jaw of the horse. The horse was guided
primarily by the rider's knees. The Plains Indians almost invariably kept a neck rope dragging when they were riding so that if
they were unseated, they could grab the dragging rope and retain
the horse."[10]

This technique, of course, enabled a warrior to use both hands for discharging arrows at his human or animal target while he kneed his horse into tight circles or on the forty-mile-an-hour gallop of a headlong charge. Coupled with his ability to lock his legs around the horse's neck during an attack, then swing down and continue to pump arrows from beneath the horse's throat, it gave him battle superiority over the white man until the introduction of Colt's revolver and the repeating rifle after 1840.

Such splendid coordination between horse and rider indicated a comradeship similar to the relationship that existed between horsemen and their mounts during the Centaur-Hyksos era. Robert M. Denhardt described this in his excellent appendices on "Indian Horse Breaking" in his *The Horse of the Americas*.[11]

"It was the Indians' custom," Denhardt wrote, "to attribute a high degree of rationality to animal life, and their attitude toward their mounts was no exception. Their relationship to the horse was one which approximated human companionship. . . . This relationship is reflected in the customary method used by the Indians in breaking horses. They were firm but, for the most part, seldom cruel.

"When the Indian had horses to be broken, the animals were rounded up, and a chosen horse roped. Several men were needed to hold the plunging horse. The first step was to accustom the horse to the Indian halter, which was very similar to our hackamore. One man worked toward the horse on the rope. This had to be done slowly, so that the horse could see he was not going to be hurt. The Indian approached the horse cautiously, continuously grunting and talking to him. Chief Long Lance writes that horse talk is a low grunt which seems to charm the horse and make him stand motionless for a moment and listen. It sounded like 'hoh, hoh' uttered deep in the chest. The cowboy says the same thing today, only he spells it 'whoa.' [Every American who could spell in 1760–1800 spelled it 'ho.']

"When the horse became accustomed to the man approaching on the rope, the Indian would then take a blanket and wave it. The first shake of the blanket probably gave the Indians holding the

rope a free ride. However, as time went on, the horse would become used to the blanket.

"The hardest job for the horsebreaker was to get his hands on
the horse. By approaching slowly and talking continually, he was
finally able to place his hand on the horse's nose. Wild horses have
always had a deadly fear of human contact and have to become
used to the human scent before they will allow anyone to touch
them. Once the horse has had his head touched, the next job is to
cautiously put on the halter, or more correctly, the hackamore.
The native hackamore was made of a narrow strip of rawhide, no
larger than a leather bootlace. It was looped over the horse's nose
and run up back of his ears and then down the other side and
through the loop. The slightest pull by the horse would tighten
the halter. It was strong and slender and put great pressure on the
nerves of the neck and nose, and the horse after one or two pulls
learned to behave. The Indian, once he had the halter on the
horse, no longer needed the extra help on the end of the rope.

"The warrior would continue handling the horse, hissing at him,
caressing him, and generally getting him to realize that he was not
going to be hurt. He would run his hands over every inch of his
head, and neck, working down to the shoulders and back. When
the area around the flanks was reached, the horse would undoubtedly begin to object more strenuously, and the Indian would have
to give a few jerks on the line to make him stand still again. When
the warrior had succeeded in running his hands over both sides of
the horse's body, he would again get his robe and gently strike the
horse with it. This was continued until the horse saw that he was
not going to be hurt.

"The most difficult task was now at hand. The warrior began
to work his hands over the horse's legs. A few well-chosen pulls
on the rawhide halter was undoubtedly needed to make the horse
stand. Not an inch of the horse's body escaped being touched and
rubbed. When this job was completed, the horse was nearly
broken, as he was no longer afraid of a blanket or a man's touch. . . .

"The actual mounting and riding were the least difficult of the breaking job for the Indians. The man would walk to the side of the horse and press down on the horse's back lightly. He kept pressing a little harder and a little harder. Finally, he would put his elbows across the horse's back and draw his body up an inch from the ground, putting all of his weight on the animal. If the horse showed fright and jumped, a jerk of the thong and the repetition of the act made him stand.

"Slowly but surely the brave would then pull himself farther and farther up until he could slip his leg over the mount. . . . Few horses broken in this manner offered to buck. The horse would usually stand perfectly still and, after a few moments of petting and urging, would trot off at an aimless and awkward gait."

This patient ritual was, of course, a repetition of human history. The Aryans and Indo-Europeans must have shown as much patience and followed a similar technique when, between 4000 and 3000 B.C., they first won mastery over the tarpans and began the Centaur rides across the Balkans and the Caucasus. The red man's Centaur re-enactment on the ancient Equidae homeland evolved a horse-economy similar to the one that Herodotus found when he visited the Scythians. Horses became the basis of wealth and prestige. Important warriors and medicine men acquired herds of fifty to a hundred horses; they controlled matings outside their herds by their stallions. The marriage dowry of a "virtuous girl" often included several horses.[12]

The horse became a symbol in religious ceremonies. Burial platforms of warriors were decorated with the heads and tails of favorite hunting and war mounts. Warriors began wearing fur or feather symbols to denote the number of horses they had stolen.

Two folkways that would account for much of the inter-tribal warfare on the plains developed during the 1750–1800 revolution: horse-thievery and the coup.

Stealing the horses of a rival tribe became a feat that won social prestige. The Sioux, especially, relished horse-thievery as a brave sport. Their warriors chanted the boast: "You must watch your horse. A horse thief often am I." One of the proudest achievements

a young warrior could dream about was to "get right into the village circle and steal the favorite horse of some important warrior."[13] The chase that followed might last for weeks, and end in
a battle between the stealer's friends and the pursuer's relatives.
The long enmity among the Sioux, Cheyennes, Shoshones and
Blackfeet was fueled by horse-stealing.

The coup seems to have been a feat of daring that originated in
the woodlands centuries before the Horse Age. But on horseback
it became an act of spectacular bravado that won social prestige
and tribal privileges. The word *coup* is French and means "a blow."
The daredevil act was to strike an enemy, or enemies, with a stick
or with the bare hands. Some warriors carried wooden poles,
adorned with feathers and religious symbols. They used these
"coup sticks" to clout enemies, or unhorse them, during battle
charges. Among the Crows, a coup striker could attach wolf tails
to the heels of his moccasins; a Sioux could add feathers to his war
bonnet; a Blackfoot could have a patch of white weasel skin sewn
on his shirt.[14]

Thus the high-plains revolution reorganized the red man's ways
of life as thoroughly as the American Revolution reshaped human
behavior along twelve hundred miles of the Atlantic Seaboard.
By 1800, horsemanship had crossed the continent. Thereafter the
Americans and the red horsemen rode toward inevitable conflict.

MULE POWER

CHAPTER TEN

THE MULE—a stoic hero in our folklore and a vital source of work-power until the 1930s—first won recognition in the United States because of George Washington's devotion to animal agriculture. Washington's promotional campaign for the mule as a cheap and durable drafter on the South's frontier farms was so timely that, within seventy years, mules on plows . . . mules in prairie-schooner harness . . . mules in pack trains, in mine shafts and on treadmills were commonplace all across the continent. On April 30, 1789, when Washington was inaugurated as the first President of the United States, his jack donkeys, Royal Gift and Knight of Malta, seem to have been the only mule sires in the new United States; the national census of 1860 reported 1,129,553 mules in the United States.

The oncoming Machine Age was a major factor in our adoption of mule power. The six events preceding it were: a virulent plague of hoof-and-mouth disease in the South's livestock herds (1760–1800); Eli Whitney's invention of the cotton gin (1795); sequential land exploitation by the "one-crop" cotton planters (1796–1860); the construction of east-west ship canals (1817–1845); and the prairie-schooner migrations west of the Mississippi (1805–1869).

Thus, the Knight of Malta and Royal Gift deserve as exalted mention in human history as the mule team—agleam in golden sandals and red harness—that drew the carriage of Nero's consort,

Poppaea, along the roads of Rome in A.D. 60. (A thorough promoter of donkey and mule excellence, Poppaea bathed regularly in milk from the royal herd of five hundred jennies and lauded donkey-milk's superiority as the lotion that kept her skin soft and allur-ing.) [1]

Mules had served mankind for at least thirty-five centuries when Knight of Malta and Royal Gift arrived at the Mount Vernon barns. Controlled mating between male donkeys and female horses is presumed to have originated among the Edomites and Hosites of Asia Minor about 2000 B.C. Both the Bible's Book of Genesis[2] and Homer's *Iliad* mention "mules." Because of its soft, sure-footed gait, the hybrid beast became the standard drafter for funeral processions in Greece. A team of sixty-four mules drew the hearse containing the corpse of Alexander the Great from Babylon to Alexandria.

During the centuries of the Roman Empire, mules made up the army pack trains and served as saddle mounts and drafters used by courtesans and by wives of the aristocrats. Most of Rome's mail carriers rode mules, too. It is probable that the first bootlike horse-shoes were invented for mules.[3]

The terms "mulish," "muley." and "mule-headed" became com-mon street language in Spain, Italy, France and Great Britain. In all of these lands the terms carried the same derogatory implica-tion.

In 1504, Christopher Columbus was crippled with rheumatism and gout. He was too ill to undertake the journey from Seville to Madrid to attend Queen Isabella's funeral. But a few weeks later he felt strong enough to begin preparations for the trip to Madrid and a possible audience with King Ferdinand. But Spanish law ruled that "the gentleman" must ride a stallion. Columbus' rheu-matism forbade this. The only carriage avaliable was a hearse owned by the Bishop of Seville. So the crippled mariner appealed to Ferdinand for a royal permit to cross Spain on muleback. The king signed the order on February 23, 1505. It was, Samuel Eliot

Morison contends, "the only favor that King Ferdinand ever granted to the Discoverer of America."[4]

Columbus had included mules among the deckloads of livestock he brought to the West Indies during his third voyage to the New World. The crossbreeding of jacks and horse mares became a profitable business at some of the studs in New Spain. The city of Gracias Con Dios in Honduras derived much of its wealth from breeding mules for pack trains and mine-cart work, as well as for labor on the treadmills powering the cane-crusher machinery at sugar mills.

There were mules at the Spanish settlements in Florida and New Mexico before 1625. The Chickasaws, Cherokees and Seminoles of the Southeast and the Apache-Navaho in New Mexico knew the secret of mule breeding by the time of the Popé Revolt. The Apache-Navaho began to breed mules for pack trains and for meat; mule steak became one of their favorite dishes. By 1750, both the Pawnees and the Comanches were mule breeders. They occasionally drove herds of the hybrids into New Orleans and the French settlements in the upper Mississippi Valley for midsummer trading.

California, too, had become a center for mule production by the time the Knight of Malta reached Mount Vernon. In 1769, Fernando di Revera drove California's first mule herd, plus cattle and horses, north from Baja California. Four years later, in a letter to Mexico City, Father Junipero Serra pleaded that "all the missions are in very great need of mules, especially the inland missions. . . . Above all, asses and mares must be sent for procreation of more mules. Otherwise, the province will never be free from trouble because of its lack of packanimals."[5] The livestock census taken at the missions that year showed a total of "from 77 to 85" mules at Monterey, San Diego and San Gabriel.

But by 1790, the eleven missions between San Diego and the Bay of St. Francis counted "more than 2,000" mules. And in 1833 California's missions owned 62,500 "horses and mules," of which not less than 10,000 were the jack-and-mare hybrids.[6]

But the mule had failed to influence the diversified-farm pioneers
of northern Europe and the British Isles. And a majority of the four
million citizens of the United States in 1787 were of North European heritage, imbued with the agricultural prejudices of their
ancestral regions. Although Daniel Gookin brought "80 asses" to
Jamestown, Virginia, in 1620, there is no evidence that this herd
was perpetuated or crossbred with horses. None of the complaints
about "wild horse" and "wild cattle" nuisances on the Virginia
and Maryland plantations between 1670 and 1720 mention donkeys,
asses or mules. In 1784 Dr. Johann Schopf found a few mules imported from Cuba in use on plantations near Richmond, Virginia,
and observed that "they are beginning to be liked because they are
so perfectly adapted for the American economy, thriving with
scant attention and bad feed."[7] But historians agree that the animal
was practically unknown elsewhere in the thirteen states.

Perhaps General Washington knew about the mules near Richmond. He had returned to Mount Vernon at the end of the Revolution determined to devote the rest of his life to improving the new
nation's farming methods. "The System of Agriculture (if the
epithet can be applied to it)," he philosophized in a letter to Arthur
Young, editor of *Annals of Husbandry*, "which is in use in this part
of the United States, is as unproductive to the practitioners as it
is ruinous to the landholders. Yet it is pertinaciously adhered to.
To forsake it; to pursue a course of husbandry which is altogether
different and new to the gazing multitude, even averse to novelty in
matters of this sort, and much attached to their old customs, requires resolution: and without a good practical guide, may be
dangerous."[8]

Washington's decision to "pursue a new and different course of
husbandry" was reached sometime during 1784 when he asked a
shipowner friend, whose vessels traded at Spanish ports, to obtain
"a good Spanish jack whose abilities for getting Colts can be en-
sured" for experimental breeding at Mount Vernon. Washington
knew that Spain's customs officials usually ordered the testicles of
all jack donkeys crushed before they were exported, "as to render

them unfit for the purpose of begetting colts." He warned the shipowner to have the animal examined carefully.

The negotiations failed. But gossip about Washington's interest
reached Spain's consul in Philadelphia, was relayed through Madrid and brought to the attention of the king. Thus, during 1785,
the king sent two jacks and two jennies to Washington as a gift. One
of the animals died en route. The remaining jack and jennies landed
at Portsmouth, New Hampshire, and were driven south over the
Post Roads to Mount Vernon.

Washington's groom, Peter, named the surviving jack Royal
Gift. The animal stood fiftten hands high—taller than most contemporary stallions and proportionately larger in the barrel and
legs. But he adapted slowly to the New World. Late in 1785, Washington wrote his brother that Royal Gift "seems too full of Royalty
to have anything to do with a plebeian race; perhaps his stomach
may come to him, if not, I shall wish he had never come from his
Most Catholic Majesty's stables."

The "stomach" returned. On February 23, 1786, a Philadelphia
paper carried an advertisement announcing that "Royal Gift—A
Jack Ass of the first race in the Kingdom of Spain will cover
mares and jennies at Mount Vernon the ensueing spring. The first
for ten and the latter for fifteen pounds the season. . . . The advantages, which are many, to be derived from the propagation of
asses from this animal (The first of the kind that was ever in North
America) and the usefulness of mules bred from a Jack of his size,
either for the road or team, are well known to those who are ac-
quainted with this mongrel race. For the information of those who
are not, it may be enough to add that their great strength, longevity,
hardiness and cheap support give them a preference of horses that
is scarcely to be imagined."[9]

By this time, news of Washington's mule hobby had reached the
Marquis de Lafayette in France. So during 1786 a jack, dubbed
Knight of Malta, and two Maltese jennies reached Mount Vernon
as a gift from Lafayette, plus a letter extolling the jacks of Malta as
the best in Europe. Was Lafayette's letter deliberately "leaked" to

a diplomatic representative of Spain? The question has never been answered. But in 1787 Washington was formally notified that a surplus of jacks and jennies existed in Spain and the animals could be delivered, in almost any quantity, to the United States at costs below the fifty dollars being asked for good draft horses.

In 1797, a year after he retired from the presidency, Washington wrote that "the Spanish jack seems calculated to breed for heavy slow draught; the others for the saddle or lighter carriages. From these, altogether, I hope to secure a race of extraordinary goodness which will stock the country."

Admiration for Washington's skills in animal husbandry caused some of his old friends in the War Department to order experimental use of mules for hauling commissary wagons and artillery caissons. Then a 1795 invention by the Yankee tinkerer Eli Whitney made the mule a logical power source on the upland cotton plantations that quickly organized across the Piedmont and backcountry.

Soon after his graduation from Yale University, Eli Whitney boarded a brig bound for Charleston, South Carolina. The widow of General Nathaniel Greene was a fellow passenger. Whitney's job search ended when he contracted to become tutor for the children on Mrs. Greene's South Carolina plantation. The manager of the plantation, Phineas Miller—soon to become Mrs. Greene's second husband—interested Whitney in development of a machine that could comb the seeds out of short-staple cotton.

The invention of spinning machines in Great Britain was enabling cotton, for the first time in history, to challenge wool and linen as a cheap cloth. But the tenacious seeds that grew in short-staple cotton bolls barred most of the South from cotton farming. Long-staple cotton produced seeds that could easily be shaken loose from the fibers. But it grew only on seashore land, hence was nicknamed "Sea Island" cotton.

Whitney devised a cotton engine after ten days of tinkering. He and Miller obtained a patent on it in 1794. But the "gin," as Southerners dubbed it, was so simple that it could be copied by a blacksmith in two hours.

Geographically, the gin enabled realtors and banks to option hundreds of thousands of acres along the eastern slopes of the Southern Appalachians, then mortgage them to planters and store-keepers as "prime cotton land." The cotton rush forced the Crack-ers and their cow-pen communities across the mountains to western Tennessee and southern Kentucky. By 1810, wagon trains of cotton planters were crossing the Georgia mountains to the rich black-top deltalands of Alabama and Mississippi.

Clearance of short-staple cotton land called for durable, disease-resistant animal power. So did the annual tasks of planting seeds, weeding the growing plants, hauling the wagonloads of ripe bolls off to the neighborhood gin, and hauling the five-hundred-pound cot-ton bales, lint and seed-cake to warehouses or boat wharves. This labor, considering the callous indifference of most "cotton opera-tors" toward the welfare of their slaves and livestock, made horse power and ox power too expensive. Furthermore, both horses and oxen were subject to the "critter plagues."

But the tough, patient mule was endorsed by President Washing-ton himself. Rumor said that the beast shook off fevers and disease "as easy as a raccoon climbs a tree." Some people claimed mules "never died until they were seventy-five or a hundred years old." A forty-dollar investment in a mule would provide power for twenty—thirty—who knows how many cotton crops! As for up-keep, the costs weren't worth bothering about. The oily mass of seeds and lint left from the cotton ginning had some nourishment in it. Gossip insisted that a mule could "get along real well" on cot-tonseed meal and grass, and could live outdoors the year around. "When I ask why mules are so universally substituted for horses on the farm," Frederick Law Olmsted wrote after his tour of the seaboard slave states in 1854–55, "the first reason given and con-fessedly the most conclusive one, is that horses cannot bear the treatment they must always get. . . . Horses are always soon foundered or crippled; . . . mules will bear the cudgeling, and lose a meal or two now and then and not be materially injured, and they do not take cold or get sick if neglected or overworked."[10]

George Washington's promotion of the mule, Spain's eagerness to sell her mule surplus, and the transformation of the South's Piedmont and deltalands into short-staple cotton plantations combined to establish the mule as the second most important work animal in the United States. After Washington's death in 1799, eight of the Mount Vernon mules were sold at two hundred dollars each.[11]

Connecticut expanded her livestock acreage markedly after the Revolution and, until the end of the War of 1812, was the largest producer of beef cattle and horses in the country. Her stud operators heard about the new market for mules in the South, and bred imported Spanish jacks to Narragansett Pacers, Canadian drafters and native mares. From 1800 through the 1820s, herds of Connecticut mules plodding south toward Virginia and Carolina sales barns were a common summertime sight on the seaboard roads.

"On observing a drove of mules passing through the streets of Washington," James Westfall Thompson wrote, "John Randolph, the witty United States Senator from Virginia, pointed them out to Uriah Tracy, the Senator from Connecticut, saying:

" 'Tracy, there go a lot of your constituents.'

" 'Ye-es,' said Tracy, scrutinizing the drove, 'going down to Virginia to teach school.' "[12]

Another tedious mule role in the development of American civilization came in after the War of 1812. Then New York, Pennsylvania and Virginia began to construct ship canals across the Appalachians. New York had the geographic advantage because of the Mohawk River gorge through the Appalachian backbone to the Great Lakes watershed. The construction of the Erie Canal began in 1817. Virginia and Maryland interests were already endeavoring to dig a Baltimore & Ohio navigation channel between the Potomac and the Ohio.

Philadelphians became fearful that the Erie Canal would lure trade to and from the West away from the Conestoga wagon routes to Pittsburgh. They lobbied appropriations through the Pennsylvania legislature for construction of an all-Pennsylvania canal-

and-railway portage system between Lancaster and Johnstown. In 1825 the Erie Canal opened and Ohio's legislature financed construction of a trans-state canal to connect its Lake Erie ports with the Ohio River.

The canal channels, only four or five feet deep, were too shallow for steamboat paddle wheels. (The invention of the screw propeller was a generation ahead.) The most practical vehicle for canal transportation was a flat-bottomed scow, drawn through the waterway by a rope. Draft animals driven along an embankment powered the rope. The mule proved to be the most economic, and durable, animal for the canalboat hauls. The folk song beginning

> I got a mule, her name is Sal,
> Fifteen miles on the Erie Canal,

is a memorial to the hundreds of thousands of mules laboring on canal towpaths between 1825 and 1900.

Thus, forty years after Royal Gift's arrival at Mount Vernon, the hybrids were a national resource. The mule was being lauded by economists as "an invaluable servant in the regions in which nature has fitted him to exist." What may be the most cogent tribute ever written about the American mule was composed by J. T. Warder of Springfield, Ohio, and published in the *Agricultural Report* of the U.S. Bureau of Agriculture in 1863.

"The mule, as an animal of burden in a rocky and precipitous country," Mr. Warder pointed out, "far exceeds the horse or any other animal; and some countries would remain separated from one another by impassable barriers were it not for the matchless sagacity, patience and sure-footedness of this creature. . . . In the mule we have the size and activity of the horse, combined with the form and hardihood of the ass, while he surpasses both his parents in sure-footedness and longevity, and has more endurance and greater power of recuperation from fatigue and exhaustion when excessively worked. Well-bred mules are as spirited, and equally active, or even quicker than horses, if perfectly broken. They will walk fast, and in the draft they pull even more steadily. Their intelligence is so great that they may be trained very readily either to the line or to the word, and many splendid large teams are driven, even over rough ground where there is scarcely any road, perfectly guided by the voice of the teamster, aided only by the loud crack of his whip, which they understand as a sign of encouragement rather than as an intimation of impending torture."[13]

Kentuckians, too, were intrigued by the mule as a source of income from their superb bluegrass pastures. Soon after 1800, the Kentucky Mule began its mighty services in our prairie, high-plain and mountain conquests.

THE BLUEGRASS

CHAPTER ELEVEN

A FEW KEGS STORED in the freight-and-livestock quarters at the stern of an Ohio River "broadhorn" or "keelboat" produced the most famous place-name in the history of the American horse. This momentous, but unrecorded, event must have occurred during one of the late fall high-waters between 1800 and 1810. Evidence indicates that the kegs were carefully packed and waterproofed by Amish-Mennonite farmers in the Conestoga Creek region of Pennsylvania, then—after the Pitt wagon ride over the Alleghenies— taken on the dangerous river trip past snags, "sleepers," eddies, Indian sharpshooters and pirates to the Louisville wharves just above the Falls of the Ohio. The kegs were filled with bluegrass seed. The world's most famous breeding center for saddle racers, harness racers, carriage horses and mules took its name from the luxuriant forage and pyramidal flower clusters these seeds introduced to the limestone-rich soils encircling Lexington.

Bluegrass (*Poa pratensis*) originated on the Black Sea–Caspian steppes where the Centaurs first domesticated the tarpan. It was first planted in North America about 1700. William Penn's interest in grassland farming plus the pastureland developments of the Amish-Mennonites suggest that the first bluegrass plantings on the continent occurred in eastern Pennsylvania. During 1685, William Penn wrote his steward at Pennsbury that "hay dust" (i.e. the chaff from the bottom of mows and stacks) "is the best for our fields." During the same year a Thomas Budd wrote that "If we sprinkle a little English Hay-seed on the land without plowing and then

103

feed sheep on it, in a little time it will so increase that it will cover the land with English grass like unto our pastures in England."

Winnowed seed from a single species of grass became available after 1785 when Hollanders invented the fanning mill. By the time of General Washington's first inaugural, many of Pennsylvania's farmers were using clover, timothy and bluegrass seed for their crop-rotation programs.[1] On limestone soil, such as that in the Conestoga Creek valley, bluegrass would grow to a height of three feet by mid-June and provide both a hay crop and June-to-November pasture for horses and cattle.

The limestone soil, mineral-rich streams and gentle terrain of north-central Kentucky lured cow-pen Crackers and Pennsylvania Germans into the trek across the Appalachians before 1780. "Everything here," wrote one of the more poetic pioneers, "assumes a dignity and splendor I have never seen in any part of the world. Here an eternal verdure reigns and the brilliant sun of latitude 39 degrees, piercing through the azure heavens, produces in the prolific soil an early maturity which is truly astonishing. . . . The fertility of the soil amply repays the labourer for his toil. . . . The ground will yield from 50 to 60 bushels of corn to the acre, and in three or four years [the] stock of cattle and sheep will prove sufficient to supply both beef and mutton. . . . By the fourth year, provided he is industrious, he may have his plantation in sufficient good order to build a better house."[2]

Gossip about this "eternal verdure" brought more than twenty thousand immigrants from Virginia, Pennsylvania, the Carolinas and Georgia into Kentucky during the seven years of the American Revolution. They packed all their goods in over the blazed trails on Chickasaw, cow-pen and Conestoga horses.

During the twenty-five or thirty years before the state's first shipment of bluegrass seed landed at Louisville, horsemanship in Kentucky created much of the social pattern that would mark the "Western pioneer." River pirates, posses of mounted Rangers, boats powered by horses walking treadmills, horse racing, horse thieves and mounted "bad men" all developed in Kentucky before 1800.

And in her forests, the red horseman and the American first met in battle.

The first legislative assembly of Transylvania, meeting in Boonesborough on May 23, 1775, passed a resolution to "preserve the breed of horses."[3] Although concrete evidence is lacking, most historians accept this resolution as evidence that descendants of the thirty-seven English "Breds" in Virginia and the Carolinas were among the horses that powered the initial American migrations across the mountains. The centers for breeding Virginia race horses had moved west into the James and Shenandoah river valleys during the 1760s.[4] Richard Henderson, George Rogers Clark and other pioneer leaders in Kentucky came from Virginia and were "blooded horse" enthusiasts.

The first court convened at Louisville on March 7, 1781, and established local price-ceilings for the "necessities of life." These included a charge of "not more than $4 a night" for stabling a horse.[5] Advertisements offering the services of stallions began to appear in the *Kentucky Gazette* in 1788. One of them read, in part: "The famous horse Pilgarlic, of a beautiful color, full fourteen hands, three inches high, rising ten years old, will stand the ensuing season on the head of Salt River at Captain Abe Irvins, Mercer County, and will cover mares at the very low price of ten shillings per leap, if the money is paid down, or fifteen at the expiration of the season; and twenty shillings the season in cash, or thirty shillings in good trade."[6]

Another advertisement, published during the last week of June in the same year, announced: "Notice is hereby given that several gentlemen propose a meeting at the CRAB ORCHARD on the 4th of July in perfect readiness to move early the next morning through the wilderness. As it is very dangerous on account of the Indians it is hoped each person will go well armed."[7]

Although horse-race meets are presumed to have been held on the outskirts of Lexington during 1787, the June 1788 advertisement is the first record of an organized horse race in Kentucky. By 1793, horse racing along Lexington's streets had become so perilous for pedestrians that the village trustees passed an ordinance resolving: "Horse racing in the streets is hereafter prohibited as being too dangerous to the citizens; but it is authorized at the west end of the Commons where stud horses are shown."

André Michaux, a consul of the new Republic of France, visited Kentucky that year and wrote that "Horses and lawsuits comprise the usual topics of conversation. If a traveler happens to pass by, his horse is appreciated. If he stops, he is presented with a glass of whiskey and then asked a thousand questions."[8]

There were a multitude of reasons for making horses and horsemanship a "usual topic of conversation." First, there were the Indian horsemen. Most of the Iroquois, Shawnees and Delawares sided with the British during the Revolution. The journals of French, Virginia and Pennsylvania officers who served on the Ohio Valley frontier during the French and Indian Wars had routinely noted the arrival of Indian war chiefs and councilors "on horseback."[9] Both the Shawnees and the Delawares were skilled horsemen before the great Shawnee chief, Tecumseh, was born in 1768 at Old Piqua, near the site of Springfield, Ohio. (Tecumseh broke a thigh when he was thrown from his horse during a bison hunt in 1787. During Tecumseh's boyhood, Ohio and Kentucky Indians organized horseback hunting parties down the Ohio Valley and across the Mississippi. At the end of the hunts, the Shawnee groups often rode south to visit their allies, the Cherokees and Chickasaws.[10])

Sporadic warfare against these Indian horsemen, their French-Canadian allies and British advisers continued until 1814. The Kentuckians organized local posses of mounted Rangers. This technique had been used on our frontiers ever since King Philip's War in Massachusetts. (John Pynchon was the captain of the Springfield Rangers. Captain Robert Rogers and his Rangers were the most famous scouts in the British-Colonial forces during the French and Indian Wars.) The Kentucky Rangers made up the bulk of the American forces in the campaigns against the Shawnees and their allies in the Ohio and Indiana wilderness. Thus Kentuckians were the first Americans to meet the red horsemen in battle.

Horse thieves, cattle rustlers, river pirates and gangs of desperadoes on the Natchez Trace kept some of the Ranger posses on the
trails for weeks at a time. The careers of Captain Samuel Mason
and the Harpe brothers at Cave-in-Rock and along the wilderness
route of the Natchez Trace make them prototypes for the "bad
men" and "gang" legends that paced American migrations into
Texas and California.

Captain Samuel Mason was the "black sheep" son of a prominent
Virginia family. After a commendable record during the Revolution, he organized a gang of cattle and horse thieves. By 1797, he
was centering his criminal skills on the "Kentucky boat" and
"broadhorn" scows that floated immigrants down the Ohio to new
homestead sites. Mason developed a syndicate of pirates that used
Cave-in-Rock, on the Illinois shore of the Ohio, as headquarters
and plunder spot. Their favorite trick was to station members of
the gang along the river in the vicinity of Henderson, Kentucky.
Presumably hunting or fishing on the shore, the gangsters hailed
immigrant boats and "hired on" to pilot the craft through the riffles,
whirlpools and deadwood barriers on the sullen swirl toward the
Mississippi. At Cave-in-Rock the "pilot" urged the immigrants to
refill their water kegs from the "real fine" springs and to explore
"the wonders" of the cavern. Mason and the rest of the gang were
waiting inside the cavern. The immigrants were murdered. The
boats and their cargoes went downstream, with a "prize crew," to
be sold at Cairo or New Madrid, Missouri.

Posses of Rangers from Pittsburgh and Louisville raided Cave-
in-Rock. Mason and most of the gang escaped downriver to Stack
Island in the Mississippi. There Mason organized a spy-and-cut-
throat system that would imperil travel on the Natchez Trace for
twenty years.

The "keelboat," rigged with sails, tow-ropes and push-poles, was
the only type of freight and passenger vessel capable of making
the upstream journey on the Mississippi. The rafts, broadhorns and
Kentucky boats that floated livestock, furs, and farm goods down
to Natchez and New Orleans were sold or abandoned at the
end of the southbound trip. Then the crews sailed back to

Natchez, bought horses to pack their purchases and "hard money," and began the six-hundred-mile trek over the Natchez Trace to head-of-navigation on the Tennessee or Cumberland rivers.

Mason secured confederates at New Orleans and Natchez. From the headquarters on Stack Island, near the present Arkansas-Louisiana boundary, Mason and the "raider" segment of the gang used spyglasses to inspect the boats heading downstream. If a cargo seemed valuable, "Slick Sam" sent word to New Orleans to have the boat's crew shadowed. The New Orleans and Natchez confederates sent estimates back to Stack Island about the sales price of the cargo and the crew's scheduled departure into the Natchez Trace. It was a simple matter then to hurry the Stack Island "raiders" overland to the Natchez Trace route in backcountry Mississippi, ambush the boat crew, hide the corpses and bring the pack-train loot back to Stack Island.

Kentucky Rangers, keelboat crews, and Spanish posses from the Louisiana shore cooperated during 1802 to uncover Mason's system. The gang broke up. A few weeks after the Louisiana Purchase in 1803, two boatmen brought a gunny sack to the U.S. Customs Office on the Natchez waterfront, dumped out Sam Mason's moldering head, and asked for a reward.

But one of the claimants was recognized to be Wiley ("Little") Harpe. Five years before, Micajah ("Big") Harpe and his "pasty-faced" brother, Wiley, had ravaged through the Kentucky backcountry with the ruthlessness of Frankenstein monsters. They, too, began stealing horses soon after they reached Kentucky from North Carolina in 1797. They murdered more than twenty settlers, including women and infants, before a Ranger posse cornered them on a Henderson County hilltop one August afternoon in 1798. Micajah "fought it out" in true desperado style, and died gasping a confession. But Wiley galloped off with his common-law wife and a few months later became "Slick Sam" Mason's lieutenant.

Wiley was brought to trial in Mississippi during 1804, sentenced, and hanged. The court ordered his head to be impaled on a stake alongside the Natchez Trace as "a warning to all outlaws." Almost six hundred miles to the northeast, at the junction of Kentucky's Henderson-Madisonville Road,[11] the skull of Micajah still leered in the tree crotch where the Ranger posse had thrust it that August night in 1798 as "a warning to all outlaws."[12]

Similar desperado acts by Joseph ("The Dandy") Hare, John A. Murrell's gang and others in Kentucky's backcountry and along the Natchez Trace continued through the 1820s. Richard Dillon in his excellent biography, *Meriwether Lewis*,[13] explores the mystery surrounding the death of the leader of the Lewis and Clark expedition at Grinder's Stand on the Natchez Trace during the night of October 9, 1809. Forcefully discrediting the legend that Lewis committed suicide, Dillon presents strong evidence that Lewis was murdered for his money and possessions, possibly by an "unknown land pirate of the ilk of the Harpe brothers."

While the river pirates, Natchez Trace desperadoes, and other lawbreakers of pioneer Kentucky forced the posses of Rangers to develop as the prototype for Texas Ranger and California Vigilante and Wyoming sheriff, three other forms of equine service to the growth of American civilization were pioneered in Kentucky: the horse boat, the Kentucky racer and the plow horse.

Upstream navigation by keelboat required a crew of boisterous, bull-strong roughnecks who would haul their craft through gorges and rapids with a "cordelling" rope or, in shallower channels, would pole the boat forward from the "running boards" that hung out from each side of the main deck. Between 1790 and 1800, a few imaginative Kentuckians began to experiment with small freight boats that would move upstream by horse power.

The principle of the paddle wheel was known. Some of the ferryboats in New York, Boston and Philadelphia harbors were propelled by a paddle wheel suspended from the stern. A boy stationed there could operate the wheel by turning a hand crank. Larger ferries, capable of carrying several horses, cows or sheep and a half-dozen humans, were powered by a treadmill built on a platform at the ship's stern. A horse, urged on by shouts of "Gee up!" and flicks of a whip, walked the treadmill. Wooden gears transmitted this horse power to the paddle wheel. The boats rarely moved faster than two miles an hour.

During 1807, at least one Ohio-Mississippi boatman installed a treadmill in a keelboat large enough for an eight-horse team. His craft splashed away from a New Orleans dock, after boasts by the "patron" that it would "break the record" into Louisville. But the vessel was wrecked near Natchez and abandoned.[14] However, the treadmill-powered stern-wheeler did succeed on freight and passenger boats, as well as on trans-river ferries across the Ohio, Cumberland, Tennessee and Mississippi. Horse boats operated at some of the river crossings until the 1920s.

The same treadmill principle worked for turning the grinding wheels at flour mills, powering the bellows at an iron furnace, operating cider presses and butter churns, and pumping water into cisterns and irrigation ditches. In effect, then, the horse boats introduced a system of horse-powered machinery to the West. The idea made its way east. During 1831, the *New England Magazine* reported an adaptation of the treadmill system for sawing wood. "A new mode of applying horsepower to move machinery," the editors wrote, "has lately been discovered by Mr. George Page, of Keene. The horse is mounted upon a band made of leather and narrow pieces of plank and this band passes round two cylinders or drums about two feet apart, the axles of which are horizontal, and one of them higher than the other. The band is supported by small wheels, which run on a railway placed under each edge. The harness of the horse is attached to an immoveable post placed near the cylinder. When made to draw, the band moves backward under him; the moving of the band causes the cylinders to revolve, and a geer [*sic*] being attached to the axle of one of them, motion is thus communicated to the machinery. . . . It has not, as yet, been applied to any purpose but sawing wood, and this it performs with great expedition. With two men to tend it, the proprietor says he can saw *thirty* cords of a mixture of soft and hard wood in a day, cutting it twice in two."[15]

Horse boats and treadmill machines, mounted posses of Rangers, and trains of pack ponies all encouraged development of a "horse-powered" society in early Kentucky. The limestone soil and gently-contoured land around Lexington plus the "eternal verdure . . . of latitude 39 degrees" made it inevitable that horse herds would supplant cattle and sheep on some of the pastures. The enthusiasm of visitors from Virginia and the Carolinas for the lithe colts developed on these pastures created one of Kentucky's first export markets to the east.

By 1792 the rush of immigrants over the Wilderness Trail through Cumberland Gap had widened it to a blazed track that could be used by Conestoga wagons, carts and livestock herds. Over it, each fall after 1795, Cracker crews herded bands of colts to the auction sales in Virginia and South Carolina. The herds averaged fifteen to thirty head. The trip from Lexington to Charleston, South Carolina, took from eighteen to twenty days. Overnight stops could be made at "drover stands," where the colts were penned in a snake-fence corral, then watered and fed cracked corn and weedy hay. At the stand-keeper's cabin, the Cracker crew could buy home-distilled whisky at "five pennies the nip," a platter of "biled taters" and venison steak for "two bits," and have the privilege of sleeping near the fireplace on the puncheon floor of the combination dining and bar room.

Likely saddle colts worth $100 at Lexington brought $125 to $150 at Charleston. Enthusiasm for "turf racing" around the mile-long circular tracks had spread north and south from the Virginia valleys. The British garrisons in New York City during the Revolution organized summer and fall schedules of race meets in Brooklyn and farther east on Long Island. In 1786, Charleston saddle-race enthusiasts formed the South Carolina Jockey Club. It was an American imitation of the English Jockey Club founded in 1752 by the group of owners and riders who gossiped, wagered and planned "plate matches" in London's Star & Garter tavern.[16]

Writing about Charleston's "golden age of racing" between 1786 and 1820, the first secretary of the South Carolina Jockey Club recalled: "Whether we consider the elevated character of the gen-

tlemen of the Turf, the attraction that the races possessed at that
time—youth anticipating its delights for weeks beforehand—the
sternness of age relaxing by their approach—lovers becoming
more ardent, and young damsels setting their caps with greater
taste and dexterity—the *quality* of the company in attendance—
the splendid equipages—the liveried outriders that were to be seen
daily on the course—the gentlemen attending the races in fash-
ionably London-made clothes—buckskin breeches and top boots—
everything combined to render race-week in Charleston emphati-
cally the carnival of the state, when it was unpopular, if not impossible, to be out of spirits, and not to mingle with the gay throng.

"The best idea we can give of the *moral influence* of race-week is
to state that the courts of justice used daily to adjourn, and all the
schools were regularly let out, as the hour for starting the horses
drew near; with one consent the stores in Broad and King streets
were closed—in fact, it was no uncommon sight to see the most
venerable and distinguished dignitaries of the land, clergymen and
judges, side by side on the course.

"Respectable strangers from abroad, or from other States, are
never allowed to pay for admissions to any of the Stands on the
Course. On their arrival they are immediately considered guests,
and provided with tickets and a ribbon which *frank* them everywhere, entitling them to the hospitalities of the club during the
whole meeting.

"The arrangements on the Course are such as to insure good
order and etiquette; refinement and high breeding characterizing
those who prefer lingering about the Grand Stand, whilst those
who wish to diversify the scene, and witness life in other phases,
can seek it out in other parts of the Course, at the booths, where
ample preparations are always made, by the different proprietors
of these restaurants, to minister, in every conceivable way, to the
tastes of the votaries of fun and frolic, and to those who also require,
in a long day, to have their inner man regaled from time to time.

"We must not omit to mention that, at considerable expense, the
Club put up a Citizens' Stand, opened to all, *gratis*—second story

arranged with rows of seats, one above the other; the lower floor divided off into different compartments, some commodiously and conveniently arranged for the accommodation of small or large parties, and fitted up in good taste."[17]

The market for "turf racing" stock in Virginia, South Carolina and New York City coincided with the need for sprightly stage-coach and carriage horses. Henry Clay, a native of Hanover County, Virginia, earned his license to practice law in 1797, crossed the Wilderness Road the same year, and "hung out his shingle" in Lexington. Within a few years, his income enabled him to develop his plantation home, Ashland, into a showplace for demonstration plots of grassland pasture, high-ceilinged barns, stallion and bull corrals, and enclosed fields of heavily manured earth that produced bumper crops of corn, oats, wheat and lucerne-grass. As intent on agricultural improvement as he was on Western expansion and protective tariffs, Clay imported Spanish jacks, Canadian pacers and English "Breds" to Ashland. He developed diets of grain and chopped hay for his brood mares and colts, and built a race track so that his stewards could keep precise running records of the crossbreds his mares were foaling. Henry Clay may have been the first importer of bluegrass seed to Kentucky.

John Breckenridge, David Meade and other early Lexingtonians followed Clay's example, developed similar experiments in grassland culture, and began crossbreeding programs. During 1797 Lexington's horsemen founded the first Jockey Club in the West. "We arrived here at exactly the right season to see the last of the spring races," William P. Fessenden wrote about an 1837 visit to Lexington with Daniel Webster. "Four horses were entered. I lost eight hailstorms [i.e. brandy juleps] on *Maria Louisa*. The Kentuckians, as you are probably aware, value themselves greatly in their breed of horses, and enter into the spirit of such an occasion, and it is not disagreeable to see such men as Clay, Crittendon, Robinson and others of that stamp apparently as much excited, talking as loudly, betting as freely, drinking as deeply and swearing as excessively as the jockeys themselves."[18]

The glamour that shimmered out of the Kentucky bluegrass region as turf racing became a national sport has all but obliterated another, and more important, contribution made by Kentucky's studs during the first half of the nineteenth century. *Poa pratensis* and the sixteen hundred square miles of limestone soil and mint-fringed streams surrounding Lexington were as important to the development of the stagecoach and carriage horse, the farm horse, and the mule as they were to the breed-up of the cavalry horses used by the Confederacy during the Civil War and the harness racers and "Breds" of the New York and New England tracks. As the "Transylvania" crossroads for the migrations to both West and South, Kentucky provided mules to the cotton growers in the Mississippi deltalands and work horses to the pioneers clearing farm-lands in Ohio, Indiana and Illinois. This trade earned greater profits for the bluegrass country's studs, between 1810 and 1860, than the "blooded" saddlers and race horses.

Sturdy Conestogans, Chickasaws and Canadian drafters were shipped to Lexington for crossbreeding. Their colts went across the Ohio to the auction markets at Cincinnati and Washington Courthouse. By 1820, horses were so plentiful in Ohio that farmers began to use them for plowing, harrowing and the dawn-to-dark labors of harvest. They found them superior in speed and intelligence to the oxen they had used "back home" in New England and New York. So the draft horse began to fix just as firmly into their way of life as the saddle horse, the "Bred" and the mule fixed into the way of life of the South. Consequently, the Ohio's snaggy channel became a socio-economic frontier between horse power and mule power and, just as clearly, between saddle racers and harness racers.

Between 1825 and 1845, the cotton planters of the South spent more than $900 million in the North for mules, other livestock, hay and farm implements. The national census for 1850 indicated that 518,990 mules were laboring in the South. Scores of thousands of them died each year from brutal treatment, scant feed, lack of wintertime shelter, and overwork. The market demands for "more

mules" were steady. Kentucky still led the nation in mule production that year, with 65,609 of the hybrids in pasture.[19]

Henry Clay died in 1852. His son, John, carried on the crossbreeding experiments at Ashland with an exciting new breed of
harness racer that had evolved in the Green Mountains of Vermont.

FIGURE'S GET

CHAPTER TWELVE

During the 1830s and 1840s, New England and New York turf-race enthusiasts cheered numerous victories by several small horses who were identical in size, color and stamina. Each was a bay with silky black legs, a black mane and a black tail. Each stood about fourteen hands high and weighed about nine hundred pounds. And each had emerged as mysteriously from Vermont's Green Mountains as Ethan Allen's men did when they captured Fort Ticonderoga.

The suspicion that a new breed of superior carriage and race horse was shaping grew into a conviction before 1850. During 1844, one of the black-pointed bays—with the track name of Fanny Jenks —pulled a sulky and driver ten miles in twenty-nine minutes and fifty-nine seconds. The following May 5, at the Bull's Head track near Albany, New York, Fanny Jenks established an all-American distance record by trotting one hundred miles in nine hours, forty-two minutes and fifty-seven seconds, then—without a break in stride or a sidelong glance toward the stables—went on to run the one-hundred-first mile in four minutes and twenty-three seconds.[1]

That same year another black-pointed bay stood at stud in Bridport, Vermont, for "$100 the leap," and had a waiting list of mares from as far south as New York City and as far north as Nova Scotia. He was named Black Hawk, and around Boston during 1840–43 he had won a score of matched-purse trotting matches. His best time for the mile was two minutes and forty-two seconds.[2]

Black Hawk's most famous son, Ethan Allen, was born on June 25, 1849. Appropriately, he was foaled at Ticonderoga. En-

24. A German coach of about 1550 A.D. The vehicle took its name from the village of Kocs in Hungary, where it was invented and first used during the 1460s. *Courtesy of the Library of Congress.*

25. Diorama of the "Flying Machine" stageline operating between New York and Philadelphia before the American Revolution. *Courtesy of the Library of Congress.*

26. Deeply chiseled lettering on the face of this Benjamin Franklin milestone is as clear as the day it was cut more than two hundred years ago. *Photo by Joseph B. Stephens, Courtesy of Yankee, Inc., Dublin, New Hampshire.*

BOSTON,
Plymouth & Sandwich
MAIL STAGE,

CONTINUES TO RUN AS FOLLOWS:

LEAVES Boston every Tuesday, Thursday, and Saturday mornings at 5 o'clock, breakfast at Leonard's, Scituate; dine at Bradford's, Plymouth; and arrive in Sandwich the same evening. Leaves Sandwich every Monday, Wednesday and Friday mornings; breakfast at Bradford's, Plymouth; dine at Leonard's, Scituate, and arrive in Boston the same evening.

Passing through Dorchester, Quincy, Wyemouth, Hingham, Scituate, Hanover, Pembroke, Duxbury, Kingston, Plymouth to Sandwich. *Fare,* from Boston to Scituate, 1 doll. 25 cts. From Boston to Plymouth, 2 dolls. 50 cts. From Boston to Sandwich, 3 dolls. 63 cts.

N. B. Extra Carriages can be obtained of the proprietor's, at Boston and Plymouth, at short notice.— STAGE BOOKS kept at Boyden's Market-square, Boston, and at Fessendon's, Plymouth.

LEONARD & WOODWARD.

BOSTON, *November 24, 1810.*

27. This poster advertising the sixteen-hour trip from Boston to the western end of Cape Cod promised a four-horse hitch of dapple-gray trotters with smartly bobbed tails and painfully tight checkreins. *Courtesy of the Bostonian Society.*

28. The driver of this coach dexterously handled six "ribbons" in guiding his matched grays over the high-plains trails. *Courtesy of the Western History Research Center, University of Wyoming.*

29. This Concord stage, with a team of four Kentucky-Morgan crosses, is reputed to have been the Russell-Majors-Waddell coach that carried Horace Greeley from St. Joseph, Missouri, to Denver, Colorado, in 1858. *Courtesy of the Chicago Historical Society.*

30. Surreys served as stagecoaches, too. This was the "express" between Meeteetse and Thermopolis, Wyoming. *Courtesy of the Western History Research Center, University of Wyoming.*

31. A Concord stage in the Wyoming hills during the 1880s, with two guards "on the deck." The teams show some Great Horse heritage. *Courtesy of the Western History Research Center, University of Wyoming.*

AN EXPRESS FREIGHT SHIPMENT OF 30 COACHES, APRIL 15, 1868
BY ABBOT, DOWNING & CO., CONCORD, N.H. TO WELLS, FARGO CO. OMAHA, NEB.

32. John Burgum's most famous painting is this scene of thirty Concord coaches rolling off toward the Union Pacific's "end of track" in 1868. There they relayed passengers between Union Pacific and Central Pacific railheads until the Golden Spike Ceremony at Promontory Summit, Utah, marked the completion of our first transcontinental railroad. *Courtesy of the New Hampshire Historical Society.*

33. Lewis Downing, the Yankee perfectionist who invented the Concord coach. *Courtesy of the New Hampshire Historical Society.*

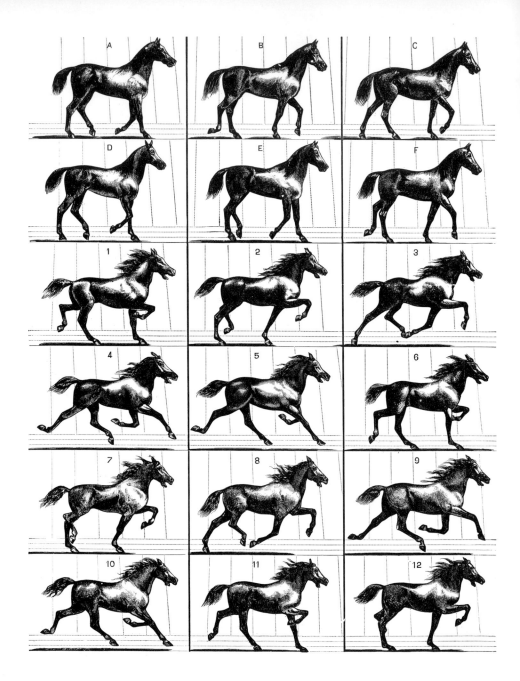

34. You can start the movie industry here with Senator Leland Stanford's curiosity as to whether all four feet were off the ground. The pictures, showing a walk (A–F) and a trot (1–12), were made with a series of cameras triggered by the moving horse, and published in the *Scientific American* on October 19, 1878. *Courtesy of F. Hal Higgins Agricultural Engineering Research Collection, University of California Library at Davis.*

35. Highlight, one of the Morgan champions at the University of Vermont's Morgan Horse Farm at Weybridge, poses with his trainer, Robert Baker, in the shadow of the memorial to Figure. *Courtesy of the University of Vermont.*

36. Kathy, one of the purebred Morgans at the University of Vermont's Morgan Horse Farm, displays the poise, deep chestnut coloration, flowing black tail and mane, and "fire" that Figure bestowed on his heritage. *Courtesy of the University of Vermont.*

37. This facsimile of the gravestone of Justin Morgan is in the Vermont Historical Society's museum at Montpelier. *Photo by Lizzari, courtesy of the Vermont Historical Society.*

38. George Harvey's painting "A Sultry Calm," done in 1840, captures the mood of a trip across New York State on the Erie Canal. *Courtesy of the New York State Historical Association, Cooperstown.*

39. E. L. Henry, famous for his painting of New York's first railroad trip, here captured the boredom of a journey through the Erie Canal. *Courtesy of the New York State Historical Association, Cooperstown.*

40. The blacksmith shop at the Pioneer Village Museum in Salt Lake City displays the hundreds of tools required for horseshoeing, farrier duties and wagon repairs. *Courtesy of the St. Joseph (Missouri) Museum.*

41. A trotter, displaying the form and color of one of Hambletonian's descendants, rolls an 1880-style buggy past the Patee House, the 1860 headquarters of the Pony Express, in St. Joseph, Missouri. *Courtesy of the St. Joseph (Missouri) Museum.*

42. Mr. and Mrs. J. I. Case behind the best matched pair to be had. Mrs. Case as a lady rider had "stolen the show" from both her husband and Abraham Lincoln at the 1859 Wisconsin Fair by winning the championship from a field of twenty. *Courtesy of F. Hal Higgins Agricultural Engineering Research Collection, University of California Library at Davis.*

43. Suburbanites of the 1890s took their "constitutionals" in runabouts like this one, with a blooded pacer or trotter in the shafts. *Courtesy of the Library of Congress.*

44. This one-hoss shay still jogs over the dirt roads of the colonial-village restoration at Old Sturbridge, Massachusetts. *Courtesy of Old Sturbridge Village.*

45. This "wonderful one-hoss shay" was owned by the Dix family of Groton, Massachusetts. *Courtesy of the Society for the Preservation of New England Antiquities.*

tered in trotting races at state fairs and northeastern tracks as a
two-year-old, Ethan Allen was declared "Champion of the World"
as a four-year-old, with a record of two minutes, twenty-five and
a half seconds for a mile run. He was eighteen years old when, in
June 1867, he established his lifetime speed record by beating
Dexter, a son of Rysdyk's Hambletonian, in three one-mile heats
with a best time of two minutes and fifteen seconds.

A search of Vermont records revealed that Black Hawk and
Fanny Jenks both carried the blood of a stallion known as Sherman.
Other splendid trotters, pacers and carriage horses out of Vermont,
and of similar stature and color, traced from stallions named Bulrush and Woodbury. The conviction grew that Sherman, Bulrush
and Woodbury were sons of a midget wonder horse who had lived
somewhere in the Vermont wilderness during the first decades of
the United States.

The first public clue to two of the most haunting, and elusive,
careers in the new United States appeared in the Albany (New
York) *Cultivator* during 1842 when Justin Morgan, Jr., a sixty-
year-old storekeeper at Stockbridge Common, Vermont, wrote an
article claiming that the founding-sire of the black-pointed bays
was a stallion named Figure whom his father had brought up-
country from West Springfield, Massachusetts. The claim was accepted by the editors of *The New England Farmer*, a magazine
published in the Connecticut Valley city William Pynchon had
founded two centuries before. During 1849, *The New England
Farmer* proudly stated that "There has never been a stock of
horses in New England which has proved so generally useful as
the Morgan stock of the original Morgan horse, raised by Justin
Morgan of West Springfield, Massachusetts."[3]

D. C. Linsley, a farmer-scholar of Middlebury, Vermont, devoted much of his time during the next decade to interviews with
Vermont grandsires and a search through family memoirs and
court records up the rocky valley of the White River and over the
hills that rear like a primordial roller coaster from the South
Royalton birthplace of Mormonism's founder, Joseph Smith, to

the granite cliffs surrounding Barre. The horse-saga substantiated by the book Mr. Linsley published in 1857 agreed with the story that the Stockbridge Common storekeeper had published fifteen years before. The stallions Sherman, Bulrush and Woodbury, plus scores of forgotten mares and stallions throughout the White River valley, were descendants of the tiny stallion that Justin Morgan, Sr., brought to his Randolph Center, Vermont, homestead from West Springfield during the summer of 1795. The Linsley book, entitled *The Morgan Horses*,[4] established the name of the new breed as "Morgans" and usurped Justin Morgan, Sr.'s name as the registry-name for the founding-sire.

Historically, this was a gross injustice. Dictionaries, textbooks, guide books, highway signs and novels have stressed "Justin Morgan" as the sire of an amazingly consistent breed of all-purpose horse. But the Randolph Center stallion who cleared woodlots, won weight-pulling and trotting matches, hauled Conestoga wagons and peddler carts, earned stud fees for twenty-two years, yet died from callous neglect in his twenty-sixth year, was named Figure. He knew no other name throughout his lifetime.

Perhaps the enthusiastic determination to give the new breed a name that actually means "sea dweller"[5] could be forgiven, if it were not for the fact that "Justin Morgan the horse" has all but obliterated "Justin Morgan the man." This situation verges on the tragic. The composer-teacher Justin Morgan is as heroic and meaningful a figure in American history as his namesake stallion.

The composer-teacher Justin Morgan was born during 1747, presumably at West Springfield. This community developed on the west shore of the Connecticut River opposite Springfield during John Pynchon's lifetime. By 1747 there were at least two Morgan families in West Springfield. Both were descended from Miles Morgan, a Welshman who settled on the Chicopee Plain near West Springfield during the 1650s.[6] Since the principal route to the West—later followed by the Boston & Albany Railroad—wound from West Springfield over the mountains to the Hudson Valley and Albany, New York, several inns and horse yards operated in the village.

Little is known about Justin Morgan's boyhood or early manhood. Many of the young men of Springfield and West Springfield marched west during 1776 and 1777 to serve under Horatio Gates, Benedict Arnold and Philip Schuyler in the series of battles that culminated in the first great American victory of the Revolution and "Gentleman Johnny" Burgoyne's surrender at Saratoga on October 17, 1777. The records indicate that these militiamen brought home several of the "Bred" and German saddle horses that British and Hessian officers had ridden during the Saratoga campaign. One of them, nicknamed Old Burgoyne, became a village pet in West Springfield.[7] Perhaps several other imported saddlers were traded off there during the late fall of 1777. Hundreds of the Hessians who had surrendered at Saratoga were marched over the Albany-Boston trail to be shipped home to Germany from Boston. They camped awhile in West Springfield. Some of the officers' horses may have gone lame during the ride over the mountains. West Springfield would have been the first logical place to trade them for fresh mounts.

Justin Morgan's occupation, and convictions, during the years of the Revolution are unknown. He first dimly appears in history during 1774 when he was twenty-six years old. He married Martha Day that year. By the time the Hessian prisoners from Saratoga marched through, Morgan either worked at, or owned, a tavern near the ferry crossing in West Springfield. A horse yard was an essential for any crossroads tavern. The Morgan tavern had one. Morgan undoubtedly traded horses, and perhaps also bred them. Highway traffic increased markedly in Massachusetts during the Revolution. Then, with the United States in prospect, hundreds of families migrated up the Connecticut Valley to pioneer homesteads in the Green Mountains wilderness. (Vermont took her name from the French name for the mountains: *Vertes Montes*, or "green mountains.")

Justin Morgan was not the ruddy-face, beer-belly type of inn-keeper popularized by the novels of James Fenimore Cooper, Washington Irving and Charles Dickens. Neighbors recalled him as tall, slim and grave, thus reminiscent of the schoolmaster in Kinderhook, New York, who served Washington Irving as the pro-totype for Ichabod Crane.

Welsh ancestry bestows a love for music. Morgan began the long, and essentially introvertive, struggle of composing melodies and verses that would express the moods of the New England sea-sons and his awe of God and Nature. This concern with the verities of life caused him to read all the books he could afford or beg. From them he accumulated enough knowledge to win the approval of neighbors as a teacher at the brief winter sessions of a "district" school.[8]

Until the 1880s, tuberculosis of the lungs was known only as "the white plague." Raw cow's milk, undernourishment, or any of a dozen sources could have infected Justin Morgan. Most of the students who have attempted to determine his life story ascribe "advanced tuberculosis" as the reason for his decision, during the summer of 1788, to move to the fresh mountain air of the White River valley, one hundred miles up the Connecticut. None of the records hint that he joined Shays' Rebellion. But a person of Justin Morgan's sensitivity would have been stirred by this farmer demonstration against bank foreclosures and the high land taxes imposed during Governor John Hancock's administration. The "hard times" finally, in 1786, caused Captain Daniel Shays to lead hundreds of farmers into Springfield for a mass protest. West Springfield was a center of the fighting that followed when Gover-nor Hancock sent General Benjamin Lincoln and four thousand of the state militia into Springfield to put down the insurrection. Many of Shays' followers fled upriver to Vermont. Perhaps both tuber-culosis and an urge for greater freedom of opportunity in Vermont influenced Morgan's 1788 decision.

The Morgans were welcomed at the hilltop community of Randdolph Center, twenty-four miles due north of the pioneer settlement of Woodstock. In 1790, Justin Morgan was elected the town clerk. Here, in a sun-dappled green wonderland, Morgan's genius as a minstrel-composer flowered. He organized singing schools, then wrote hymns and chorales for the community sings that provided much of the neighborhood's entertainment during the long winters. Some of his compositions became so beloved that they were carried downriver, accepted by compilers of songbooks, and published. Frank J. Metcalf, author of *American Writers and Compilers of Sacred Music*, lauded Morgan's "Judgment Anthem" as "remarkable." Morgan's tune "Montgomery" was still being republished in 1849. In 1953, Professor Thomas Canning of the Eastman School of Music at Rochester, New York, expressed his admiration for the musical genius of Justin Morgan by composing *Fantasy on a Hymn by Justin Morgan* on a theme from Morgan's haunting folksong "Amanda."[9]

But the frontier evil of "childbirth fever" brought disaster. On March 10, 1791, Martha Morgan gave birth to their third daughter, Polly. On March 20, Justin Morgan was a widower with four children. Justin, Jr., the first born, was only nine.

The father struggled on for two years to rear his youngsters at the Randolph farm. He was too grieved to court a stepmother for them. In 1793 he consented to put the children "our for boarding" with neighbors. By then the tubercular coughing spells were a night and morning torture. But he drove himself relentlessly in farm work and musical composition. He found a slight new source of income by organizing a class to teach penmanship to the children of Randolph Center. Still, throughout the winters, he rode the Woodstock-Randolph circuit to give afternoon singing lessons and lead the evening community sings.

Creditors still owed him money in West Springfield. Sometime during the spring of 1795, possibly riding a log boom down to the Springfield sawmills, Morgan returned to his native village and attempted to collect the debts. Details of the settlements never have been clarified. All that is known is that Justin Morgan returned to Randolph Center that fall riding a three-year-old gelding and leading a chunky bay-colored two-year-old stallion.

During the winter of 1795–96, most researchers agree, Morgan rented the young stallion out to a neighbor who was clearing trees from a piece of land in preparation for the "stumping" and plowing. The folklore of the American lumberjack's transcontinental swagger into Paul Bunyan legendry was shaping at these winter "clean outs." Tree trunks were skidded over the ridges to a creekside, then stacked for the "boom" ride on the spring's freshets to White River Junction, Brattleboro or Springfield mills.

The tiny stallion may have earned his name that winter. Woodlot horses hauled the skids of logs up hills, then braked them "cat sure" down gullies to the creekside stacks. The name of Figure would have seemed appropriate to a crew of lumberjacks for either of two reasons. A midget stallion stepping proudly through the woods with a haul of logs that weighed twelve times as much as he did would have "cut quite a figure!" Similarly, the art of applying an even, steady pull to skid such a load over a hilltop, then the quick transfer of strength from uphill pull to cautious downhill "holdback," required in 1796 parlance "considabul figurin' by a dumb brute." Whatever the source of his name, Figure earned such a favorable reputation on the winter log-skids that he was entered in matched weight-pulls and then in quarter-mile races. Legend has it that he won all of them.

Justin Morgan's cough became more rasping, his face more ashen. Sheriff Rice had become a devoted friend. Perhaps Rice insisted during December 1797 that Morgan join his family at Woodstock for Christmas and the New Year gift-giving and visiting. It is known that Morgan spent the last weeks of his life in the Rice home. He died there on March 22, 1798. His estate totaled $160 in assets, plus a book of unpublished hymns and folksongs and the tiny stallion Figure. Morgan willed Figure to Sheriff Rice to defray medical bills and funeral expenses. Sheriff Rice sold the horse to a lumberman during 1801 or 1802.

In the remaining eighteen or nineteen years of his life, Figure
had ten more owners. He worked as a lead horse on a Conestoga
wagon hitch. He plowed. He skidded logs again. He hauled a
peddler's cartload of tin pans, nutmeg graters, pewter porringers,
copper roasting pans and iron skillets up the draws and over the
rotten corduroys to farm houses throughout the Green Mountains.
He paid the bar bills for most of his owners by "leaping" at stud
for fees of two dollars to five dollars the mare.

D. C. Linsley concluded, in 1857, that Figure stood "about
fourteen hands high and weighed about nine hundred and fifty
pounds." (Later researchers estimate Figure could not have
weighed much more than eight hundred pounds.) "His color was
dark-bay with black legs, mane and tail. He had no white hairs on
him. His mane and tail were coarse and heavy—the hair of both
was straight and not inclined to curl. His head was good, not ex-
tremely small, but lean and bony, the face straight, forehead broad,
ears small and fine, but set rather wide apart. His eyes were medium
size, very dark and prominent, with a spirited but pleasant ex-
pression. . . . His chest was deep and wide, projecting a good deal
in front. His legs were short, close joined . . . with muscles that
were remarkably large. . . . He was a very fast walker. In trotting,
his gait was low and smooth, and his step short and nervous. . . .
He was a fleet runner at short distances."[10]

No physical description, however, could explain the genetic
dominance that enabled Figure to pass his intelligence, his do-or-
die willingness, his "bright but pleasant" eyes on to most of his
offspring, plus those trade-marks of small stature, big chest, and
jet-black legs, mane and tail.

Figure was tugging a Conestoga wagon as a forgotten twenty-
year-old when his son Sherman began winning quarter-path races
and weight-pulling matches in townships across Vermont, New
Hampshire and Maine. Sherman's stud fee rose to ten dollars . . .
twenty dollars . . . fifty dollars. He is reputed to have bred more
than fifteen hundred mares. But his owners failed to trace his
parentage—or didn't care.

In 1819 Figure was twenty-six years old. Harness marks welted his shoulders. His flanks were tinged with gray. At the end of a long pull, his head drooped while he drew in great wheezing breaths. His wagoner-owner sold him to a farmer named Bean near Chelsea. To Bean, Figure was a worn-out nag, fit only for spring plowing or the onerous task of hauling the manure wagon. Figure wasn't even given winter shelter.

Sometime during the spring of 1822, Bean rode out across his woodlot to round up the horses he had wintered there. He found most of them. But all that was left of Figure was the skeleton and the few scraps of hair the wolves had left.

The scholarly data Linsley presented in *The Morgan Horses* persuaded sports writers to refer to Figure as "the Justin Morgan horse," and then, simply as "Justin Morgan." They similarly re-named Sherman, Bulrush and Woodbury as the Sherman Morgan, the Bulrush Morgan and the Woodbury Morgan. The few thousand stallions and mares whose descent from Figure could be proved were admitted to stud books as Morgans.

Enthusiasm for the new breed by 1861 caused the First Vermont Cavalry to be outfitted, from colonel to ambulances, with eleven hundred mounts of "proven Justin Morgan" heritage. The audacity and thoroughness of the regiment's charge against a Confederacy entrenchment during the Battle of Gettysburg was acclaimed, by the press of New England, as "one of the most gallant cavalry charges of the War." Throughout the four years, the First Vermont fought in seventy-five battles. Only two hundred of its Morgans lived to prance in the 1865 victory parades.[11]

Morgan admirers tingled again during October 1864, when the newspapers reported that "the marvelous history-making ride of General Philip Sheridan up the Shenandoah Valley of the Battle of Winchester" was made on his favorite horse, Black Hawk Rienzi. (The fact that sculptor-painter Thomas Buchanan Read was a Pennsylvanian possibly accounted for his failure to identify Black Hawk Rienzi as a Morgan in his gallop-cadenced, but inaccurate, poem *Sheridan's Ride*.)

During the Civil War, the stallion Ethan Allen was owned by a Boston syndicate of merchants and bankers. He took daily airings in his private exercise-yard and was "handled" by a staff of grooms, stable boys and drivers, plus a consulting physician. Fourth- and fifth-generation descendants of Figure and his woodlot mares were shipped to Kentucky and Virginia to mate with "blooded" turf racers and saddle horses. Others took steamboat journeys to Galveston, Texas, during the 1870s to mate with the mustang-Virginia-Illinois hybrids who had become famous on the quarter-path race tracks outside Dallas, Fort Worth and El Paso.

Between 1870 and 1900 the flawless persistence of Figure's traits enabled outbreeding with the English "Bred," Chickasaw, Narragansett, Canadian and Mexican-dun blood lines that perfected our modern breeds of American Saddle Horse, Tennessee Walking Horse, and Quarter Horse. Morgan clubs were established, coast to coast. The U.S. army established a Morgan stud near Middlebury, Vermont, to assure a sufficient stock of "pure Morgans" for its cavalry and staff officers. (The bay ridden by George Armstrong Custer at the Battle of the Little Bighorn in 1876 was Vic, bred in Kentucky. The probabilities are that Vic carried at least "a dash" of Morgan blood.) Many of our staff officers during the Spanish-American War and World War I learned horsemanship on Morgans.

Devotion to the Morgan breed survived the Auto Age. A National Horse Show of Morgans is held each year. Scores of horse farms, especially in Vermont and Maine, specialize in "registered Morgans." A breed magazine, later renamed *The Morgan Horse Magazine*, began publication in 1941 at Woodstock, the village where Justin Morgan died. House Bill 106 of the 1961 session of Vermont's General Assembly resolved that "the state animal shall be the Morgan horse." It passed easily and became a state law that fall. (But no memorial exists in Vermont for Justin Morgan, the genius composer!)

After 1860, the legend grew that Figure was a "Thoroughbred" and had been sired by a famous "Maryland-bred Thoroughbred" known, in 1793, as Beautiful Bay. A Colonel DeLancey of a Tory cavalry troop, the Westchester Horse, the story "allegends," owned the "Thoroughbred" during the early years of the Revolution. The animal was then named True Briton. Continental soldiers from Connecticut kidnapped True Briton, smuggled him through the British patrols, and hid him on a stud farm near New London. In 1793, when he must have been more than twenty years old, True Briton was known as Beautiful Bay and under contract to stud at a livery stable in West Springfield. Presto! Figure was sired by the "Maryland-bred Thoroughbred" on a "powerful black Barb mare," then was turned over to Justin Morgan in settlement of a farm debt.

It is a delightful story. Promoters of the Kentucky Thoroughbred must have had fun concocting it. The Thoroughbred, as a breed or even as a proven blood line, did not exist in America in 1776 or in 1793. The consistent compactness of the Morgan breed, plus the black legs, mane and tail points, the valiance and the adaptability to stagecoach, wagon, sulky or saddle all suggest the heritage of Figure as a chance hybridization of Canadian horses and Narragansett Pacers with, perhaps, some Chickasaw and British cavalry-horse infusion.

The presence in West Springfield of Old Burgoyne and other English "Breds" looted or traded from British and Hessian officers offers another clue to the possible parentage of Figure. So does the fact that the Canadian and Narragansett Pacer trail drives by Benedict Arnold and other New England jockeys during 1763–64 went through West Springfield and probably used one or more West Springfield taverns for overnight "stands."

Hybrid ancestry for Figure would be proper. His breed became the most beloved all-purpose "family horse" in the United States. Morgans powered the country doctors in their desperate races against "the Angel of Death." Morgans delivered the stagecoaches on precise schedules over the new Post Roads and pikes. Morgans paced the new cast-iron and steel-faced plows of the 1840s across cropland from Maine to Iowa, then, hitched to the family buggy after dinner, jogged leisurely and unerringly on when "Junior" knotted the reins around the whipsocket and engaged both hands in "spooning" the night's adored one.

The first turnpike in the United States, the Philadelphia-Lancaster Toll Road, opened the year Figure was born. Marietta, Ohio, the first trans-Appalachian settlement by New Englanders, was five years old. Thousands of covered wagons, carts, carriages and shays formed the summer-long rushes across the West Springfield–Albany Pike and the Mohawk Trail toward the "New West." During Figure's twenty-six years, hundreds of inter-city and east-west toll roads were built as far west as Indiana. State-operated lotteries or legislative appropriations financed some of them. But the majority were launched by the sale of shares of stock, with the salesmen promising "lavish dividends" from freighter, stagecoach, carriage and drover toll fees. (Hundreds of the ventures "went bust.")

The obvious influence of the new roads was to make a horse and carriage a necessity for lawyers, doctors, ministers and other "professionals," as well as for the families of store owners, ship captains, factory executives, politicians and saloonkeepers. Toll roads, and the network of dirt lanes beaten out to them, encouraged the development of the tin peddler, the scissors man, the journeyman-blacksmith, the patent-medicine hawker and other migrants who earned precarious—and often dubious—livelihoods by wagoning their wares and "slick tricks" from farm to farm and hamlet to hamlet between March thaws and November blizzards. Our national census for 1860 reported 16,594 "peddlers" on the roads that year.

Into this medley of new roads, new vehicles and new journeyman professions cantered the compact get of Figure. They were as "gentle as a hobby horse" and snickering-grateful for every proffered apple core, biscuit crumb or lump of brown sugar. They were abubble with courage. They were quick and shrewd-as-could-be. The conviction spread that "You can breed with almost a certainty for matched drivers, and with never a fear of bull-headed, ewe-necked, long-backed, coarse-jointed, cow-hipped, rat-tailed off-spring!!! . . . The Morgan does not claim perfection, but the highest excellence; not the track-record but the road-record; not to bike but to buggy; not one mile out and repeat, but ten miles out and repeat, in from 40 to 60 minutes."[12]

Even the coachmen tipped their beaver hats to the Morgans.

THE STAGERS

CHAPTER THIRTEEN

THE CONGRESS of the United States realized the importance of the horse revolution and its potential for home industry. By 1800 it had imposed a 45 per cent tariff on all vehicles imported from abroad.[1] This action encouraged cabinetmakers and master carpenters to experiment with designs for various new types of "waggons." The wainwrights and their assistants—the wheelwright, joiner, blacksmith and whitesmith—were soon operating at county-seat towns from Damariscotta, Maine, to Lexington, Kentucky. The big dream for many of these specialists was to design a speedier and more comfortable stagecoach.

Our stagecoaches in 1800 were rigid copies of the springless wagons used on the "Flying Machines" that jolted between New York and Philadelphia during the 1770s. Dr. Johann Schopf rode one in 1783 and grumbled that they were "in reality only large wooden carts with tops."[2] The four-horse team of his vehicle was treated so brutally, he added, that "two of them died in harness."

Josiah Quincy, mayor of Boston and president of Harvard University, detailed the discomforts of the post-Revolution stagecoach passenger in a description of his 1795 trip from Boston to New York.

"We generally reached our resting place for the night, if no accident intervened, at 10 o'clock," he wrote. "After a frugal supper went to bed with a notice that we would be called at three in the morning—which usually proved to be half past two. Then, whether it snowed or rained, the traveler must arise and make ready by the help of a horn lantern and a farthing candle and proceed on his way over bad roads—sometimes with a driver showing no doubtful symptoms of drunkenness, which good hearted travelers never failed to improve at every stopping place by urging upon him the comforts of another glass of toddy. Thus we traveled eighteen miles a stage, sometimes being obliged to get out and help the coachman lift the coach out of a quagmire or rut; and arrived at New York, after a week's hard traveling, wondering at the ease as well as the expedition with which our journey was effected."[3]

The Irish poet Thomas Moore was more pungent. "Such a road as I have come! and in such a conveyance!" he wrote his mother from Baltimore on June 13, 1804. "The mail takes twelve passengers, which generally consist of squalling children, stinking negroes and republicans smoking cigars." ("Jim Crow" and other manifestations of racial prejudice were introduced *after* the Civil War.) "How often it has occurred to me that nothing can be more emblematic of the *government* of this country than its *stages*, filled with a motley mixture, all 'hail fellow well met', driving through mud and filth, which bespatters them as they raise it, and risking upset at every step. God comfort their capacities!"[4]

The capacities persisted. A few wainwrights began to build enclosed coaches with windows and leather springs. A type produced in Salem, Massachusetts, had one side door with a small window. Passengers called it "the Hen Coop." Congress encouraged more coachlines by authorizing the U.S. Post Office to subsidize lines that would agree to carry packets of mail. These mail contracts were so generous that they usually paid a line's operating costs.

The bulk of travel developed on routes connecting the three largest cities—Boston, New York and Philadelphia. British blockades along the Atlantic coast during the War of 1812 turned more travelers to them. By 1815, a score of competitive lines operated out of the three cities. And by 1829, Boston alone was the "hub" for seventy-seven coachlines.

Travel in commercial vehicles had profound influences on the nation's hotels and inns. Etymology provides a clue. The word *stage* is from the Medieval French *estage*, and originally meant "a building." The English picked up the word, discarded the initial *e*, and applied it to the inns and taverns where wagonmen and travelers stopped for meals or a few hours' sleep. So the word *stagecoach* means a "coach that travels between inns." Both the word and its English meaning migrated to America.

As our pikes opened and the coaches creaked American civilization on toward highway departments, Chambers of Commerce, traffic laws, signal lights, and the Interstate Commerce Commission, hundreds of stage-stands opened. Social status determined the four types of inns that developed. "Stage-stands which catered to stagecoach passengers," wrote the astute Stevenson W. Fletcher, "were at the top of the social ladder; usually teams were changed at these inns. A great gulf separated them from the 'wagon-stands' which were patronized only by wagoners, who slept on bags of oats or hay spread on the taproom floor."[5] Still lower, in both public esteem and "conveniences," were the "drove-stands" where livestock drovers rested. The "tap house," filthiest of all, derived its income from watered whisky and flat beer. It offered sleeping facilities only to "the drunks" who collapsed over the sawbuck-and-plank tables.

Whatever the type of hostelry, a traveler forsook privacy the instant he, or she, left home. The usual sleeping arrangement at a stage-stand was six to ten beds, arranged like dormitory bunks, in each upstairs room. Overnight guests were not expected to undress. Hand-lettered signs requested that they "Remove Boots before retiring." Male and female passengers were democratically assigned to the same room. A stage-stand described by a British traveler in western Pennsylvania during 1807 was only a little worse than the accommodations imposed on Boston Post Road travelers: "The scene in the tavern was truly novel. It was a large, half finished log house, with no apparent accommodations for any traveler who had not his own bed and blanket. It was surrounded on the outside by wagons and horses; and inside the whole floor was so filled with people sleeping, wrapped in their blankets round a large fire, that there was no such thing as approaching it to get warm until some of the travelers who had awoke at our entrance went out to feed their horses, after doing which they returned, drank whiskey under the name of bitters, and resumed their bed on the floor—singing, laughing, joking, romping, and apparently as happy as possible."[6]

Any shred of privacy that a traveler managed to retain was stripped away by the cross-examination that prefaced a request for "lodgings." Newspapers were a rarity; anyway, not more than 20 per cent of the adults in the United States could read. The traveler, then, was "fair game" for news as well as for tidbits of biographical data that might prove useful for family gossip or exaggerated recital to the "regulars" in the taproom. The probe into the traveler's destination, profession, family life, religious beliefs and political convictions began when he entered the stage-stand. Unless promptly satisfied, it could persist through the taproom's fellowship, the dining alcove's two-hour repast, and the return to the taproom for a "nightcap."

A folk tale relates that young Ben Franklin devised a formula he punctiliously followed for a half century, with only minor changes and spectacular success. Upon arrival at a stage-stand, the legend claims,[7] Ben sought out the proprietor and boomed a request that all of the proprietor's family and helpers be assembled. This set off bellows to the kitchen, yard, taproom and family quarters while Ben posed in haughty silence. When everyone was in attendance, he proclaimed: "Worthy people, I am Benjamin Franklin of Philadelphia, by trade a printer. I have some relatives in Boston to whom I am going to make a visit. My stay will be short and I shall then return and follow my business, as a prudent man ought to. This is all I know of myself and all I can possibly inform you of. I beg, therefore, that you will have pity on me and my horse and give us both refreshment."

Poor Richard's insistence on "pity" and "refreshment" for his horse as well as himself was typical of his humaneness. Also, it sounds like a sly innuendo that the horse might be neglected without this polite insistence by its owner. Repeated references to "bad

food" . . . "rooms swarming with buggs" . . . "filth" in the diaries
and letters of travelers in the early United States—from President
Washington to the embittered Englishwoman, Frances Trollope
—suggest even shabbier conditions at the stables and feed-
yards of the inns. Available evidence indicates that most innkeepers were as indifferent to the welfare of their four-legged guests as
most of Figure's owners were to his health and winter shelter.
Horses were plentiful, they must have reasoned, and cheap, and
could always be replaced! Conestoga wagonmen included feed-
troughs and rations of oats, barley and corn as standard equipment
on their vehicles. These were needed, of course, for the midday
meals beside the turnpikes. But they were also available when
the driver found it necessary to "put up for the night" at a wagon-
stand where the hay was moldy and the grain was peppered with
rat-droppings.

Evidence of callousness toward their horses by stage drivers
between 1790 and 1830, such as Dr. Schopf's mention that "two of
our team died in harness," suggests that the owners of the coaches
were, by and large, equally indifferent to the quality of their drafters and the care given them along the routes.

Then technology forced improvements. Steamboat lines began
to operate on major rivers. In 1825, completion of the Erie Canal
opened a waterway from New York City through to Chicago's
prairie wilderness. Railways were built west from Baltimore,
from Charleston, from Albany. The steamboats, the canalboats, and
the steam car threatened the stagers' monopoly in public transportation.

The birthplace of the vehicle that would enable stagecoaches to
compete was the small wainwright factory founded by Lewis
Downing at Concord, New Hampshire.

Lewis Downing was an introvertive tinkerer. His father became
a blacksmith in Lexington, Massachusetts. The new horsemanship
of the 1790s was the most profound influence of Lewis' childhood.
He migrated to New Hampshire's capital city during 1813 and,
despite the depression caused by Great Britain's blockade of New

England seaports, earned and saved enough to open a shop for the repair of wagons. The first buggy he built was sold, on November 8, 1813, to Benjamin Kimball, Jr.; the price was sixty dollars.[8]

Within three years the shop earned Downing enough profit to finance a tract of land and a larger plant. But he was a cautious perfectionist. While he pondered the details of wagon design and the most durable materials for each part, his factory paid its way by producing hardwood chopping bowls, maple and birch mixing spoons, white-pine forms to preserve the shape of beaver hats, curtain poles and almost any household item that could be sawed, carved or polished from New Hampshire's hardwood and pine forests.

Intent on the "perfect horse-drawn vehicle," Downing fashioned a code of principles. He concluded that the wheel hubs for his wagons must be fashioned from elm, the frame for the box from oak and the wheel spokes from hickory. All of these materials must be unblemished wood that had been slow-cured. He was equally adamant about the quality of the prime ox and horse hides, tannin-cured, then softened with neat's-foot oil, that his workmen proc-essed into cushions, trim, and the annealed strips of bullhide that would suspend the body of the buggy between the wheels. (The bullhide sling enabled a spring-like absorption of bumps and sways as the buggy traveled over the rough roadbeds.)

The folk tale persists that Downing periodically left his office, hammer in hand, for a cat-nervous tour of the factory. If he saw a wagon part that did not meet his standards, he smashed it, lectured the workman who had "failed his duty," and stalked on.[9]

By 1826, Downing shays, buggies and wagons were famous in New Hampshire and Massachusetts. Some time that year Downing hired a young craftsman named Stephen Abbot, the most promis-ing pupil of the Salem, Massachusetts, artist James Frothingham. Frothingham, also, earned his living building carriages, but he derived his professional satisfaction from portrait painting.

Historians are still arguing as to whether Downing or Abbot conceived the idea of the Concord Coach. Since it combined Downing's standards for flawless materials and Abbot's instinct for sleekness and bright colors, it is reasonable to assume that the creation that first took shape on the assembly floor of the factory during the spring of 1827 was a Downing and Abbot invention. (Abbot became a partner in 1828, and the name of the firm was changed to Downing & Abbot.)

Basically, the design of the Concord was similar to the egg-shaped coach created, thirty-five years before, for General Washington's inaugural journey from Mount Vernon to New York City. The cabin was U-shaped and would comfortably hold six passengers on its two leather-cushioned cross-seats. The flat top was edged by metal racks that enabled hand trunks, hat cases, portmanteaus, valises and packages to be strapped on. The oval bottom was suspended in a cradle of bullhide straps, similar to the ones Downing built into his buggies. As in the Conestoga wagon, the rear wheels were a third taller than the front ones. The driver's seat was a leather-and-wood superstructure built into the front end of the U and projecting above the front wheels. A long pole extending from the center of the front axle made it possible to use a four-horse hitch.

John Shepard of Salisbury, New Hampshire, bought the first Concord coach in July 1827.[10] The price was in the neighborhood of four hundred dollars, a most reasonable payment for the privilege of inaugurating the vehicle that, during the next sixty years, would be renamed, by local promoters, admirers and authors, the Butterfield coach, the Colorado and Overland stage, the Ben Holladay, Wells-Fargo and Deadwood stages, the California mud-wagon, and the rockaway.

No comprehensive description of the first Concord has been discovered. It is impossible to state whether a scene typical to Salisbury, New Hampshire, or a symbol especially endearing to Mr. Shepard was painted on its doors. If not, the idea pulsed through to Stephen Abbot a few weeks or months later. At Abbot's insistence, the firm hired a young English artist named John Borgum. Borgum devoted the rest of his long career to painting bucolic local scenes, or symbols, selected by the purchaser, on the molded lindenwood doors and front panels of the cabin of each Concord.

A coach operating between Boston and northern New Hampshire would be enhanced by paintings of Mount Washington and the profile of the "Old Man of the Mountain" at Franconia Notch. A coach destined for the "rockaway" from Philadelphia to Pittsburgh displayed John Borgum's green, blue and brown concept of the Ohio River's headwaters. The federal government's symbol of the bald eagle, clutching a bundle of Indian arrows, was a Concord favorite. So were portraits of George Washington, Benjamin Franklin and Thomas Jefferson. Borgum and his apprentices framed each picture in scrolls, curlicues and bows of gold leaf, scarlet, canary yellow and green.

The "Gee up" and "Lo-ow b-ridge" shouts on the towpaths of the Erie, Baltimore & Ohio, and Potomac canals, the growing clang of cast-iron rails pushing west out of Boston, Charleston, Baltimore, Philadelphia and Albany ended the stagers' resentment against investing a thousand dollars in a "Concord outfit." (The cost of a coach with Borgum's decorations rose to $500. Harness cost another $100. Four-horse teams of matched Morgans, Narragansetts or Canadian Pacers could be purchased at the studs for $325 to $400.[11] A diet of hay and oats then cost twenty-five cents —"two bits"—a day per horse.) Road tests made by Downing & Abbot demonstrated that a Concord, drawn by a four-horse hitch, could average ten miles an hour. No railway engine could equal that pace, hour after hour, in 1827. Canalboats averaged only three miles an hour.

Congress finally approved appropriations for the construction of a National Pike to connect Washington, Baltimore and Philadelphia with the Ohio-Indiana "Far West." During the 1830s the right-of-way, ninety feet wide, was built through Columbus and Indianapolis to the east shore of the Mississippi opposite St. Louis. The Cumberland, Maryland, to Wheeling, Virginia, section, across the Alleghenies, opened on August 1, 1817.

By 1830, more than 4,300,000 Americans lived west of the Alleghenies. The phrase "Far West" began to mean Missouri . . . Arkansas . . . Texas . . . even the "distant Pacific shore." Traffic over the National Pike became a day-long-night-out jangle. Stageline owners contracted with innkeepers to feed and properly house relay-teams of horses, and began to exercise some control over the quality of food and sleeping accommodations for their passengers. The "express" coaches changed horse teams every tenth mile. The Downing & Abbot factory had to be enlarged in 1830 and again in 1832. The payroll eventually grew to six hundred employees. So the Concord coach and its imitators established the Ox-bow trail, the Overland Trail, and other throughways in the race of American civilization to the Pacific.[12]

"The arrival of the stage was a much more important event than that of railroad trains today," the Pennsylvania historian W. J. McKnight wrote of the 1840s. "Crowds invariably gathered at the public houses where the coaches stopped, to obtain the latest news. The passengers were of decided account for the time being. . . . There were no tickets sold. The fare was six cents a mile, in advance, to be paid in hard money. The coaches were made in Concord, N.H., and were called 'rockaway coaches'. Each coach had heavy leather belt-springs and was a handsome vehicle, painted red, with gold stripes and letters, and was drawn by four horses.

"When nearing a relay or postoffice, the valleys and hills were made to echo and re-echo to the 'er-r-rah, er-r-rah, tat, tat, tah' of the driver's horn. The driver carried a whip with a hickory stock and a buckskin lash ten or twelve feet long, with a silk cracker on the end. These whips were handled with a marvelous dexterity, and were made to crack over the horses' heads like pistols. The roads in spring, summer and fall were a succession of mudholes, with an occasional corduroy. The male passengers usually walked up the hills."[13]

Thomas B. Searight recalled in reference to the same decade that "teams were changed almost in the twinkling of an eye. The moment [the coach] came to a halt, the driver threw down the reins, the incoming team was detached, the fresh one attached, the reins thrown back to the driver—and away again went the coach at full speed."[14]

So the sturdiness, improved comfort and gay decorations of Downing & Abbot's Concord coach enabled the stagers to compete with the early railway. As the railroads improved and tracks were laid into Chicago and St. Louis during the 1850s, Eastern stagelines became subsidiaries. Stages adjusted their schedules to those of the trains, changed their terminals to the "train depots," and began to service suburbs and rural areas. The "hack" and the "jitney" that "met all trains" to offer individual, or group, transportation to hotels, homes and "across town" railway stations were technologic stepchildren of the Concord coach, as well as the sires of the modern taxi and airport limousine.

By the 1840s, the stage driver was a spectacular figure. His symbol of office was a stovepipe hat, made from felted beaver fur. He often tucked important letters and receipts inside it to assure protection from the weather. His winter costume was a bulging raw-wool cloak, usually gray or black, topped by a shawl collar. The cloak was swathed by a woolen cummerbund dyed in the colors of the line, or, if he was a veteran with a reputation for daredevil driving, a driver was permitted a flaming red, Kelly green or gold sash. (The gold service-chevrons awarded veteran railroad conductors may have descended from this show-off.) Gleaming below the cloak were black or tan knee boots, custom-made from calfskin or cordovan leather and meticulously cleaned with biweekly buffings of lard or neat's-foot oil.

As reinsman, conductor, guard and mail bearer, the stager became a hero figure to children, a dashing Beau Brummell to village maidens, and a symbol of "evil worldliness" to preachers. Some drivers played all three of these roles with the ease of trained actors. Redding Bunting, one of the most picturesque drivers on the National Pike runs between Pittsburgh and Philadelphia, stood six feet six inches tall, weighed 250 pounds, and perfected a basso growl that was as impressive as the blasts from his brass trumpet. One day, running late out of Pittsburgh and possibly exhilarated by "sour mash rye," he gave passengers a lifelong memory by racing the teams 131 miles over the Allegeny ridges in twelve hours. Another National Pike driver named Homer Westover established a trans-Allegheny record by lurching his Concord twenty miles in forty minutes.

Headlong runs through the forests and rock cuts of the Allegheny crests were sound strategy, rather than "show-off." Gangs of robbers infested these areas. Stagecoaches occasionally carried shipments of gold or bank notes, and the Conestoga freighters brought the payments for their hauls back to their terminals in brass-studded leather chests. Stagecoaches and Pitt wagons lurching through narrow passes at a gallop stood a better chance of running down any highwaymen attempting a blockade. There are numerous stories about "stick-up" attempts in the 1830–50 wilderness between the Monongahela headwaters and the Susquehanna Valley, when the stager's blacksnake whip slashed out at hooded bandits and the Conestoga wagonmen's rifles, or "hoss pistols," flamed in the gloom.

A few stage drivers were excellent executives, as well as derring-do folk heroes. Ginery Twichell, born near Worcester, Massachusetts, in 1811, operated stagelines across Vermont and western Massachusetts by the time he was twenty-five. He drove so skillfully and administered his line's schedules and drivers so pleasingly that he became a favorite of Cornelius Vanderbilt, was elected to Congress, and in 1857 was elected president of the Boston & Worcester Railroad. During the 1870s, Twichell became a director of the Atchison, Topeka & Santa Fe Railroad, as well. He was so beloved by the time of his death in 1883 that the U.S. Postmaster General and several ex-governors of New England states attended his funeral; the sermon was delivered by the distinguished teacher-author the Reverend Edward Everett Hale.[15]

Harvey Parker, a quiet, determined farm boy from Paris, Maine, left home in 1825 with a dollar in cash and "all of his worldly possessions" wrapped in a handkerchief. He hired on as a stableboy at a livery stable and coach-stand near Boston, became an apprentice coachman and then the private coachman for a dowager in Watertown, Massachusetts. Wandering through the melee of coach terminals around the Faneuil Hall market and Scollay Square, Parker resolved to establish a restaurant, and perhaps even an inn, that would provide clean "home cooking" and friendly service. He lived frugally and, by 1832, had enough saved to purchase a restaurant for four hundred dollars. By 1854, his Tremont Restaurant earned him enough to finance the construction of the first five-story marble-faced Parker House.[16] So Parker House rolls, the gracious décor and hospitality of the Walnut Room and Oak Room restaurants in Boston's present-day Parker House, and the best tripe and "baked cod cheek" dishes proffered in New England are still delightful by-products of the coachman.

Improvements in the quality and endurance of stagecoach teams were inevitable, too, after the 1828 introduction of the Concord coach. Line owners began to patronize studs and auction barns. Some of them financed outbreeding programs for the development of fifteen-hand horses that could trot, or pace, the ten to eighteen miles between stage-stands at an average ten miles an hour. Again, the Morgans proved their adaptability. Matched teams of Morgans became standard equipment for many lines in New England and the Midwest. Heavier animals were obtained by outbreeding Morgans, Canadian drafters and Conestogas. The coach horse that evolved by 1860 for use on the mountain and hill-country relays along the Atlantic coast had an average weight of thirteen hundred pounds and stood about fifteen hands high. Crossbreeding with the heavier coach horses from Germany, France and Great Britain began after the Civil War.

The piston-like precision of stagecoach teams as they cantered the Concords toward their Far West destiny during the 1840s and 1850s popularized two styles of running "in harness." Both styles became as fashionable as a Duncan Phyfe settee or a nickel-plated, mica-windowed stove on a parlor hob. Even the North's clergymen approved the trotter and the pacer.

THE HARNESS RACER

CHAPTER FOURTEEN

THE INSTINCTIVE RUNNING GAIT developed by the Equidae during evolution was, and is, the leaping stride called a "gallop." Slow-motion photographs reveal its similarity to the running gait of the dog and the rabbit; all four feet leave the ground simultaneously. Like many of the words associated with the horse, *gallop* derives from the French. It originally meant "to run very fast."

Probably the Hyksos, and certainly the ancient Greeks, Egyptians and Assyrians, noted that some horses vary the gallop with two other kinds of peculiarly precise gaits, A chariot's stallion would lift a "near" foreleg and "off" hind leg at the same time, and never depart from this tread-and-push unity during the frenzy of a battle charge. His mate might run, just as instinctively, by lifting the front and rear legs on the same side in perfect unison, and thus surge across a field with a slightly rocking motion.

These gaits could be taught, the stable slaves learned, by tying hobble-ropes around the legs of colts. A patient system of reward and punishment conditioned the horses to use a gait consistently, and even to switch gaits in response to a slight tug of the reins or a subtle knee pressure by a rider. By 500 B.C. it was fashionable in Athens, Thebes, Babylon, Jerusalem and Rome to drive matched teams of the off-leg "treaders" or the piston-like "rockers."

By A.D. 1600 the off-leg runners were being called *trotters*. This, too, was derived from a French word, originally meaning "to tread."

The horses that ran by moving their legs in lateral pairs were named *pacers*, a word borrowed from the Latin *passus*, meaning

141

"a step." Challenge races between trotters and pacers were popular in many sections of Europe and Asia when the Virginians
pushed their first deckloads of horses overboard into the James
River.

Horse racing had devotees in early Massachusetts as well as in
Virginia. Matched races between trotters and pacers, and between
gallopers, were held in forest clearings, but with spectators carefully chosen. The early Puritan clergy condemned such "wicked-
ness." Court records in Plymouth and Salem during the 1630s report that "certain evill and disordered persons" were fined, or
sentenced to the pillory, for riding horses in races, or watching
races "with favour."[1] But the excitement of a trot or pace match
between three or four mounts in a forest clearing stimulated young
Puritans as much as a quarter-path race fascinated young Virginians. The diary that William Pynchon wrote during his term as
Massachusetts Bay Colony treasurer in Salem mentions saddle
races between pacers and trotters.[2]

The "freedom of conscience" advocated by Roger Williams made
it possible to hold horseback sports events openly in Rhode Island.
New England's first public race track was, it seems, a sandy course
laid out at Little Neck Beach, near South Kingston. Pacing and
trotting matches were held there "several times a year," beginning
soon after 1700. The owners of winning horses were awarded engraved silver tankards. Thus the Reverend James MacSparran,
hearty pastor of the Narragansett Church after 1721, could report
that he saw "some of these horses pace a mile in a little more than
two minutes and a good deal less than three."[3]

Circumstantial evidence suggests that the development of the
jockey-ship trade with the West Indies after 1648 was a motivating
factor in removing pacer and trotter matches from the New England clergy's list of "damnable sins." The growth of a premium
market for smart, proud saddle horses to be sold to plantation owners and overseers in the West Indies necessitated, as an 1833 resolution by Pennsylvania's General Assembly stressed, that the

"speed and bottom of horses be tested by means of legalized racing."[4] New England shipowners, stud keepers, rum makers, sail-loft and rope-walk operators and others directly concerned with the West Indies trade approved such tests and exerted economic pressures and neighborly argument to win the consent of the clergy.

Meanwhile, the work routine imposed on the clergy—and perpetuated by the circuit-riding systems used throughout the eighteenth and nineteenth centuries—made ministers keenly aware of the advantages in owning a speedy "square-gaited"[5] pacer or trotter. The urgency increased after the horse-and-turnpike revolution of the 1770–1810 era made at least one horse and buggy essential equipment for every parsonage and manse. Most ministers were farm-reared, hence knew and admired "good horseflesh." It was natural to "slap the reins and cluck a bit" during the afternoon rounds of home visits to parishioners and on the harried trips to and from the services at out-appointments, "come hell or high water," every Sunday afternoon and evening.

These realities served to win approval—even though it was rarely admitted publicly—of pacer and trotter matches among most of the clergymen in New England, New York and New Jersey. The air-of-approval moved west to the prairie and high-plains, and became a major factor in the popularity of harness racing over the "evil saddle racing" throughout the North and West.

The importance of the preacher's horse during this writer's childhood may unduly condition him to the conclusion that unspoken preacher approval was one of the strongest motivations for the popularity of harness races at state and county fairs and private tracks throughout the North and West after 1830.

The Reverend C. J. Howard was pastor of the Methodist Episcopal "charge" at Edenville, New York, during 1915–16. Edenville is in Orange County, only ten miles from the Good Times Track at Goshen. In those days, onions, celery, and harness racers were the three major products of the area. (An Orange County Special was a delectable concoction of cold baked beans, sliced onion and chili sauce between lavishly buttered slices of whole-wheat bread.)

The Reverend Howard strode brusquely up the Wesleyan glory road. A deck of cards for playing Old Maid or Hearts was as vicious a devil's tool as a roulette wheel. Only "savages" and "lost souls" distorted their bodies in the lewdness of the waltz and two-step. Alcoholic beverages, *any* proof, were skidways to hellfire. (The manufacturers of cough syrups and "elixirs" maintained pious silence about the 30 to 50 per cent base of alcohol in *their* products!) The saddle races at Saratoga and Belmont were trap doors to the Inferno.

But Whitey, like the Narragansett Pacers and Morgan and Hambletonian trotters, was sound economics, hence a most ethical beast. Whitey was the parsonage power source for visits to parishioners, shopping trips to Warwick, funerals, home weddings, and the Sunday-afternoon drives to and from the "out-appointment."

In his stall, or sleepwalking through the clover, skunk-cabbage and wild-onion mélange of the parsonage pasture, Whitey looked like a stage prop for *Don Quixote*. He must have been twenty years old. In youth, he may have been a bay. In 1915 his coarse hair had the tint of great-grandmother's ivory pickle fork. A gaping, orchid-tinted eye socket enhanced the sepulchral air; years before, the Reverend explained, some "drunken lout" had gouged out Whitey's eye with a pitchfork.

Whitey usually walked with his head down, his feet shuffling and his ribs threatening to collapse into the gaseous torment of his pendulous belly. But, given a cluck, a rein slap and an open road, Whitey could pace like glory-in-the-morning. Then his head came proudly erect. His belly tightened. The ribs arched back to cantilever. The "tata tat tat" of his hooves, the sudden blur of the wheel spokes into a solid shadow flitting across the stone walls and dirt banks, the metronome sway of the buggy seat were, to an eight-year-old boy, comparable only to Christmas morning, a

Barnum & Bailey circus poster, or Mother's organ rendition of "The Road to Mandalay."

The Reverend owned a vest-pocket, snap-case watch. It was railroad-accurate. The out-appointment church was in a village three miles away, and services there began promptly at three o'clock each Sunday afternoon. The preacher drove Whitey up to the parsonage horseblock between two-forty and two forty-five those afternoons, then sat, watch in hand, while his wife and son climbed into the buggy. When the second hand swept past two forty-five, he dropped the watch back into his vest pocket, nodded to his passengers, slapped the reins against Whitey's hips, and clucked.

The buggy took the turn into the Warwick Pike on two wheels. Whitey's nose pointed at the hilltops. The wheel shadows glided up the stone walls. The metronome creak of the springs, the cadence of the tawny-ivory hooves were hypnotic. Every minute or two the Reverend grunted "Now, boy."

The echo of the hoofs and spring squeaks heralded the vehicle as Whitey charged down the hilly curve to the driveway of the out-appointment. Two or three men—sometimes a half dozen—were sauntering from their carriages to the church steps. They turned, with expressionless stares. As Whitey reached the horseblock and collapsed into his *Don Quixote* stance, they pulled out their watches and snapped them open. With the same Greek-chorus precision, they bowed to the Reverend's wife as she hurried up the steps and rustled on toward the organ bench.

The writer's Sunday show-off, at age eight, was the task of clucking Whitey back to life and persuading him to stagger the final fifty feet to the church carriage-shed. The Reverend bestowed the reins, beamed his approval at the porch chorus, then, as he strode up the walk, pulled out his watch and barked, "What time have you got, Brother Williams?"

The chorus grinned and tucked their watches back into vest pockets. Brother Williams—sometimes the formality was bestowed on Brother Farris or Brother Armsbrucker—pronounced

it to be "Two fifty-eight and twenty seconds," or, rarely, "Two
fifty-seven on the nose." When it was "Two fifty-seven on the
nose," he added, "Purty good, Reverend!" and the rest of the
chorus nodded an "Amen!"

Now and again in the intervening half century, the thought has
occurred that Whitey was an important factor of male attendance,
and possibly of "regular tithing," at that out-appointment. If this
is a just presumption, it helps to vindicate the decision, by a majority of the North's clergy, to set the trotter and pacer apart from
the "sinful" saddle racer.

The "harness" part of the folk name "harness racer" originated
with the sleigh more than 150 years before carriages were used.
The winter freeze of lakes and rivers provided smooth highways.
Before 1700, priests at the French parishes in the St. Lawrence
Valley were voicing concern about the dangers of the horse-and-
sleigh racing that occurred on the river ice during the rides to and
from Sunday Masses. "The Canadian engages in racing, even at the
close of divine service," a visitor from New England observed
during the 1840s. "The practice endangers the safety of persons
on foot, and the law now ordains that no fast driving shall be permitted within a certain short distance of the sacred edifice. As
many of the churches stand near the rivers, and the worshippers
pass upon the ice, . . . the trials that take place in returning from
service are interesting to witness. The mode of handicapping, when
one horse is allowed to be more powerful or fleeter than another,
by transfer of a passenger, perhaps a woman or child from the
weaker to the stronger team, is really comical in a high degree. The
Canadians drive single, that is only one horse to a sleigh; a mode
which gives at once the most perfect control of the animal, and
taxes his powers to the utmost."[6]

Similar challenge races were common during the colonial era on
the frozen Charles, Merrimac, upper Connecticut, Thames and
Hudson rivers, especially on the Saturday-afternoon drives home
from town or during moonlit "sparking" outings by young couples.
The trot and the pace were safer gaits than the gallop on glare ice.

Also a driver gained satisfaction, and group acclaim, by holding his horse to the gait throughout a contest. The sport moved naturally out to the new highways after 1790. Challenge races, with impromptu spectator wagering, were held on straight stretches of country road wide enough for two shays or gigs to pass one another.

The first trotting race of record on a professional track was run, as an "added attraction," over the Union Course on Long Island on May 27, 1823. The winner was a stallion named old Top Gallant. But it was a saddle race. The first harness races were run on New York and New England tracks during the early 1830s. No standards for the racing vehicles were established until the eve of the Civil War. Light four-wheel wagons vied against ponderous two-wheel gigs; each weighed eighty to ninety pounds.

The superb Fanny Jenks, Black Hawk, Ethan Allen and other descendants of Figure were responsible for the popularization of the harness racers. During the late 1840s, enthusiasm soared as a long and bitter feud for harness-race supremacy developed between the Morgans and the descendants of an ill-tempered gray stallion named Messenger.

An English "Bred," Messenger was a descendant of the Darley Arabian. Foaled in 1780, he won several races as a three- and four-year-old at tracks near London. Then he became a terror of the stables because of his cold eagerness to maim any groom or jockey who came within range of his hooves or teeth. Legend states that he stamped one of his grooms to death. In 1788, Messenger was sold to a Thomas Benger and shipped to Philadelphia. Benger's effort to establish the stallion at stud, at a fee of sixteen dollars the mare, was a failure. Pennsylvania law forbade "racing by horses"; all of the colts would have to be trained as carriage horses. So Messenger was driven to New York and sold to a brother of the ex-butcher and nouveau-riche fur merchant John Jacob Astor. (Butchers were important in the popularization of harness racers. They owned many of the famous trotters and pacers of the pre-Civil War era.)

The Astors kept Messenger at stud on their Long Island and Hudson Valley estates until he breathed his last vicious gasp at Oyster Bay, Long Island, on January 28, 1808. His daughter Miller's Damsel was famous as a winner of saddle races at New York and Connecticut tracks. His son Mambrino was siring excellent pacers and trotters. Messenger was buried in a separate plot near the Astor stables, and honored with a headstone.

Old Top Gallant, winner of the first professional trotting race in 1823, was a great-grandson of Messenger. He had been led up from a Philadelphia livery stable, where he worked as a carriage drafter. He returned to the livery stable a few days after his victory and hacked out an undistinguished career. But other Messenger descendants earned grandstand cheers during the next two decades. One of them was a chestnut named The Dutchman who earned his oats and clover at a Philadelphia brickyard until a foreman noticed his persistence in delivering loads of bricks at a proud trot. Under saddle, The Dutchman trotted a mile in two minutes and thirty-three seconds. A year or two later he lowered his record to two minutes and twenty-eight seconds.

The first harness trotter to race a wagon and driver over a mile-long course in less than two and a half minutes was a great grand-daughter of Messenger named Lady Suffolk. She began her career by powering a butcher's cart around Smithtown, Long Island. She established her harness record (actually 2:29½) at a Long Island track during 1845 when she was a twelve-year-old.

Direct rivalry between the descendants of Figure and Messenger began during the early 1840s when Black Hawk, the most famous son of the Sherman Morgan, repeatedly beat the Morse Horse, a great-grandson of Messenger, at the New York state fair and at several New England tracks. But a climax of the feud loomed in 1849 when Black Hawk sired Ethan Allen and the crippled Kent Mare foaled Rysdyk's Hambletonian.

William Rysdyk was the broody, illiterate stableman on a livestock farm owned by Jonas Seeley near Goshen, New York. Like most of the farmers in Orange County, Seeley raised cattle, sheep and horses. His wife and daughters manufactured the cheese and butter he traded at neighborhood stores. Every year or two he drove a herd of fat-cattle down the Hudson Valley to the foul sales pens operated by Daniel Drew at the Bull's Head Tavern on New York City's Third Avenue. Seeley traded in horses, too, and dreamed of producing a saddle racer, trotter or pacer that would become famous.

During a trip to the Bull's Head Tavern in 1847, Seeley bought a horse named The Kent Mare. She had been so severely injured during a team runaway that she was permanently lame. But her record showed that she had once trotted a mile, in harness, at 2:41 and that she was a descendant of both Messenger and a family of English race horses known as the Norfolk Trotters. A few months later, Seeley drove The Kent Mare into Goshen and paid twenty-five dollars to have her bred by a twenty-five-year-old stallion named Abdullah, also a descendant of Messenger.

The bay colt produced by this mating was born, without human attention, some time during the night of May 4–5, 1849, under a clump of oak trees in Seeley's horse pasture. William Rysdyk had grown fond of the mare and was boasting that she would produce "a great foal." He discovered her and the still-damp son soon after dawn on the fifth, then spent the rest of the day caring for them. Within the week, Rysdyk decided that the colt would fulfill his boast. He spent so much time admiring and caring for it that Seeley scolded him. Rysdyk replied by asking Seeley to name a sales price for the mother and son. The bargaining continued for a week. Seeley finally agreed on a price of one hundred and twenty-five dollars, with fifty dollars down and the balance in time payments to be deducted from Rysdyk's wages.

Rysdyk owned a small farm near the village of Sugar Loaf. As soon as he had worked off the rest of the sales price, he resigned and took The Kent Mare and the colt off to his farm. The origin of the name he bestowed on the young stallion has never been clarified. Rysdyk never explained; reporters and friends apparently never dared to ask. The suspicion is that Rysdyk was an admirer of the great New Yorker, Alexander Hamilton, and meant to name the stallion The Hamiltonian. But when he wrote the first announcement offering his stallion at stud in 1852, he spelled the name Hambletonian. And thus it remained.

The stallion's initial fees were twenty-five dollars the mare. Rysdyk financed a trip to Long Island, where he entered Hambletonian in a harness match at the Union Course. The stallion clocked a commendable 2:48½. But Rysdyk did not enter him again. He was too busy luring horse breeders to Hambletonian's stall, pointing out the stallion's sleekness and physique, and talking up the animal's potency. He was a convincing salesman; Hambletonian's fee rose to one hundred dollars the mare.

By 1855, Hambletonian's get were proving to be as splendid harness horses as Rysdyk had promised. The stud fee rose to two hundred dollars . . . three hundred dollars . . . five hundred dollars. During his twenty-four years as a breeder, the beautiful bay sired 1,331 colts and earned Rysdyk more than $300,000. The get included George Wilkes, Dexter, Dictator, Happy Medium and scores of other trotters and pacers whose names became familiar on race cards and in the advertising sections of agricultural magazines and racing journals.

Races between the sons and daughters of Rysdyk's Hambletonian and those of Fanny Jenks, Black Hawk and Ethan Allen grew into the most popular events at the harness races. New Englanders huzzaed the Morgan horses. New Yorkers bragged about the "obvious" superiorities of the Hambletonians. Ohioans and Indianans outbred and inbred Morgan, Hambletonian, Kentucky Saddler and likely mustangs in a feverish urge to produce a hybrid that would outrun both of the master breeds. The Standardbred that evolved during the 1880's was a cross between descendants of Figure and Messenger, plus Kentucky Saddlers and high-plains duns.

The carriages drawn by the harness horse during races underwent technologic hybridization, too. The wagons and gigs used during the 1830s, plus the driver, gave the horse a 225-pound to

250-pound "drag." A lighter cart with two high wheels appeared about 1840. It enabled Ethan Allen and his rivals to run the mile in 2:30 . . . 2:20 . . . 2:15. But the two-minute mile remained the "Magic Two" until the 1890s, when ironmongers and bicycle designers produced a fifty-pound cart with wire wheel spokes and pneumatic rubber tires. Equipped with this, Lou Dillon first trotted the mile in two minutes (in 1897) and the legendary Dan Patch broke the "Magic Two" (in 1902) for the pacers.

Four-wheeler or two-wheeler, the harness racer's cart took the name *sulky*. It is an Anglo-Saxon word that means "to be slothful" or "sullen," and it was first used as a sneer-term by race fans. But in 1900 dictionary editors admitted *sulky* to standard American speech as a word meaning "a light two-wheeled carriage for a single person." The Midwest's farmers developed a hearty enthusiasm for harness racing, too. When the machine manufacturers began producing a two-horse plow equipped with wheels and a driver's seat, farmers promptly dubbed it the "sulky plow."

The harness racer exerted momentous influences on American cities. The trotter and the pacer became the executive's horse. A matched team of Morgans or Hambletonians high-stepping a carriage along a city street was as certain an indication of "a personage" as a Cadillac or Continental or Rolls-Royce with a low-number license plate is today. The harness racer also enabled the executive to develop his home "in the countryside" two . . . four . . . even ten miles from his downtown office; the trotters and pacers in his stable "commuted" him between home and office at gaits averaging six to eight miles an hour.

Clerks, factory workers, and others who could afford the delights of harness-horse transportation only by fifty-cents-an-hour rentals from livery stables were, until the advent of the horsecar, forced to live in the box-like houses and somber three- and four-story tenements that encircled the downtown area. By the time the Civil War began, this pattern was so firmly established that "mid-city blight" was already the most challenging problem of American cities.

The telephone and the electric dynamo were the "scientific miracles" on exhibit at our Sesquicentennial Exposition in 1876. Early on the morning of that March 26, a groom went to the paneled stable of Rysdyk's Hambletonian to begin the morning cleanup and rubdown. But some time during the night, as unobtrusively as he had tumbled out on Seeley's pasture twenty-six years, ten months and nine days before, the beautiful bay had died from a heart attack. He was history. William Rysdyk had died in 1874, leaving instructions in his will that the corpse of the horse was to be "fitted in new blankets, his legs drawn up against his body and strapped there, and the remains buried in a casket" beside the Rysdyk home at Chester, New York.

Hambletonian's admirers were as devoted as the breeders, race fans and New England families perpetuating the Morgan as "the American wonder horse." The Hambletonian Society was formed in 1924. In 1926, its members inaugurated the annual harness race for the Hambletonian Stakes. This race remains the annual classic of harness racing.

"OH, SUSANNAH"

CHAPTER FIFTEEN

MOST OF THE TOOLS and techniques used in the Americans' 1865–1900 conquest of the trans-Mississippi West were perfected between 1822 and 1860. This significant age of adaptation to environment began with the development of the Santa Fe Trail by trains of pack horses and ended with the unique communications system of the Pony Express. The wagon train, the bullwhacker, the wagon-circle defense against Indian raiders, the transcontinental trails, the Western stagecoach, the scout and the Missouri mule all evolved during these thirty-eight years. In this pageantry, the horse resumed his old knighthood role as the power source for the warriors and the socially important. But oxen and mules performed the menial power tasks, and outnumbered the horses in service ten to one.

The instructions given to Captain Meriwether Lewis and William Clark by President Thomas Jefferson during May 1803 stressed the necessity for day-by-day journals. The observations of Indian folkways scrawled into the record books of the 1804–6 Lewis and Clark Expedition prove that between the 1660s and 1805 the horse revolution had swept across all of the trans-Mississippi West and transformed the attitudes and habits of most red-man tribes.

The Mandans and Sioux in the upper Missouri Valley had re-designed their wintertime lodges and, by 1804, were adding lean-tos to provide shelter for horses, or partitioning off sections of the lodge interiors as horse stables. The Mandans had also learned that

153

their mounts could survive the severe winters of the upper Missouri Valley on a diet of bark from cottonwood limbs. "The Indians in our neighborhood are frequently pilfered of their horses by the Ricaries, Sioux and Assiniboines," Meriwether Lewis noted during the winter of 1804. "They make it an invariable rule to put their horses in their lodges at night. In this situation, the only food of the horse consists of a few sticks of cottonwood, from the size of a man's finger to that of his arm."[1]

The horse had become so revered among tribes in the northern Rockies that the boys selected to guard a village's herd composed chants that they sang to the animals. One of these translated to a singsong reiteration of "You are my gods. I will take care of you." These youngsters had discovered, too, that a horse's faith in a rider can be won by riding the animal out to a spot in a lake or river so deep that the horse is forced to swim. There the young rider petted him and crooned assurances. (This system works so well that it was used in England during World War I at a reclamation camp for artillery and officers' horses who became "unmanageable."[2])

The importance of the horse as the warrior's escort to "the Happy Hunting Grounds" became as pronounced as the gory rituals observed by Herodotus on the Black Sea steppes twenty-five hundred years before. A warrior's favorite horses were killed as soon as his death was proclaimed. Their heads, tails, hoofs and ornaments decorated his grave. This custom spread throughout the high-plains and mountains. In a letter to the editor of the *Western Christian Advocate* in May 1841, from the "Indian Country" of Kansas, the Reverend James M. Jameson related, "We . . . took our course through the Shawnee settlements. Nothing of interest transpired during the day except that as we passed through the prairie, we saw . . . what proved to be the grave of a Kansas Indian who had died there last fall. The body had been laid on the sod, and probably surrounded and covered with stone, after which a heap of sods had been raised over it, and the whole surrounded with a pen of small logs, within which were set up two poles. On the one was placed two scalps, taken from the heads of the enemy by the deceased young man, and which now wave over his grave as monuments of his bravery. On the other were some of the ornaments of his horse."[3]

During 1834, Prince Maximilian of Wied and the gifted Swiss artist Karl Bodmer rode the American Fur Company's steamboat *Yellowstone* up the Missouri to Fort Union, at the mouth of the Yellowstone River. Maximilian's book about the adventure[4] and Bodmer's glowing paintings of the West and its Indians are among our best sources for details of wilderness life during this era. West of Fort Union, Maximilian and Bodmer were permitted to observe the funeral ceremonies for a chief of the Blackfeet. A total of 150 horses were slaughtered to honor the chief's grave and accompany him to the Hereafter, Maximilian reported.

Both the Cayuse and Nez Percé, Lewis and Clark observed, were practicing selective breeding in efforts to develop superior stallions for warfare and the hunt. The Cayuse became so successful in this endeavor that early American immigrants gave the name "Cayuse" to the sturdy fourteen- and fifteen-hand horses they found running feral in Oregon.

Meriwether Lewis was so favorably impressed by the horses of the Nez Percé that he devoted a paragraph to them in his daily journal for February 15, 1806. "Their horses appear to be of an excellent race," he concluded. "They are lofty, elegantly formed, active and durable; in short many of them look like fine English coarsers [sic] and would make a figure in any country. Some of those horses are pided [sic] with large spots of white irregularly scattered and intermixed with the black, brown, bey [sic] or some other dark color; but much the larger portion are of a uniform color with stars, snips, and white feet, or in this rispect [sic] marked much like our best blooded horses in Virginia, which they resemble as well in fleetness as in form and color."

Dr. Francis Haines, an authority on Nez Percé history and on the Appaloosa breed of horse, deduced, a century and a half later, that Captain Lewis' description of horses "pided with large spots of white irregularly scattered and intermixed with the black, brown, bey or some other dark color" indicates that the Nez Percé of 1806 possessed, or had bred up, Appaloosa horses.[5]

The Appaloosa breed was named for a type of spotted horse found along the Palouse River of northwestern Idaho during the 1840s and 1850s. Again, the mystery of the influence of the French *coureurs de bois* on Indian horsemanship raises intriguing questions. The word *Palouse* is Canadian-French; it means "jagged rock." Since the name of the river is French, French traders knew the area well enough to bestow place names. Captain Lewis' 1806 description of the Appaloosa-type horses owned by the Nez Percé is remarkably similar to drawings of Canadian horses made at Quebec about 1700. Did *coureurs de bois* introduce "spotted horses" to the Nez Percé during trading expeditions west from Lake Superior between 1700 and 1760?

A horse discovery that impressed Captain Lewis as much as the Nez Percé stud skills was the surgery performed by the Flatheads and other tribes in castrating stallions. Lewis conceded the technique to be "superior to both American and English practices."[6] Assumedly, the operation was entrusted only to a medicine man. But it was performed on adult animals as well as colts. Geldings, the Flatheads explained, "did not tire out so easily."

Another operation, developed by the Sioux or perhaps borrowed by them from the Comanches, was the practice of slitting the horses' nostrils "up to the grissel of thare head"[7] so that they could breathe more freely during battle charges and bison hunts.

The first American introductions of Chickasaws, Conestogas, Virginia Saddlers and other types of Atlantic Seaboard horses to the trans-Mississippi West began while the Lewis and Clark Expedition was struggling over the Rockies. Between 1804 and the mid-1850s, six huge infusions of our Eastern breeds were driven and shipped into Missouri, New Mexico, Texas, Oklahoma, Idaho, Utah, and finally across the continent to California and Oregon.

The influences of these animals on the wild horse herds and on the horse stock of the high-plains and mountain tribes of the red man must have been great. Most of the "Easterners" ran in unfenced pasture after they reached their new homes. They were free to seduce, or be seduced by, the herds of feral horses. Thousands of the imports never reached the rangeland intended for them but were stolen en route across the plains by red raiders or were "spooked" into a feral state by thunderstorms, wolves or some other violence.

Were the majestic stallions that led the wild horse bands of Texas, New Mexico, Nevada and Montana during the 1870s and 1880s pure Andalusian inbreds? Or were they outbreeds of Spanish and perhaps French-Canadian strains free-mating with Virginia-Kentucky-Carolina-Vermont animals stolen, or escaped, from the 1805–60 imports? Were the get of Figure and Messenger, of Chickasaw horses, Virginia racers and Kentucky Saddlers the sires and dams of some of the horses that carried the warriors of Red Cloud, Sitting Bull, Chief Joseph, and Geronimo to the Indian Wars? The records of trans-Mississippi horse shipments between 1805 and 1860 make these questions valid.

"They have come from regions thousands of miles apart," the Reverend Timothy Flint wrote of the immigrant boats anchored along the Mississippi River's Missouri shore in 1815. "They have floated to a common point of union. The surface of the boats cover some acres. Dunghill fowls are fluttering over the roofs, as an invariable appendage. The chanticleer raises his piercing note. The swine utter their cries. The cattle low. The horses trample, as in their stables. . . . The immigration to this country pours in a flood, the power and strength of which could only be adequately conceived by persons on the spot. We have numbered a hundred persons passing through the village of St. Charles in one day."[8]

The Kentucky and Tennessee wandering by the parents of Samuel Clemens ("Mark Twain") before they settled in the Pike County hill country behind Hannibal, Missouri, was typical of the search for "good land" that impelled the Americans' rush into the new Louisiana Territory. As in Kentucky, many of the first wave of settlers were natives of Virginia or the Carolinas. These were soon followed by Pennsylvania Germans, who introduced their bank-barns and Conestoga-type horses. The Germans promptly began to deep-plow the Missouri prairie and plant crops of grain, clover and bluegrass.

The depression caused by the British blockades during the War of 1812 first sent New Englanders to Missouri. In 1815–16 more than fifteen thousand residents of Maine went "to the West."[9] In 1818, a settler told English traveler William Faux that "hundreds of wagons with droves of beasts, four or five hundred in a drove, and at least five thousand souls bound for Missouri from Kentucky had passed his house since the last harvest."[10]

Hundreds of rafts, Kentucky boats, broadhorns and arks floated families down the Ohio each spring and summer. Horse boats became increasingly popular until about 1820, when steamboats began to establish regular schedules between Pittsburgh and St. Louis. The horse boats proved particularly useful for bucking the current of the Mississippi between Cairo and St. Louis, and for trips up the Missouri. A horse boat, built from two keelboats with the horse-treadmill suspended between them, delivered the first details of U.S. troops assigned to build and man forts on the upper Missouri.[11]

The second wave of Eastern horses into the West was a product of the cottonland development made possible by the Whitney gin. Moses Austin, a native of Durham, Connecticut, migrated to Virginia soon after the Revolution and became a promoter of lead mines in the Blue Ridge. He obtained permission to settle in Missouri in 1797, six years before the Louisiana Purchase, and prospered as a trader in lead from the mines near Ste. Genevieve. The price drop for lead in 1817–20, following the end of the War of 1812, caused him to investigate the potential of American colonies in Texas. He persuaded the new Republic of Mexico to grant Texas land for settlement by three hundred Americans, but died before the colony could be organized. His plans were carried out by his son, Stephen, then a twenty-eight-year-old law clerk in New Orleans.

Development of the Austins' colony in Texas coincided with a "last stand" against the cotton planters by the cow-pen operators of western Tennessee, Mississippi and Alabama. Between 1822 and 1830, many of the Southeast's Crackers migrated to the Austin colony.

A majority of the founders of the Texas Republic were Southeasterners who, directly or indirectly, had been evicted by the development of cotton plantations. The Bowie brothers came from Georgia. Sam Houston and Davey Crockett were Tennesseeans. Colonel William B. Travis, commander of the Texans at the Battle of the Alamo, was a native of Edgefield County, South Carolina. (The late, and great, Texas editor-historian Stanley Walker summarized the migration by saying, "Tennessee is the mother of Texas.")

Horse-wise and cattle-wise, these First Families of Texas not only brought the century-old Cracker skills into the Southwest, but jogged along some of their best horses, too. The cowboys who rode up the Chisholm and Goodnight-Loving trails after 1865 were, in effect, profession-hybrids of the 1700–1820 skills of the Crackers crossed, because of environmental necessity, with the 1525–1820 skills of the Mexican *vaquero* and *ranchero*. During the 1825–65 period of the Cracker-*vaquero* blending, Spanish names, such as lariat, chaps, mustang, and remuda, were substituted for the Old Carolina cow-pen terms of rope, brush-britches, wild critters, and horse herd. Only the basic know-how of the Crackers enabled them, and their sons, to adapt so quickly to high-plains and desert ranching techniques and to the work tools that the Spanish pioneers had developed. Even so, the herdsmen who surged up from Texas after 1865 retained the Irish name "cowboy," as well as the Cracker's deftness with a blacksnake whip, and the Virginian's studious concern about quarter-path horses.

East-West hybridization took place in the Texas breed-ups of horses between 1822 and 1860. Mustangs were so plentiful, and bison so scarce, that early immigrants lived on stallion steak and mare stew until they harvested their first crops and fattened up their cattle and lambs.[12]

During 1839, President Sam Houston of the Republic of Texas had three stallions imported to Galveston from Pennsylvania to "improve the native breed of horse." One was an eleven-year-old chestnut from Lancaster named Copperbottom and alleged to be a descendant of Diomed. All three animals survived the trip, were put to stud and stayed on duty in various sections of Texas until the eve of the Civil War.[13]

Other Eastern horse imports reached Texas with every wagon train that crossed its borders. Two of the great Quarter Horse sires were Steel Dust and Dan Tucker. Each came into Texas from Illinois, jogging beside immigrant wagons. Both Morgans and Hambletonians were imported to Texas, before and after the Civil War, to "improve the breed." So were scores of valuable trotters, pacers and "Breds" from Kentucky.

Both Figure and Messenger evolved their breeds during stud stands over twenty-year periods; Rysdyk's Hambletonian mated with 101 mares during his fourth year, and, in all, sired 1,331 foals. Comparable virility by the Eastern horses imported to Texas between 1825 and 1860 must have produced scores of thousands of hybrids. Every horse has the potential of running wild, given the opportunity. And multiple opportunities existed in early Texas, especially during the 1836–37 War for Independence and the 1847–48 War with Mexico. Also, thousands of horses were stolen by the Comanche, Apache-Navaho, and other tribes during their raids across west and central Texas.

The third Far West introduction of Eastern horse stocks entered future Oklahoma during the 1830s when the Chickasaw, Creek, Choctaw, Seminole and Cherokee tribes were evicted from ancestral homelands in the Southeast. This exodus, too, was an aftermath of the cotton gin. The land greed of upland cotton planters was a major motivation for the regional "politicking" that pressured the Removal Act of 1830 through Congress and created the high-plains west of Fort Smith, Arkansas, as the "Indian Territory" home of the "Five Civilized Tribes."

The Chickasaws, Cherokees, Choctaws and Seminoles were all

veteran horsemen. More than six thousand Chickasaws were in the wagon-train processions that crossed Arkansas to the new homeland during 1837. In 1838, more than fifteen thousand Cherokees began the infamous "Trail of Tears" march, guarded by U.S. troops under the command of General Winfield Scott. (More than fifteen hundred died from pneumonia and starvation during the journey.) The Cherokees had operated prosperous cattle and horse ranches throughout the Great Smokies. They employed thousands of Negro and mulatto herdsmen and farmhands. Many of these servants accompanied them west. Thousands of saddle and harness horses were introduced to the mid-continent by the Five Civilized Tribes between 1831 and 1840. They crossbred with the feral herds of the Texas-Oklahoma-Kansas ranges, and the horses owned by the Comanche, Pawnee, Kansas and Apache-Navaho tribes.

Two other introductions of Eastern breeds went to the northern high-plains. One began with the supply trains driven from St. Louis to the Mountain Man rendezvous in Wyoming during the 1820s. Then during the 1840s, Eastern horses accompanied the wagon trains of the Oregon Trail pioneers. The impact on the get of the wild horse and Indian horse became massive during the 1847–50 marches of the Mormon pioneers to the valley of the Great Salt Lake and the 1849–60 "rushes" by gold seekers, immigrants and freighters to California, Nevada, Wyoming and Montana.

The "outfit" assigned each family of five for the Latter-day Saints' 1847 march from Winter Quarters, Nebraska, to the "Land of Deseret" was one wagon, three yoke of oxen, two cows, two steers and three sheep, plus "one, two or more saddle horses for the men to ride on guard duty."[14] The first company of 143 men, three women and two children that reached the site of Salt Lake City on July 23 had a train of seventy wagons powered by sixty-six oxen, fifty-five mules and ninety-three horses.

A horse-breeding program soon began. "In the early days, the Mormon Church invested thousands of dollars in stallions and brood mares," according to Frank C. Robertson. "They were turned loose on Antelope Island, in the middle of Salt Lake. Here, reports tell, they became 'nimble, wiry, and sure footed by continually travelling over the rough trails of the island from the time they were foaled until they were grown. It became second nature for them to jump up and down precipitous places four or five feet high.' . . . Porter Rockwell—the legendary commander of the Nauvoo Legion—is said to have imported Kentucky mares and stallions. Some escaped to the desert and bred with mustangs. Their offspring were being caught on the Nevada desert as late as 1900."[15]

Corroborating evidence comes from George E. Stewart, an attorney at Roosevelt, Utah, and a great-grandson of the Tennessee horseman Riley Stewart, who made the epochal march from Nauvoo across the Rockies. "There were four Stewart brothers, Levi, Riley, William Jackson, and Urban Van," Mr. Stewart reported. "Their birth and rearing were in Tennessee and it seems that two of them were horsemen, not the ordinary kind but the professional kind. Each of them crossed the plains with horse teams, and not with ox teams. It has been told me that my great-grandfather, Riley Stewart, was forever impatient with the daily progress made by the train and, on several occasions, wanted to forge ahead because his stock were faster and in better condition than most. The leadership of the train prevailed and in the end he plodded westward with the others until he reached the place where the trail forked. To the right was Salt Lake, to the left was California. Riley went to California. . . . He had to kill one of his horses en route to eat for they ran out of food due to the early autumn storms.

"Riley and his brother William were not particularly interested in work horses. They had a love for fast horses, in other words, hotbloods. My father told me that wherever these two went . . . they took with them the nucleus of a race-horse string. These horses were not bums, but were a pure strain of an old Tennessee-Kentucky kind. If thoroughbreds existed at that time, I assume that is what they were. My father said Riley had a colt shot because he suspected the mare had been bred by a wild stallion, and he would take no chances on coming up with a mixed strain at a later date. I feel that such a story points authentically to the quality of the horses owned by these people."[16]

During the 1849–60 Gold Rush to California and Silver Rush to Nevada, Salt Lake City became a trading center for fresh horses, mules and oxen. Between twenty-five and thirty thousand people began the overland journey to California in 1849. More than eighty thousand of the two hundred and fifty thousand settlers in California in 1852 had migrated there by wagon. Many of them refused the advice from scouts and veteran Mountain Men to "use mules or oxen," and started up the trails with Eastern horse teams. Thousands of the horses foundered and were abandoned. Other thousands were stolen by Indians or ran away. The teams that did reach Santa Fe via the southern route or Salt Lake City via the central route were in pitiful condition. The Mormons bought "jaded oxen and horses at one-fifth their cost, often blooded stock which needed only rest," Hubert Howe Bancroft reported.[17]

Some of the Eastern horses reached California, after rests at Santa Fe, Albuquerque or Salt Lake City, then mated with the splendid animals that had been bred up at the missions and ranchos. But this did not satisfy the American ranchers developing "spreads" of cattle, sheep and horses in California, Oregon and Washington. During the 1850s they imported Morgans, Hambletonians, Kentucky Saddlers and "Breds" for experimental outbreeding with native California horses—duns, blues and grullos—to obtain better cow ponies, carriage horses, coachers and drafters.

Thus, by the time the Civil War loomed, Eastern horses were influencing domestic, feral and Indian herds all across the trans-Mississippi West.

But the horse traffic was not all east-to-west. The export of Spanish horses to the United States began, insofar as the extant records related, with the questionable hunts made by Philip Nolan between 1794 and 1801. A young Kentuckian, reputed to be the son of an army officer, Nolan organized a gang of whites and Indians to smuggle horses out of the Spanish West. His gang reached the vicinity of San Antonio, Texas, some time during 1795, rounded up 250 "duns, blues and grullos," and succeeded in getting most of them back to Natchez. A second raid in 1797–98 netted a thousand horses. But when Nolan and twenty-five Americans attempted a third raid in 1801, they were ambushed. Nolan was killed. The few members of his party who survived the fight were jailed.

Sporadic efforts to steal herds of California horses and drive them across the deserts into Texas or New Mexico were made by traders and Mountain Men during the 1830s and 1840s. But, so far as records reveal, only a few hundred animals survived the trips.

The principal export of horses and mules from west to east migrated over the Santa Fe Trail into Missouri. On January 29, 1822, Captain William Becknell rode into a Missouri River valley settlement with the news that the Republic of Mexico was permitting Americans to trade at Santa Fe. Three months later, Becknell led the first pack train of trade goods back to the Great Bend of the Arkansas, west along the banks of the river to the southern Rockies, thence southwest over the tortuous causeway that would be named Raton Pass. His route established the Santa Fe Trail. The great distances between water supplies and the summer parch of grasslands across Oklahoma and eastern Colorado caused Becknell and those who followed him to heed the advice of the Santa Fe officials and switch to mule or ox power.

The first New Mexican mules for Missouri are reputed to have been driven east over the Santa Fe Trail during 1825 or 1826. "Before the importation of [Eastern] jacks into Missouri and Arkansas," James Westfall Thompson reported, "these areas relied almost wholly upon New Mexico for mules."[18] Thus trail-wise Spanish mules and jackasses, whose ancestors had powered freight across the Southwest deserts for three hundred years, became the nucleus of Missouri's mule farms. The stockmen from Pennsylvania and Maine adapted as readily to mule production as the Connecticutmen and Kentuckians had adapted a generation earlier. By 1850, the national census reported, there were 41,667 mules and jacks at breed-farms and livery stables in Missouri. During the next decade, these herds doubled; the 1860 census reported a total of 80,941. Thus the term "Missouri mule" became standard American.

Herds of Mexican oxen and Spanish saddle horses mingled, too, with the wagon trains creaking pueblo-loomed blankets, beaver and otter pelts, leather, wool, piñon nuts, Oriental silks, Spanish lace and strongboxes filled with Mexican silver home from the Santa Fe and Albuquerque markets. Most of the horses were sold to immigrants and Indian traders for use by the scouts, captains and night-guards of wagon trains. But the "likeliest" went into stud-pens to contribute to that ceaseless search for "better horses" or, prayerfully, for a new breed that would be as distinctive as the get of Figure and Messenger and "those British hot-bloods."

The oxen, like the mules, became a dependable power source of the mile-long "trains" of prairie schooners.[19] "Oxen could pull heavier loads than mules, especially through sandy or muddy tracts," James Westfall Thompson explained. "But they generally fell off more than mules as the prairie grass became drier. Another disadvantage of the ox was the tenderness of his feet. Good ox-shoers were few on the plains. Sometimes oxen were shod with moccasins made of raw buffalo hide, which worked well as long as the weather was dry, but soon wore out if they became wet with rain or, what was more usual, in fording streams. Most mules, on the other hand, traveled the whole distance from Missouri to New Mexico without being shod at all."[20]

Thus, between 1822 and 1840, the Santa Fe Trail served as a laboratory for the development of the transportation equipment, routines, work animals and specialist skills used on the Oregon, California, Oxbow, Bozeman, and other Far West trails between 1840 and 1880. The basic materials were at hand, and commonplace. The *scout* had been used as an advance trail lookout for centuries. The *ox* had been a favorite power source of the New Mexicans since 1598 and of the New Englanders since 1620. The *mule*, while a hee-haw-come-lately in the United States, had packed

Spanish expeditions across the West since the 1540s. The *prairie schooner* was a simplified Conestoga wagon, with somber camouflaging paint substituted for the Pennsylvanians' gay red-white-and-blue, and the boat-like bed trimmed down from sixteen to ten or twelve feet. The *bullwhacker's whip* was the beloved old name-giver of the Carolina Crackers. The *wagon train* was borrowed from the army's ancient technique of carrying equipment and foodstuffs on columns of wagons moving in single file. The *train captain* was just what the word implied; the commanding officer of the train. The *wagon circle*, imperative to the midday rest as well as the overnight encampment, was borrowed from the military strategists of Greece and Rome who had discovered that soldiers organized in a hollow square could effectively protect themselves from surprise attack in any direction.

The terminals developed by professional prairie freighting firms at Independence, Westport Landing, St. Joseph and other towns in the mid-Missouri valley depended largely on oxen and mules. During the 1850s, Russell, Majors and Waddell won the U.S. War Department's contract to haul supplies to all army posts west of Missouri. They used five hundred wagons to deliver the twenty-five hundred tons of food, clothing, guns and tools annually furnished to the frontier forts. The wagons were powered by seventy-five hundred oxen and several hundred mules. The remuda of horses that went out with each train was reserved for the use of train captains, scouts and night-guards. The bullwhackers walked.

Eastern horses and the Southwest's mules shared the task of hauling the first stagecoaches across the West. In 1857 John Butterfield ordered Kentucky horses used on the Missouri, Kansas and Arkansas sections of the Butterfield Company's runs over the Oxbow Trail to and from Los Angeles and San Francisco. But mules powered the dangerous runs of these Concords across Indian Territory and the Southwest.

In 1859 William Russell, always an extravagant showman, bought several hundred Kentucky, Tennessee and Morgan horses to power the Leavenworth & Pike's Peak Express Company. But wise Ben Finney and Alexander Majors supplemented them with herds of Missouri mules. The mules proved more dependable.

All of this evidence of horse importations from the East to every American colony and commercial project in the trans-Mississippi West between 1805 and 1860 testifies to a tremendous influence by Chickasaw, Conestoga, Narragansett, Virginia, Kentucky and Tennessee strains, plus Morgans and Hambletonians, on the range herds, feral mustangs and Indian horses. In all, a total of not less than two hundred thousand Eastern horses must have crossed the Mississippi and the Missouri during these fifty-five years. While the angry political campaigns of 1860 increased the threat of Civil War, descendants of the Great War Horses of the knights were being readied for still another horse revolution throughout the West.

THE DRAFTERS

CHAPTER SIXTEEN

A SEARCH FOR BREEDS of domestic animals to improve the scientific husbandry of America began during the 1790s and reached a zealous climax in the 1840s. More than eight out of every ten Americans lived on farms. More efficient types of sheep, cattle, pigs and horses were essential. On the prairies west of Ohio, the new iron tools were demonstrating that a family farm could easily expand to two hundred or even three hundred acres of cropland—when stronger work horses became available.

In 1785, bankers, physicians and gentleman farmers of eastern Pennsylvania organized the Philadelphia Society for Promoting Agriculture. Similar organizations were formed in every large city. They sponsored the searches through Europe, Africa and Asia for crops or animals that could be adopted for farm production in one or more of our climatic regions. The importation of the Spanish mule was followed by the introduction of Spanish Merino sheep, Hereford, Holstein and Brahman cattle, and various breeds of chickens and ducks.

The skill of Norman, Flemish, German and British farmers along the shores of the English Channel and North Sea, abetted by the generous rainfall and succulent foliage, had evolved the Jersey, Guernsey and Holstein breeds of milch cows as well as superior breeds of sheep and beef cattle. These same Lowlands were also the homeland of the Great War Horse that had been developed to elephantine proportions during the centuries of struggle between the knight, the longbow and the gun.

American agents were sent to Normandy, the Netherlands,

South England and the Channel Islands to examine the regional livestock. They learned that several breeds of work horse had been bred from the Great War Horse stocks. These horses ranged from fourteen hundred to more than two thousand pounds in weight, and from fifteen to seventeen hands in height. Yet from the Clydesdales of Scotland through the Perche-Normans of Normandy to the Belgians, each breed perpetuated the Great War Horse traits of a massive neck, ribs "rounded like a barrel," and "feathers" of curly hair on the lower legs.

The French called this type of horse Cheval de Gros Trait. They used him on farm wagons, plows, mail coaches and freight vans. (Legend insisted that the graceful white horses used by the cowboys in the delta plains of the Camargue were descendants of Chevaux de Gros Trait mated with Moorish stallions and mares during the thirteenth and fourteenth centuries.)

The English gave the name "draft" to all of the Great War Horse breeds. The word came from the Anglo-Saxon *dragon*, meaning "to draw or haul."

The first American import of drafters was made in 1839 when Edward Harris of Moorestown, New Jersey, had two mares and a stallion "of a Norman breed" shipped to his farm.[1] His neighbors were impressed by the animals' size, the surprising lightness of their walk, and the ease with which they pulled sledge-loads of stone during field tests. But, like the Hereford cattle John Clay had imported to his Kentucky plantation, the Norman drafters failed to attract cash customers. The animals were "too big," Harris' neighbors argued, to breed with native horses. Moreover, they would cost too much to feed, harness and house.

Yet adaptations to technology on the farms and in the cities were making the draft horse inevitable. The generation span between 1830 and 1850 marked the American farmers' transfer from wood and leather tools, usually homemade, to iron tools that were factory-made and so had to be purchased with trade goods or cash. The first successful grain-reaping machines appeared between 1832 and 1840. The first patents for disk harrows, grain drills, grain binders and threshing machines were granted between 1840 and 1850. The transition from cumbersome wooden beam plows to armor-steel moldboard plows quickened, too, with a series of inventions during the 1830s and 1840s.[2]

The new tools, the need to produce larger crops in order to pay for them, and the transportation facilities offered by the new railroads and canals all influenced agricultural expansion of crop acres and better work-animals. An average farm in the thirteen original states at the close of the Revolution totaled one hundred acres, of which only twenty-five or thirty produced grain or vegetable crops in any year. But by 1850 the size of the average American farm had increased to 202 acres. Many farmers, especially in the Midwest, tilled fifty to a hundred acres each year. "Fifteen years ago," a writer for *Appleton's Cyclopedia* wrote in 1861, "the writer required twenty men to cultivate properly a garden of thirty acres; now, by the use of a few judiciously chosen horsetools, he cultivates many times that area, with but eight farm-hands, four of whom are boys."[3]

Like many European writers during the first half of the nineteenth century, James F. W. Johnston toured as far west as Cincinnati, then hurried back to England to write a book about the United States. Of our work horses he warned: "They are, in reality, too light for heavy farm work; and when the period arrives for deep-ploughing, and the more extensive cultivation of heavy land, a heavier and stronger stock of horses, still preserving a quick step, will gradually take the place both of the oxen, which, in many States, are now extensively employed, and of the limber-horses, with which they are sometimes yoked in the same team."[4]

Similar needs for bulky, but quick-stepping, horsepower confronted the managers of street railways, freighters, construction firms and iron foundries in the city areas. New York City opened its first horsecar railroad on Fourth Avenue in 1832. Its cars, shaped like oblong boxes with small windows, were jolted over strap-iron and wood rails by two-horse teams between City Hall and Murray Hill (i.e. the present location of Grand Central Station and the

Pan-Am Building).⁵ Boston and Philadelphia soon imitated. By 1860 more than five hundred miles of horsecar lines operated in major cities between the Atlantic and bumptious Chicago.⁶ Again, as with the horse-and-carriage appearance after the Revolution, one social result was the development of new suburbs, with unpaved streets of row houses, open sewage and tiny yards. Nevertheless, the horsecar's jolting six miles an hour enabled factory craftsmen, bank tellers and clerks to move their families away from the fumes, filth and noises of the city's downtown area. In effect, the horsecar was phase two in the sprawl of the cities out toward modern suburbia.

Other urban draft-horse needs loomed from the mountains of cargo unloaded at city terminals by canalboats, railroads, steamships and sailing vessels. The vans that were used to transfer this industrial and farm wealth to warehouses, or across town to another shipping terminal, were fifteen and twenty feet long and often carried loads of ten tons gross. Ox teams were too slow and clumsy. Mules were moderately good. Drafters would be best of all.

Reasons for the failure to adapt the Conestoga horse to these needs have never been adequately explained. The record of the Conestoga as the power source for army commissary trains as well as the trans-Allegheny Pitt wagons testifies that the breed was a superior draft horse.

But, by 1840, the Pennsylvanians had built a roller-coaster canal and cableway between Lancaster and Pittsburgh. The jangle of Pitt-wagon bells changed from an 1820 crescendo to a few lonely notes tinkling counterpoint to the calls of bobwhites, cardinals and chickadees along the National Pike. The Pennsylvania Dutch farmers shrugged and abandoned their efforts to perpetuate the breed. By 1863, the Conestoga had deteriorated to a few Amish plow and wagon horses in the vicinity of York and Lancaster.⁷

Even less is known about a second breed of American drafter reputed to have been developed in Vermont during the lifetime of Figure. James Westfall Thompson reported that they were

"models of what drafthorses should be, combining immense power
with great quickness, a very respectable turn of speed, fine show
and good action." They may have been descended, Thompson believed, "from horses brought over by the Scotch-Irish, . . . the
result of crossing Lanark mares with Irish ponies, although the
absence of feather on the legs is difficult to account for unless the
Irish blood in them threw off this appurtenance."[8] But the Vermont
drafter disappeared soon after railroads built up the river valleys
in the 1830s. It never achieved a breed name.

The possibility of Canadian ancestry for the Vermont drafters
is emphasized by the memoirs about the brisk trade in Canadian
draft horses, as well as trotters and pacers, during the 1830s. The
first American importation of drafters from Normandy seems to
have been influenced by admiration for Canadian work horses.
Edward Harris compared his new Norman drafters in 1838 to "the
thorough-bred Canadian horse."[9] Four years later, in a letter to
the editor of *The Farmer's Cabinet*, Harris praised French-Canadian horses as "well known and highly prized in this section of the
country, and still more to the north, where they have undoubtedly
given that stamina and character to the horses of Vermont, New
Hampshire and the northern section of New York, which makes
them so highly valued all over the Union as road horses."[10]

Droves of Canadian drafters, all of them freebred descendants
of the Cheval de Gros Trait brought from Normandy and Brittany
during the seventeenth and eighteenth centuries, were bought by
American dealers and driven south along the same routes used
by Benedict Arnold before the Revolution. "So great was the demand at Quebec in the 1820s," Robert L. Jones reported, "that the
multitudes of horses for sale were a feature of the market place."[11]
Montreal's horse market, known as The Tattersall's of Montreal,
operated in a hotel yard near the center of the city. George Barnard, writing in 1846, declared that "yearly, ever since my recollection, the northern residents of the United States have been tak-
ing away numerous droves of the best Canadian horses, but mostly

for draft and recently the fastest trotters. . . . Many of our best, and some of our largest horses in this district are out of common mares of less than 15 hands; and got by Canadians of 14. The offspring of such often grow to 15½, and sometimes to 16 hands, and are both heavy and agile. The loss of the coarser marks of the parents in these crosses is sometimes amazing."[12]

Canadian drafters were brought into Ohio and the "Illini" country during the 1830s. Gray coated, they stood about fourteen and a half hands high and carried the leg feathering traditional to the descendants of the Great War Horse. Hundreds of prairie frontiersmen during the 1830s were veterans of the William Henry Harrison and Andrew Jackson campaigns of the War of 1812; resentment still smoldered against the "Canucks" and their Indian allies. So the gray drafters took the derogatory nickname of "Canucks." Many farmers and freighters refused to have anything to do with the "enemy" breed.

But Isaiah Dillon was a philosophic exception. A Quaker blacksmith, and blessed with the practicality that prevails among members of that sect, Dillon was one of the first settlers in Ohio to sense the need for sturdier horses to work the prairie's sticky black soils and horizon-big fields. Between 1820 and 1830 he bred up the heaviest stallions and mares he could buy in Cincinnati and Washington Courthouse. With their get, he developed a freighting business as a side-line venture. Naturally, too, he drilled his seven sons in the intricacies of horse care, crossbreeding, and wagoning. By the time each boy was old enough to sing baritone or bass at a husking-bee singalong, he was a horse expert and professional freighter.

The lure of the deep black loams of Illinois brought Isaiah Dillon and his family to Tazewell County, near the new port city of Peoria. There Isaiah first saw the "Canuck" horse. He had already created an equine law of "Breed to the largest horse thee can find." He bought several of the feather-legged gray stallions and mares and again established a blacksmith shop, a draft-horse stud and a freighting service. By 1850 the Dillons were famous as breeders of "big ones." Their "Canuck" hybrids made them the most dependable freighters in the upper Illinois River valley.

A. P. Cushman of Waynesville, Illinois, drove his Norman stallion over to the Dillon farm one afternoon in 1857. Two Ohio horse traders had imported the animal six years before from The Perche, a hilly midland region of Normandy. A shimmering dapple gray, the drafter stood sixteen hands high and weighed sixteed hundred pounds. But, like the New Jersey farmers and freighters of 1838, Ohioans had regarded the horse as a "freak"; Cushman had been able to buy him for a thousand dollars.

The Dillons examined the stallion minutely, then asked if they could "drive around a bit." That evening they offered Cushman one thousand dollars for a half-interest, provided the horse stayed at the Dillon stud and that their Canuck-hybrid mares had the first "leaps." Cushman agreed, but insisted that he was to have a choice of any of the Canuck-Perche colts.

Named Louis Napoleon and shrewdly promoted at county fairs and auctions, the stallion soon earned a profit. His foals were so promising that the Dillons decided to risk some of their freighter profits on a stud and demonstration farm devoted entirely to popularization of Perche-Norman drafters. They selected the rich grainlands around Bloomington, Illinois, as the logical location for the stud. Ellis and Levi Dillon moved their families there in 1863. More drafters from The Perche could be purchased in Ohio. Farmers and businessmen there had finally sensed the values of the drafter, so formed an organization to import Perche-Normans.

Farmers in the Bloomington area initially complained that Louis Napoleon and the other Dillon stallions were "too big for any mare around here" and that the offspring were "too fussy." It was only farmer caution. By 1865, colts sold for two and three hundred dollars at weaning time. In 1870, the year before he died, some of Louis Napoleon's colts sold for fifteen hundred dollars. (During his twenty-three years, the stallion sired more than fifteen hundred foals—four hundred stallions and eleven hundred mares.)

Ellis and Levi Dillon made the family's first drafter-hunt through Normandy in 1870. Each summer thereafter until 1885 one or more of the seven brothers searched farms and sales barns between Paris and Alençon. In all, the family imported six hundred stallions and one hundred mares. They favored the brawny, quick-stepping horses bred by the farmers in The Perche, and began promoting their imports as Percherons. The purebred and half-blood colts became so popular that the Dillons began to publish an annual sales catalogue. They built a show-barn and reception center in downtown Bloomington. Each spring, railroads ran Percheron Tour excursion trains down from Chicago. "Five well-equipped farms were devoted to the raising of horses," Jessie M. Dillon recalled. "Large barns with abundant stall room and storage room for supplies were erected on these farms. The barn on the Isaiah Dillon farm was 98 feet long, 42 feet wide and 52 feet high. A basement and two floors above provided stall room for 60 horses. There was a large number of box stalls. Granaries and shops were also provided."[13]

The hazards of bringing the Percherons across the Atlantic were almost as great as they had been for the eighteenth-century Virginians. "For the first few importations," Mr. Dillon told, "the horses were placed on the upper deck in narrow padded cells which were much like shipping crates. In the small stalls the horses had no opportunity to move and adjust themselves to the motion of the ship. As a result the flesh became bruised and sore. In some cases the scars from these sores remained through life. It was learned that on the upper deck of a ship there is more motion than on the lower decks. . . .

"Horses were placed on one of the lower decks. The stalls were made large enough to allow the horses opportunity to sway with the motion of the ship and to adjust themselves to the sudden or severe rolling. In preparation for the trip, the stalls were arranged so that the horses' heads were toward the center of the ship. The floors and partitions of the stalls were reinforced with heavy lumber. Strong wooden cleats were nailed to the floor so that the horses might place their feet firmly on them and thus keep themselves from being thrown down by the rolling and pitching of the vessel.

"During the journey the horses were constantly and anxiously watched and cared for to make sure that all was well. The stress and strain on those in charge was indeed severe. When a storm occurred, the situation was something terrible to contemplate. In the first place, fresh air was kept out by the necessary closing up of the hatchways. The rolling and pitching of the ship threw the horses about in their stalls and they had to exert themselves to the very limit while the storm lasted to keep from being thrown down. There was no rest during a storm for either horses or men. At times one or more horses lost their footing and fell. Then the attendants had to exert all their strength and ingenuity to get them to their feet again.

"By thoroughness and painstaking effort the Dillons were particularly successful in their ocean shipping. One of the smaller importers in 1882 started over with seventeen head of horses and encountered a storm at sea. The stalls broke down. The horses were thrown about amidst the broken partitions, against each other and upon each other in the center of the ship, until only two out of seventeen survived. In contrast to this experience E. Dillon & Co. during the same year brought 103 horses and a cousin, Mr. Ed Hodgson, brought about 50 more on the same ship with the same kind of care without the loss of a horse and without an accident to any of the herd."[14]

As deft in showmanship as they were in steamship precaution, the Dillons leased special trains of padded boxcars to carry each year's importation of Percherons from New York City—or sometimes Boston—to Bloomington. The cars were decorated with life-size drawings of the horses edged by garlands of bunting. Copies of the French tricolor and the Stars and Stripes were painted above the doors of each car. These Percheron Specials used the New York Central's route across New York State, switched to The Big Four at Cleveland, and crossed the corn country to Bloomington. A brass band, a parade of decorated carriages and wagons, and scores of dealers and farmer-customers invited in from Iowa, Wisconsin, Missouri and Indiana were waiting at the Bloomington depot. The brothers held open house for a week.

Thus Bloomington and her sister city, Normal, became nationally famous as a center for Percheron and half-blood drafter breeding. In 1885 more than a hundred studs and sales barns specializing in Percherons, Normans, Suffolks, Clydesdales and their hybrid get operated within a few miles of Bloomington.

It was not a monopoly. More than a thousand drafter sales barns, studs and auctions flourished throughout the Midwest. Typically, a Perche stallion named Success, imported to Chicago in 1868 by W. J. Edwards, then sold to the Fletcher Horse Company of Wayne, Illinois, founded the famous line of Dunham-Percherons.[15] Careful supervision by veterinarians enabled stud operators to breed drafter colts that matured at twenty-one hundred pounds and seventeen hands.

Thousands of Germans migrated to the Midwest during the 1850s. St. Louis, Milwaukee and Chicago developed big German-American colonies. The breweries followed, and perpetuated the Old World custom of delivering their lager and ale to saloons in gaily-painted wagons drawn by teams of six drafters. The spotless beer wagons and matched gray, brown or black teams, each horse agleam with 110 pounds of leather, steel and brass harness, became a city and county-seat tradition. The brewers had a second reason for this show-off. The word *draft* and its Medieval English twin, *draught*, have a score of meanings. One of the commonest is "Drawing from a cask or keg on order; as beer on draught." The form *draught* is the preferred spelling for "a drawing of beer." Brewers called their delivery teams "draught horses."

The saloons brought the meat packers into product promotion via drafter teams. The "free-lunch counter" at the corner saloon of the 1880s and 1890s was a Gargantuan outlay of sausages, liverwursts, baked hams and cheese, flanked by hillocks of sliced breads, crackers, pickles, slaw, and smoked herring filets. (All thirst-inducing!) So saloons were the meat packers' best customers for bratwurst, knackwurst, braunschweiger, bologna, salami and the other protein delights the Germans, Italians, Greeks and Austrians had learned to process for their pre-refrigerator and surplus-of-bulls economies. The huge meat vans, often twenty feet long and ten feet high, wafted odors of hickory smoke, pepper, cinnamon, clove and cardamom as they clattered through downtown areas. Department stores realized the promotion value of drafter teams and adopted them for their delivery vans.

All of this led to a form of competition that became as fashionable in the Midwest as "The Season" at the Saratoga races was in the East. The Union Stockyards opened in Chicago the year the Civil War ended, and became the home of our largest horse auction. The International Livestock Show, held there each November, grew into our largest competitive display of meat and work animals. The annual show-off and judging of champion teams of drafters owned by each meat packer, brewery and department store became a satin-and-white-tie event of the International's week-long evening contests in the stockyard's amphitheater.

This tradition persisted into the 1960s. A few brewers and meat packers still maintain draft-horse show teams. Anheuser-Busch of St. Louis and Wilson & Company of Chicago compete at stock shows and state fairs. (Thomas E. Wilson, the founder of Wilson & Company, was a Scotchman. Heritage bade Tom Wilson develop show teams of Clydesdales, the Scotch breed-up from the Great War Horse.)

During World War II, the Wilson & Company six-horse hitches were placed at the disposal of the War Finance Committee and the Treasury Department for showing at War Bond rallies. "It was a star attraction in parades in more than 150 cities and towns," a company executive told me. "The Treasury Department estimated that the horses were responsible for the sale of $15 million in War Bonds. . . . In the Thanksgiving Day Santa Claus parade of 1947, staged in Philadelphia by Gimbels, the hitch took over the lead position. It took the place of honor at the Mardi Gras in New Orleans and hauled the carriage of King Rex. Still a most powerful advertising medium, it is conservatively estimated that, in the course of a year, our hitch is seen by between six and seven million people.

"The horses average over two thousand pounds each. Their shoes require three and a half pounds of steel for each foot, compared with the eleven-ounce shoe of the saddle horse. When the driver is putting the hitch through maneuvers, he has about sixty-five pounds of rein pressure on his two hands. When he starts a left turn, for example, he must start the lead-horses by exerting greater pressure on the left reins of these two horses and lessening the tension of the right reins. At the same time, through his wrist and hand movements, he will hold the reins of the next two pairs tight and pull them slightly to the right. As the hitch gets well into the turn, he will bring his swing-horses to the left and finally the wheel-horses. If he had tried to turn the hitch by guiding just the lead-horses, or pulling all the horses to the left at the same time, they would come around too fast, get tangled in the traces or tip over the wagon. To make a right turn, this procedure would be reversed."[16]

The wagons still being used by Wilson's exhibition team are identical with the ones used to deliver meats in 1900. Each weighs 4,400 pounds empty and has space for 12,000 pounds of meats—a 2,750-pound draw for each drafter, assuming a 125-pound weight for the driver.

Bulk loads like this made the Percheron and other European families of the Great War Horse an essential migrant to America after the Civil War. The introduction of low-cost steel during the late 1860s hastened our technologic revolution of farm machines and city wagons. The impressive bulk, glossy coats, and ponderous cadence of the drafters made them model show horses on city delivery vehicles. Their strength, quick step, and normally placid dispositions won the favor of farmers when the great plow-up began for the corn, wheat and sugar-beet belts.

In 1900 the various trade associations promoting breeds of drafters reported a total of twenty-seven thousand purebreds in the

United States. But this revealed only a small percentage of the genetic change the drafter had created in the American horse during the thirty-three years since A. P. Cushman drove Louis Napoleon up to the Dillon hitching post. Crossbreeding had transformed the farm and city work-horses to an average fifteen and a half hands height and twelve to fifteen hundred pounds weight. At least half of our 13,537,000 horses during the first month of the twentieth century carried from 10 to 50 per cent of Great War Horse blood.

47. Overwork and brutal whippings were the lot of most work-horses. *Courtesy of Dr. J. F. Smithcors and the Iowa State University Press.*

48. The patent-medicine brag "Good For Man and Beast" became a farm folk-saying. The use of *good* to indicate a state of health began appearing in our literature about 1820. *Courtesy of Dr. J. F. Smithcors and the Iowa State University Press.*

49. Wagon train on Denver streets, 1860s. *Courtesy of the Denver Public Library Western Collection.*

50. Mule teams dominate this drawing of a Rocky Mountain wagon train made by Tavernier, the magazine illustrator, during the 1870s. *Courtesy of the National Archives.*

51. The Best Friend. *Courtesy of the Western History Research Center, University of Wyoming.*

52. Home-on-the-range couldn't be without the plow teams. The identity of this sodhouse family is unknown. The costumes indicate the photo was taken during the 1870s. The presence of the mule team and the size of the horses hints that the family came into Nebraska from Missouri. *Courtesy of the Nebraska State Historical Society.*

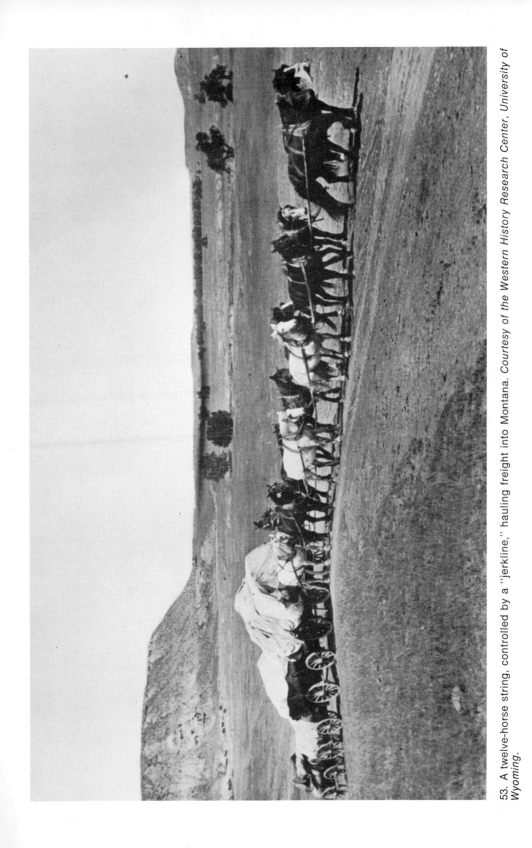

53. A twelve-horse string, controlled by a "jerkline," hauling freight into Montana. *Courtesy of the Western History Research Center, University of Wyoming.*

54. A sixteen-horse string, with a "spare" ambling beside the second team, hauls freight into the South Pass gateway-town, Lander, Wyoming. The traditional sheepwagon home of the freight crew is the caboose of the three-wagon train. *Courtesy of the Western History Research Center, University of Wyoming.*

2000 ARMY HORSES
WANTED!

I want to purchase immediately at the Government Stables at this station,

TWO THOUSAND ARMY HORSES!

For which I will pay the prices named below, IN CASH. Horses must pass inspection under the following regulations, to wit:

FOR HORSES

Sound in all particulars, well broken, in full flesh and good condition, from fifteen (15) to sixteen (16) hands high, from five (5) to nine [9] years old, and well adapted in every way to Cavalry purposes—price

160 DOLLARS!

FOR HORSES

Of DARK Color, sound in all particulars, strong, quick and active, well broken, square trotters in harness, in good flesh and condition, from six [6] to ten [10] years old, not less than fifteen and one half [15 1-2] hands high, weighing not less than ten hundred and fifty [1050] pounds each, and adapted to Artillery service,

170 DOLLARS!

N. B. VAN SLYKE,
CAPT. & A. Q. M.

Assistant Quartermaster's Office, Madison, Wis., March 22, 1865.

55. Horse fatalities were so great during the Civil War that, by the spring of 1865, army buyers offered as much as $170 each for sound cavalry and artillery animals. *Courtesy of the Chicago Historical Society.*

56. A portable smithy and farrier crew during the Civil War. *Courtesy of the Library of Congress.*

57. Six-horse teams, with riders on the off-horses of each team, raced artillery into battle during the Civil War. This battery is galloping into action at the Battle of Gettysburg. *Courtesy of the W. A. Cooper Company.*

58. These four "young fellows willing to risk death daily" were Pony Express riders . . . but their names have been forgotten. *Courtesy of the St. Joseph (Missouri) Museum.*

59. Ranch wives favored pony teams when they went "gadding" to town or to a neighbor's. *Courtesy of the Western History Research Center, University of Wyoming.*

60. Most of the "swing" and "relay" stations built across the West during the winter of 1859 to 1860 for the desperate gamble of the Pony Express looked like this one in Gothenburg, Nebraska. *Courtesy of the St. Joseph (Missouri) Museum.*

61. Rigs like this gave the head-man of a trail crew the standard nickname "wagon boss." *Courtesy of the Western History Research Center, University of Wyoming.*

62. Chow time! The T-7 Ranch crew at dinner beside their chuckwagon near Gillette, Wyoming, in 1895. Courtesy of the Western History Research Center, University of Wyoming.

63. Judges and champion riders paraded through Main Street to ballyhoo the "death-defying" rodeo show. *Courtesy of the Western History Research Center, University of Wyoming.*

64. Rodeo's broncho-ride event has a five-thousand-year heritage. The first wild-horse "busting" must have been attempted on the Black Sea or Siberian steppes before 3,000 B.C. *Courtesy of the Western History Research Center, University of Wyoming.*

65. Steamboat, the famous bucker, with Guy Holt, one of rodeo's greatest, aboard. The photo was taken in 1903. *Courtesy of the Western History Research Center, University of Wyoming.*

Union Pacific R.R. Views
Across the Continent,
West from Omaha.

A.J. Russell, Artist.

No. 94--Supply Trains, Last Siding, C. Peck's Outfit.

66. Donkeys, mules, range-ponies, as the power-source for the first conquest of the Continental Divide and high-plains by the "iron horse," pose with a construction train's crew for this A. J. Russell photo taken in Utah's Promontory Mountains a few days before the Golden Spike Ceremony. *Courtesy of the Union Pacific Railroad.*

67. Brigadier General Jack Casement, construction boss of the Union Pacific, spent most of his workdays on horseback. *Courtesy of the Union Pacific Railroad.*

68. This is the only known photograph showing "Blind Tom," the horse reputed to have hauled every rail the Union Pacific laid during its epochal race from Omaha to Promontory. *Courtesy of the Union Pacific Railroad.*

"BRED'S" PROGRESS

CHAPTER SEVENTEEN

WHILE THE STEEL AGE popularized the draft horse, an equine aristocracy was evolving in Kentucky, New York, New Jersey, Virginia and California. But the transition of the "Bred" horse to the "thorough-bred," the "thorough-blood," and finally the "Thoroughbred" did not take place in the social or economic spheres of the work horse, the mule, the family horse, or even the trotter or pacer.

Saddle racing became a favorite public sport and skill exhibition for millionaires, paupers and all the status levels between. A horse who consistently won races was as valuable a property as a flawless fifty-carat diamond—and infinitely more delicate. The breeding and ownership of saddle racers became an expensive hobby for the wealthy. A horse carrying the "Bred" pedigree of descent from Herod, Matchem or Eclipse merited a pampered environment with regulated diet, medical supervision, a personal groom and a padded box-stall.

Eventually other types of the American horse profited from the meticulous care lavished on saddle racers. The "Bred" studs and stables developed saner and more scientific practices for the welfare of all horses. Our national acceptance of veterinary medicine, more humane treatment and better housing was partly due to the demonstrations of response to these factors made by the generations of saddle racers between 1830 and 1860.

Despite the public rancor against "Mother England" that echoed out of the Revolutionary War and the War of 1812, American promoters of the saddle race accepted the dictum by England's Jockey

181

Club that the descendants of Herod, Matchem and Eclipse were the most wonderful horses on earth. Importation of English "Breds" and English advice continued. During the 1820s, John Lawrence's book, *A Philosophical and Practical Treatise on Horses and on the Moral Duties of Man towards the Brute Creation*, was read as avidly in Louisville, Lexington, New York City and Richmond as it was in Great Britain.[1] Lawrence managed, in his two-volume work, to combine "the phenomenon of blood" with rationalization for bold experiments in "thorough-blood" breeding and humane treatment. "Fine and delicate horses, the natives of warm climes, excel in swiftness," he believed. "The most perfect of these were originally found in Arabia, but they are improvable in their descendants by a more fruitful country. The Arabians tried in England have never proved themselves in any respect equal upon the course to the English racers, the descendants of their blood. . . . Although amongst horses equally well-bred, superior external conformation well generally prevail in the race, yet racing can in no sort be said absolutely to depend on good shape; it depends entirely on blood. . . . This principal is so universal that perhaps it would be altogether impracticable to find a thorough-bred horse in England sufficiently bad to be beaten by the speediest and best common bred hack. . . .

"Hot, eager and speedy horses are fittest for a short race [but] are usually beaten by horses with less speed, but stouter, at the distance of four miles, or, as it is called, over the course. . . . After all, what is the cause or basis of that superior speed, endurance and strength which distinguish the southern horse? Doubtless a peculiar innate quality of body which some attribute to the dry and elastic air of those countries where he is bred, but which appears not to me altogether satisfactory. The game, or wild animals of northern climes, possess the peculiar qualities of the race-horse, which they lose in a few generations, on being domesticated; their bones become soft and spongy, like those of tame animals in general. The race-horse is much stronger than the cart or command horse, weight for weight, his substance being of a much finer, closer and more solid contexture. The bones of the two species have been very aptly compared to steel and iron; the sinews of the racer are stronger and more capable of extension than those of the other, in proportion as a rope of silk is endowed with more strength and elasticity than a hempen one of the same weight or bulk.

"Since it has been shown that a horse does not race from the excellence of his external form merely, the grand principle of blood may be said rather to subsist in the flexibility of his sinews, and we may compare the skin of the racer to silk, his bones to steel and his fibrous system to the solid but ductile gold.

"I have enlarged on this particular, for the use of those gentlemen chiefly, who may be ambitious of still farther improving our racing breed by an import of real and thorough-shaped Arabian stock; and must farther add, that to make the experiment complete, it would be absolutely necessary to provide Arabian mares as well as stallions. The produce of these nourished, enlarged and invigorated by the fruitful soil of England must indubitably, at one or other period, attain the highest degree of excellence. Curious comparative experiments might also be made by crossing the new with the English blood. The emoluments derived from the stock of those celebrated Arabians above mentioned, might be far exceeded in these times, from the possession of horses of equal goodness."

John Lawrence's convictions not only reveal the probable origin of the physiologically meaningless terms "hot blood" and "cold blood" but demonstrate the fixations that both British and American breeders were developing about the "Bred" get of Herod, Matchem and Eclipse.[2] The first races at England's Newmarket Course were run in 1744; England's Jockey Club was founded in 1752; Eclipse died, during his twenty-sixth year, in 1790, only twelve years before Lawrence's book was published.[3] Yet, by 1830, saddle-race enthusiasts on both sides of the Atlantic had enshrined the happenstance of three Arab or Barb stallions mating with English, Scotch—and possibly Flanders?—mares under the regimen of new, hence still experimental, enclosure techniques. The blind faith in the "fruitful soil of England" establishes the emergence of the English "Bred" as one of the most lavish demonstrations of national snobbery in world history.

America's saddle-race breeders knew, as even the most patriotic members of the Jockey Club must have known, that no comparable breed of horse succeeded the British importations of Arabs and Barbs during the Crusades or the introduction of "high-class horses from the Continent"[4] to the Royal Stables of Henry V, Henry VIII, Elizabeth I and James I. A natural deduction, thus, is that the enclosures techniques of controlled breeding plus persistent experimentation in diet and housing, generation after generation, were the real reasons for the fleetness and endurance of the English racers. As for the English climate and soil, Kentucky's bluegrass region excelled any region of England in agreeable climate, rich soil and mineral-rich water. And so did sections of New York, New Jersey and Virginia.

As for those "curious comparative experiments by crossing the new with English blood," America was fabulously rich in horse-types. The chunky Chickasaw ponies possessed greater "powers of continuance" than any of the thirty-six "Breds" imported to Virginia before the Revolutionary War. Trotters and pacers imported from Canada were daisy-fresh after ten- and fifteen-mile runs. The Narragansett Pacers had proved a capacity for both speed and endurance. And, by the 1840s, both the Morgans and the Hambletonians were creating furors at Eastern tracks.

So the dream of evolving the swiftest, tallest saddle racers on earth grew across Kentucky, Virginia and New York's Long Island. The importation of English "Breds" quickened. A. Keene Richards made two journeys to Arabia and brought several Arabian mares and stallions home to Kentucky. Another large consignment of Arabians was brought to America in 1838 by a U.S. Navy squadron commanded by Commodore J. D. Elliott. The first volume of the Bruce *American Studbook*, published in 1868, listed forty-two Arabian stallions, twelve Arabian mares, four Barb stallions and two Barb mares in America.[5]

"Breds" named Sarpedon, Glencoe, Leamington, Bonnie Scotland and Australian proved to be the most distinguished racers and producers of the two hundred to four hundred imported from England between 1830 and the outbreak of the Civil War. Both Arabians and "Breds" were experimentally mated with Chickasaws, Canadians, Narragansetts, Morgans and any other horse who seemed likely to produce speedy offspring. Prescribed rations of oats and corn plus bundles of sun-cured bluegrass replaced the "daily hot breads" advocated by the eighteenth-century sportsmen. Fresh air, daily rubdowns, gentler exercises and a more cautious use of blankets were accepted; the smoky "tropical heat" once believed critically important in preserving the "fire of this desert breed" were discarded. So were many of the foul nostrums advocated by Gervase Markham and other farriery authors. But the sordid practice continued of bleeding horses "until they fall" as a prerequisite of health. In 1871 the magazine *Horseman's Friend* advised that the foot inflammation called "founders" could be cured by bleeding the afflicted horse "until it falls, then pour boiling lard over the hoof."[6]

New Georgian and Federal mansions in Kentucky's bluegrass region and on New York's Long Island became the hubs of miles of whitewashed paddock fencing, hay barns, stables and exercise tracks. Each "Bred" stallion had a full-time groom. Trainers, stable boys, jockeys, farmers and "hands" were deemed equally essential. But the production was minute in comparison to the other horse breeds. By 1900 only twenty-five thousand horses were listed in the Jockey Club's Stud Books.

Yet the dream was being realized. The height of the average American saddle racer increased from fourteen to fifteen hands; the average weight rose from nine hundred to one thousand pounds. Conformations smoothed out toward long, strongly-muscled hindquarters with slanting pasterns, carried at an angle of about forty-five degrees, and a circular body "with a depth at the withers rather less than half the height and a length equal to the height at withers and croup."[7] Decade by decade, too, new track records were established during the fashionable "race seasons" at New Orleans,

Charleston, Long Island and, beginning in March of 1851, at the Mission San Dolores Course near San Francisco. During the great North-South challenge race of 1822, the best time made in any of the three heats was seven minutes thirty-seven and a half seconds for the four miles. In 1855, the Kentucky-bred Lexington ran four miles in seven minutes, nineteen and three-quarters seconds. One-mile runs pushed steadily, over the 1830 to 1860 era, from two minutes down to 1:45.

The etymological transition from *Bred* to *Thoroughbred* moved more slowly. The Oxford English Dictionary cites John Lawrence as the first writer to apply the word *thoroughbred* to horses. He stated that "thoroughbred hacks are the most docile and quiet and least liable to shy." In the 1828 and 1843 editions of Webster's Dictionary only the general sense of "completely bred or accomplished" was used in defining *thoroughbred*. "In the next, 1847, edition," the editors of G. & C. Merriam relate, "appears *for the first time* an added sense, 'In *horsemanship*, bred from the best blood as horses.' This definition was retained with no major semantic alteration in the editions of 1864 and 1890 though the 1890 added a noun, 'A thoroughbred animal, esp. a horse.' "[8]

When the secession of Southern states and the creation of the Confederate States of America placed Kentucky on the battle front of our Civil War, more than five hundred stud farms operated in the bluegrass countryside. The habits of British sportsmen were Kentucky tradition. Owners and trainers dressed in English woolens, rode on English saddles, imitated English pronunciations of equestrian terms, rode to hounds in English-type pink coats and caps, preferred Episcopal rectors for the blessing of the hounds before each chase, and relaxed afterward by drinking mint juleps from silver-plate goblets patterned on the English Pimm's Cup. Charles E. Trevathan aptly demonstrated the fixation in the first chapter of his book *The American Thoroughbred*, when he alleged that "the American turf is only the English turf transplanted, with some alterations to a new soil. Our whole instinct for racing comes from our English and Irish ancestry. . . . We owe [the thoroughbred's] early and prominent existence in America to the coming of the first gentleman."[9]

Kentucky in 1860, Trevathan reported, "was full of foreign stallions of the purest blood. Two close relatives of *Sir Archy* stood within a few miles of Lexington. One of them, *Hephestion*, was at that time the only living son of *Buzzard* and was out of the best mare ever on this continent. . . . *Bertrand, Cherokee, Saxe Weimar, Sumpter, Kosciusko* and several others of the first sons of *Sir Archy* stood within less than a day's ride of Lexington. His brothers *Hamlintonian, Florizel, Cashier* and *Eclipse* had numerous progeny in Kentucky. No part of the United States produced perhaps so large a number and kindred of that first and noblest of American horses as this state and this part of it. Kentucky's stock of horses of other bloods than the *Diomed* or *Archy*, or only remotely related, was very fine. *Blackburn's Whip* was a son of the imported *Whip*, and was, except a defect in the withers, a most beautiful horse. His brother, *Rees's Whip*, his sons *Tiger, Paragon, Whipster, Kennon's Whip* and others were fine horses."[10]

Two other equine families destined to play critical roles in the breed-up of both the Thoroughbred and the American Saddle Horse were also "at the leap" in the Lexington countryside. The English stallion Hedgeford, foaled in 1825, was brought to New York in 1832, then shipped to Kentucky. There, during 1838, he was mated with a mare named Betsy Harrison. The foal produced of this mating was named Denmark. This stallion, mating with a mare known only as "Stevenson's mare," sired Gaines' Denmark, Muir's Denmark and Rob Roy. The get of the Denmark family, together with that of John Dillard and Tom Hal—both of direct Canadian descent—and at least two Morgan stallions, became the foundation stock of the American Saddle Horse.

Meanwhile, at the Woodburn Stud, the blind champion Lexington began his mighty contribution to the improvement of the saddle racer. Woodburn's two thousand acres of woodland and bluegrass pasture on the bank of Elkhorn Creek was, Kentuckians bragged, "the largest breeding estate in the world." It had been pioneered between 1790 and 1800 by Robert Alexander, former private secretary to Benjamin Franklin and a relative of a powerful Scots family, the Earls of Stirling. Robert Alexander inherited the Scottish skills in livestock production. He built up herds of pure-bred cattle, flocks of black-faced Highland and Cheviot sheep, and one of Kentucky's finest stables of "Bred," Canadian and Narra-gansett horses. Robert Aitchison Alexander carried on his father's livestock program, and is credited with inaugurating Kentucky's tradition of auction sales of yearling horses each spring.

En route to England in 1856 to buy more stallions for Woodburn, R. A. Alexander learned that Lexington, the Kentucky-bred stal-lion who had recently established a world's record of 7:19½ for the four-mile gallop, was going blind and would be retired to stud. Alexander purchased the horse for fifteen thousand dollars and brought him to Woodburn. By the spring of 1861, Lexington's sons and daughters were winning races; his stud fee was doubled to two hundred dollars.

Woodburn and all of the bluegrass horse farms became essential prizes to the warring armies. The forty-eight-month struggle be-tween the Confederacy and the Union was critically dependent on horsepower—and the horses were more expendable than the men who rode and drove them. The cavalry of J. E. B. Stuart and the guerrilla raiders of John Hunt Morgan rode some of the best of the South's "Breds" and Quarter Horses. Every raid left dead horses sprawled along its route; every battlefield screamed the agony of horses suffering from shrapnel, musket-ball or bayonet wounds.

Sometime during the spring of 1863, the whisper reached Robert Alexander that Confederacy raiders were riding against Wood-burn. Their orders were to capture every horse, including the blind Lexington, and drive them into Tennessee.

Alexander ordered out all available wagons, then sent his most trusted stablemen down to the Ohio River to organize a flotilla of barges and rafts. After a night-long drive over country lanes, one of the most significant cavalcades in the Thoroughbred's history reached the Ohio's shore, was loaded on the rafts and poled to the safety of Illinois.

The Woodburn herd remained in central Illinois until the final months of the war. Then Lexington and his stablemates returned to the bluegrass pastures beside Elkhorn Creek and resumed the task of making Kentucky's dream come true. The six hundred foals Lexington sired before his death in 1876 became the fruition of the dream. One of his sons was the great Kentucky, owned by Sir Winston S. Churchill's grandfather.[11] And Lexington's most famous great-great-grandson was Man O'War.

THE CONQUERORS

CHAPTER EIGHTEEN

WHEN GRANT'S CINCINNATI and Lee's Traveller finally met in the dooryard of Major Wilmer McLean's home at Appomattox Courthouse on the afternoon of April 9, 1865, a new era began for the seven to eight million horses and mules who survived the Civil War. The first "heat" of commercial steel ever made in America had been prepared at the Wyandotte Iron Works in Michigan only eight months before. Construction crews of the Union Pacific and Central Pacific were laying the first transcontinental railroad out of Omaha and Sacramento. The virgin soils of Kansas, Nebraska, and Dakota territories pushed up buffalo grass and spring flowers in deceitful welcome to the new homesteaders. Architects were drawing plans for the seven . . . ten . . . even fifteen-story buildings that would be possible with steel framework and the new steam-powered Otis elevators. The United States Veterinarians Association prepared for its third annual convention.

Low-cost steel . . . transcontinental railroads . . . homesteaders . . . skyscrapers . . . veterinarians would become keys in the pioneering the horse and mule must undertake between 1865 and 1900. The challenge was the conquest of the trans-Missouri wilderness, the expansion of our cities, the establishment of our wheat, corn, and sugar-beet belts, and the hauling of supplies for a population that would more than double during thirty-five years, all of which required the work-power of the horse and mule. The veterinarians, aided by a growing awareness that humane treatment of work-animals is "sound economics," would meanwhile develop

190

sanitation and diet standards and principles of scientific breeding that would enable our horse population to double.

The companionship and interdependence developed between soldiers and their horses and mules during the Civil War must have contributed to the greater consideration shown our work-animals after 1865. From Bull Run to Appomattox, it was a horse- and mule-powered war with every army dependent on field artillery and cavalry columns, every company of infantry dependent on commissary wagons, every wounded or sick fighter praying for the arrival of the ambulance wagon.

Horse and mule mortality during the four years was twice as great as human mortality. The death toll of soldiers, sailors and marines is estimated at 618,000: 258,000 Confederates and 300,000 Union fighters.[1] Between 1,200,000 and 1,500,000 horses and mules died "in service." Horses were primary targets on the battle fronts. Union commanders reported that Confederate sharpshooters killed or wounded an average of five hundred Union horses a day. More than 100,000 horses and mules died during a virus plague in 1862–63. Only two hundred of the one thousand Morgans who carried the First Vermont Regiment to the front in 1861 survived the war.[2] Battlefield photographs and sketches show horse carcasses sprawled every few feet. Epidemics of pneumonia, influenza and glanders ravaged the herds of the opposing forces from Vicksburg to the Virginia Wilderness during 1863 and 1864. Many of the horses sold by the Army during 1865–66 had glanders and were later destroyed—but not in time to prevent a major epidemic in the Midwest.[3]

Nevertheless, the medical services provided army work-animals show more concern about diet, shelter, medicine and surgery than had been given to the horses, mules and oxen of the Revolution, the War of 1812 and the War with Mexico. The Union's War Department created the rank of veterinary sergeant during 1861. Each "V.S." supervised the farriers and handlers assigned to three battalions of cavalry. During 1863, the rank was replaced by regimental sergeant majors. These appointees, with a salary of seventy-five dollars a month, supervised all the farriers attached to a cavalry regiment, and were assumed skillful enough to serve as regimental surgeons for wounded and infected animals.[4]

The relationship that developed between Ulysses S. Grant and Cincinnati, and between Robert E. Lee and Traveller, is representative of the humanitarianism and abiding friendship nourished by the rigors of long marches and countermarches, the dangers shared at the front, and the abject dependence of the armies on horse and mule power.

Both Cincinnati and Traveller stood between fifteen and sixteen hands high; each weighed about twelve hundred pounds. Both were hybrids with "Bred," Morgan and, probably, Narragansett, Canadian and Chickasaw heritage. A St. Louis admirer presented Cincinnati to General Grant in 1863, alleging that the dark bay stallion was a son of Lexington, the great Woodburn sire, out of a Kentucky mare. The friendship between General Grant and Cincinnati continued through Grant's election to the presidency. Until 1874 Cincinnati occupied a private stall in the stables of the Executive Mansion. Then he was retired to the Maryland farm of Grant's close friend Rear Admiral Daniel Ammen, where he died.[5]

General Lee fell in love with the "fine muscular proportions . . . deep chest and short back . . . quick eye, small feet and black mane and tail"[6] of Traveller when he first saw the gray gelding during the spring of 1861. The horse, then five years old, was foaled on a plantation near Blue Sulphur Springs, Virginia (now West Virginia), and was at first named Jeff Davis.[7] Later he was renamed Greenbriar. Efforts to trace his heritage decades later revealed that Traveller carried some "Bred" blood via the Sir Archy strain but had a predominance of Morgan on his mother's side. General Lee purchased the horse for two hundreds dollars in gold, and a few weeks later bestowed the name Traveller because of the long, nervous stride the gelding began to display when Lee rode him. For the rest of General Lee's life, Traveller remained his favorite mount. The horse became a legendary figure to both Secesh and Yank. From Appomattox, Traveller carried General

Lee to Richmond and then to Lexington, Virginia. There during the General's presidency of Washington College, the two were almost daily companions on long, aimless trips over farm roads and forest trails. A few weeks after General Lee's death in October 1870, Traveller developed lockjaw and had to be destroyed.

Records of similar devotion that developed between "Stonewall" Jackson and his Little Sorrel, J. E. B. Stuart and his Chancellor, Virginia and Maryland, Sheridan and Rienzi, Sherman and Old Sam testify to a humanitarianism that did not exist a century, or even half a century, before when New Englanders failed to provide winter shelters for their horses, Carolina planters fed work-animals on dried cornstalks and weeds, and "Flying Machine" coachmen beat and raced teams until the animals dropped dead in harness.

Such sociological change was critical to the challenge of technologic and geographic conquest that confronted our work-animals on April 9, 1865. Neither the Andalusian ponies of Ponce de León, the Irish-English ponies of John Pynchon, nor the semi-feral hybrids the Apache-Navaho stole from New Mexico could have performed the tasks assigned to the horses and mules of the 1865–1900 period. The Percherons and Clydesdales were essential. But like the Morgan and the evolving Thoroughbred, the drafters could not have achieved sixteen- and seventeen-hand stature or maintained moderate health without the humanitarianism expressed through improved diet, better housing and more scientific medical supervision.

The breeders of saddle racers, pacers and trotters had demonstrated the advantage of such "sound economics." The Dillons and other Midwest promoters of the Percheron and other Great Horse breeds were proving it through careful supervision and humanitarian treatment at their studs and sales barns. The affections generated between animal and master during the emotional crises of the Civil War further heightened the American's regard for his "dumb creatures."

In further evidence, the medically-trained veterinarian replaced the farrier and "horse doctor" as the trusted guardian of the work-animal's health. And our horses repaid "with interest" by producing sounder foals, increasing their average height and weight, and turning out more work-power per unit.

An exceptional demonstration of humanitarianism contributed to the success of the Pony Express in 1860–61. Alexander Majors was a devout Kentuckian whose integrity and drive built Russell, Majors & Waddell into the largest freighting firm in the West. Majors preached at two- and three-hour religious services for the bullwhackers and train captains before departure of each of the firm's wagon trains from Leavenworth. He also composed a good-conduct oath that every bullwhacker, train captain, scout, groom and stableboy had to memorize and then recite aloud, with his right hand pressed against an open Bible. It read:

"While I am in the employ of Russell, Majors & Waddell, I agree not to use profane language, not to get drunk, not to gamble, *not to treat animals cruelly*, and not to do anything incompatible with the conduct of a gentleman. I agree, if I violate any of the above conditions, to accept my discharge without any pay for my services." (Italics mine. R.W.H.)

When the Pony Express was organized during the winter of 1859–60, Majors made his oath a prerequisite for every "young skinny wiry fellow, not over 18 . . . willing to risk death daily"[8] who passed the physical examinations. The memoirs of Pony Expressmen and subsequent research by historians indicate that adherence to Majors' rule against treating animals cruelly was an important factor in maintaining the corps' two-hundred-miles-a-day schedule, despite Indian ambushes, blizzards, cyclones and prairie fires.[9] The Pony Express herds of Morgans, "Breds" and mustangs were treated as companions and essential individualists rather than as "dumb brutes." Every swing-station across the plains and mountains was equipped with horse shelters, exercise yards, cabinets of the best available liniments and medicines, and lavish supplies of oats, corn, sweet hay and bedding. Except in emergencies, the mail-run of each pony was limited to twenty-five miles. Hostler crews were required to cool down, currycomb, and finally water each mount promptly after a mail-run.

During the spring, summer and fall of 1861, Pony Expressmen passed hundreds of mule and horse teams hauling loads of wood posts, fist-size insulator caps, and bales of finger-thick zinc wire for construction of the first transcontinental telegraph line. The line's completion—with a ceremony at Brigham Young's home in Salt Lake City during late October 1861—ended the need for the Pony Express.

The telegraph line was only a few months old when cavalcades of surveyors and engineers rode out from the remote little river-port of Omaha to establish gradients for "The Union's Pacific Rail-road and Telegraph Company." These field surveys were carried on from 1863 to 1865, usually without cavalry protection, despite the Indian terrors triggered by the Sioux Rebellion, the Sand Creek Massacre and the plots of Confederate agents in Colorado and Dakota territories.

Construction of the Union Pacific finally hit its stride during the spring of 1866 when Major General Grenville Dodge became chief engineer and Brigadier General Jack Casement and his brother, Dan, assembled their massive work train, "Hell on Wheels," at Omaha. The race to lay fifty-pound rail up the Platte Valley to the 100th Meridian transformed Omaha into a day-and-night bedlam of wharf gangs unloading steamboats and loading supply trains, mechanics assembling locomotives and boxcars, and endless lines of horse and mule teams straining wagonloads of cottonwood and swamp-hemlock ties through the settlement's hub-deep ruts toward end-of-track. "Hast ever been to Omaha," John G. Saxe asked in a poem published in *Harper's* in September 1869, "where rolls the dark Missouri down, and four strong horses scarce can draw, an empty wagon through the town?"

More than twenty-five thousand horses and mules powered the dump-carts and supply wagons as "Hell on Wheels" ironmen averaged a mile of new track each day. Bridge builders and blasters worked more than one hundred miles in advance of the construction train; they could be supplied only by wagon train. Gangs of "tie hacks" wagoned out to the headwaters of the Platte to raze valley forests and transform them into desperately needed ties, telegraph and semaphore poles, and warehouse framing. Squads of U.S. cavalry patrolled the right-of-way—but usually arrived too late to prevent horse-stealing raids, ambushes and train derailments by bands of Sioux, Crow and Cheyenne horsemen.

North Platte, Nebraska, was born as the 1866–67 winter quarters for "Hell on Wheels" and its columns of work-animals, wagons and teamsters. Cheyenne was similarly founded a winter later. Laramie sprang to slabside and rut hubbub during the spring of 1868 as the western division-point between the haul across Lone Pine Pass and the Red Desert crossing of the transcontinental divide.[10]

In the same months thousands of horse-carts, more than fifteen thousand dollar-a-day Chinese laborers, and a bootleg supply of nitroglycerine—manufactured at a jerry-built factory near Lake Tahoe, then transported by horse-cart to the tunnel faces—powered the track of the Central Pacific Railroad over the Sierra Nevada from Sacramento.

The titanic task ended on May 10, 1869, when Union Pacific and Central Pacific tracks met in a field atop the Promontory Mountains, seventy miles northwest of Salt Lake City. A guest of honor not listed in the telegraph dispatches that day was the blind gelding led to the scene of the golden-spike ceremony by a crew of Union Pacific ironmen. The horse had become a byword since that spring morning in 1866 when he first hauled a flatcar loaded with rails and spikes from "Hell on Wheels" to the ironmen waiting at end-of-track. The question "Where's Blind Tom today?" was crew-semantics for "How much rail did we lay yesterday?"

During the twenty-seven months when weather permitted track-laying, Blind Tom is reputed to have hauled every rail of Union Pacific's eleven hundred miles into position for the final clamp-down by the ironmen, spikers and gandy dancers. Standing patiently on the Promontory plateau while the telegraph signaled a transcontinental celebration of parades, speeches and grand balls, Blind Tom was official delegate for the horses and mules who conquered the United States's last great wilderness, by hauling the rock, dirt, iron, timber, "Patent Blasting Oil," and hand tools that made possible the iron highway.

Second and third armies of conquest already rolled across Kansas and Colorado territories. Horse- and mule-powered carts and wagons were shaping the Kansas Pacific Railroad from new Kansas City to Denver, and the Atchison, Topeka & Santa Fe southwest across Kansas prairie to the ruts that Santa Fe traders, Kearney's Army of the West and the Mormon Battalion had scuffed across Raton Pass.

Each railroad proved a catalyst for change in its right-of-way countryside. Texas cattlemen launched drives of longhorns and range horses up the trail that Jesse Chisholm's trader wagon had pioneered across Indian territory a few years before. Thousands of coal miners migrated from Wales, Cornwall and central Europe to harvest the veins of coal that geologists had discovered in the Wyoming hills and the dour cliffs at the east approach of Raton Pass. Trainloads of lumbermen roistered out from Chicago and Kansas City to transform the camps of the tie hacks into year-round operations that would provide construction materials for the new towns, new factories, new iron and gold and silver and copper mines.

The Texans drove their longhorns northwest up the high-plains to fatten on Nebraska and Wyoming grass. Oregon and Washington cattlemen drove their herds of chunky Durham cattle and hybrid horses across Montana and down the plains to the new stockyards at Omaha and Kansas City.

The homesteaders rattled close behind, their wagons heavy with tools and seeds that would change the prairie from a primitive sea of grass to a chessboard of plowland, fenced pasture and scrawny hillside orchards, where the castles were built with blocks of sod, the knights rode the swaying steel seats of planters and harvesters, the queens wore homemade calico dresses and sunbonnets, and the

occasional bishop jogged his circuit on a mustang, carried his vest-
ments in saddlebags, and feasted on antelope stew, sage-hen, roast
bison hump and ground-cherry pie after The Preachings.

Nebraska, with a population of less than 30,000 in 1860, held
123,000 homestead, ranch and townsmen residents in 1870. Kansans
swarmed from 107,000 to 364,000. Missouri found ample space for
another 550,000. Utah's population grew from 40,000 to 87,000,
and Nevada's from 7,000 to 42,000. California added another 200,000.
Arizona, Montana, Idaho, the Dakotas and Wyoming all made first
bows in the 1870 Census. The trans-Missouri West of 1870 held
more than four million settlers.

All of them depended on horse and mule power. The railroads
could highball trains brimming with wheat, cattle, coal, copper
and timber to processing plants in Chicago, Kansas City or the
East. But railroad locomotives could not haul loads of coal out of
a pit and down a mud road to town. Nor could railroad locomotives
pull plows or harrows or planters or threshing machines, then—
after a night's rest, a rubdown, and a measure of oats and corn—
haul the harvest over twenty-five or fifty or a hundred miles of
miserable trail to a wholesaler's elevator. Neither locomotives nor
cabooses nor boxcars could herd cattle, pull sheep wagons, pack-
load a prospector's supplies up a canyon, plow an irrigation ditch,
haul a windlass, skid a log, or even run a quarter-mile race. These
follow-throughs of the Far West conquest were chores for *Equus
caballus*, cousin donkey and stepbrother mule.

Two developments assured these follow-throughs. The Percherons had created such a favorable impression with Midwest farmers
and city freighters that hundreds of purebred mares and stallions
migrated to Denver, Cheyenne, Salt Lake City, San Francisco and
Portland and began crossbreeding with local horses.

Simultaneously, medical science began winning the battle
against the farrier's deadly nostrums. By 1870 Philadelphia, New
York and Chicago had veterinary colleges. In 1868 President
Andrew D. White of Cornell University recruited Dr. James Law,
Professor of Anatomy and Materia Medica at the University of

Edinburgh, to organize a Division of Veterinary Medicine on the new campus at the foot of Lake Cayuga. Dr. Law's contract stipulated that Cornell would pay him a salary of two thousand dollars a year "until such time that his independent or outside income totalled $500, when his Cornell salary would be reduced in proportion".[11] The Division offered the degrees of Bachelor of Veterinary Science and Doctor of Veterinary Medicine. So, 350 years after Ponce de León, the horse and his welfare were formally recognized by American educators.

THE GOLDEN AGE

CHAPTER NINETEEN

In HIS REPORT for 1869, Horace Capron, Commissioner in charge of the six-year-old U.S. Department of Agriculture, urged "the establishment of a Division of Veterinary Surgery in connection with this department. . . . Simple humanity would dictate that the services of useful animals should be rewarded by proper care and attentions. . . . It would seem to be the duty of the government not only to direct the attention of the agricultural community to the want of care of stock and to the general ignorance of appropriate treatment, but also to encourage the establishment of institutions where veterinary medicine and hygiene, in their widest application, may be taught, and a class of practitioners be produced capable of solving the problem: How to preserve domestic animals in good health under conditions not natural to their species."[1]

Sixty-two years before, on November 2, 1807, Pennsylvania's famous statesman-physician Dr. Benjamin Rush made a similar plea during a lecture to medical students of the University of Pennsylvania. "Domestic animals," Dr. Rush pointed out, ". . . live only for our benefit . . . so that there is constantly due, to them, an immense balance of debt from us.· . . . By studying the diseases of domestic animals, we may rescue them from the hands of quacks, who add to the mischievous and unsuccessful efforts of nature, the evils of absurd, painful, and destructive remedies."[2]

Dr. Rush's plea went unheeded. The task of improving the breeds and researching saner and healthier methods for livestock care was left to private groups such as the societies for the improvement of agriculture, to individuals like the Dillons, and to sportsmen intent on developing the "Bred" into the world's speediest saddle racer.

But Commissioner Capron's 1869 plea was tardy acknowledgement by a federal executive of a popular movement in science-based humanitarianism. Cornell had already pioneered with its Division of Veterinary Science. Iowa and Illinois were debating similar innovations financed by state taxes. New York's Jockey Club had recently established the *American Stud Book* as the official registry for "thoroughbred" saddle racers. The owners and breeders of purebred trotters, pacers, Morgans and Percherons were considering the same restrictive listing for their breeds. And both farm and city were becoming more and more dependent on horsepower, hence on horse health.

"Nineteen hundred patents were issued during the past year on agricultural tools and equipment," the 1870 *Report* on agriculture stated. "There are as many applications for improvements now as when there had been but 500 patents issued." More than thirteen hundred of these inventions called for additions to, or new forms of, horse-drawn machines: cotton pickers, cultivators, drills, diggers, harrows, harvesters, mowers, reapers, planters, plows and rakes. The Department's engineers noted a strong tendency toward "wheel plows, gang and sulky, in the prairie country west" and "considerable activity manifested in machines for sowing seeds and fertilizers."[3]

The check-row corn planter, the vibrator threshing machine, barbed wire, the all-metal prairie windmill, the railroad refrigerator car and storage silos were all introduced to our rural economy before 1875. So was the jouncing seat for the driver on seed planters, hay rakes, mowing machines and harvesters—even though it added another 150 to 200 pounds to the machine's haul-weight. All of these technologic innovations influenced the breeding and care of horses. So did the larger horsecars, omnibuses and freight wagons in the cities.

Between 1867 and 1869, our horse population increased by 37

per cent and our mule population by 32 per cent. Despite this, the national average price for a horse rose from $75.16 in 1867 to $81.38 at the end of 1869, and the average price of mules rose more than 40 per cent from $77.61 to $109.01.[4] Illinois studs and sales barns met the demands of farm, homesteader, and city growth so promptly that the state's horse total rose from 651,262 in 1867 to 881,500 in February 1870. The horse population of Kansas tripled during the two years; Nebraska's doubled. By 1870, one fourth of all the horses in the United States were in Indiana, Illinois, Missouri, Kansas and Nebraska.

New York and Pennsylvania dominated Eastern markets. New York's horses increased from 446,119 in 1867 to 600,000 in February 1870—only 22,000 fewer than the total reported from Texas. Pennsylvanians bred and imported enough horses to increase their total from 404,555 in 1867 to 501,000 in 1870.

The 1865–75 growth of the Studebaker Wagon Works at South Bend, Indiana, was typical of those horse-plus-steel changes. John Studebaker, a Pennsylvania Amish blacksmith, settled in the prairie village of South Bend during 1852. His five sons developed the father's smithy and wagon shop into a prosperous family business that built carriages and peddler carts and farm wagons.[5] They promoted their trade-mark by stenciling *Studebaker* in bold yellow block letters on the side of every vehicle they produced.

During the Civil War the firm expanded by developing a chain of subcontractors who built the wheels, axles and bodies for the artillery carriages, commissary wagons and ambulances assembled at the South Bend plant. Like Lewis Downing of Concord, John Studebaker had been mercilessly intent on quality materials and flawless workmanship. The sons maintained his standards and were so prompt in delivering equipment to army purchasing agents during the desperate Mississippi Valley and Potomac campaigns of 1862–63 that the Studebaker Wagon Works became one of the largest wagon factories in the Union.

A grave problem was posed for the Studebakers when Sherman's ravage across Georgia in 1864 and Grant's bludgeons against the

Army of Virginia indicated the collapse of the Confederacy—and the end of federal wagon contracts. The Studebakers began to fill out their assembly lines with hundreds of light, two-wheeled "Red River" carts, prairie schooners, ore wagons, dump-carts, and the huge two-wheeled trucks used by lumbermen. Then Peter, as the glibbest salesman in the family, rode to St. Joseph, Missouri, rented a building near the Missouri River waterfront, and transformed it into a display room.

The gamble proved to be as shrewd as the block-letter *Studebaker* trade-mark. In 1865, the Hannibal & St. Joseph Railroad was the westernmost rail line on the continent. Until 1867, when trans-Iowa connections with Chicago were completed, most of the equipment needed for Union Pacific's construction out of Omaha was freighted to St. Joseph over the "Hannibal & St. Joe," then transferred to steamboats that "grasshoppered" the sandbars and snags of the Missouri River's 150-mile channel to Omaha and Council Bluffs.

Also, because of the Hannibal & St. Joseph, the Wells-Fargo stagecoaches on the Denver, Salt Lake City and San Francisco route maintained an eastern terminal at the stables that the Pony Express had used. Thousands of families venturing to homestead claims in the high-plains and mountains outfitted their wagons at St. Joseph. The Studebaker showroom made so many sales that the South Bend Works had to expand. Other showrooms were opened in Chicago, Kansas City, Salt Lake City and San Francisco. By 1872 there were 325 Studebaker employees; the year's production totaled 6,950 vehicles. In 1874 more than 500 Studebaker workers lined up at the cashier's window on payday; production totaled 11,050 vehicles.

The Studebaker gross reached a million dollars in 1875. The Works covered twenty acres. Five railroads ran spur lines in to the loading platforms.[6] The firms' exhibit at the Centennial Exposition in Philadelphia during 1876 featured a moving sign, operated by clockwork, that boasted, "Largest wagon and carriage builders in the world." Their special Centennial Wagon, available for seven hundred dollars (f.o.b. South Bend), had a body of solid bird's-eye maple, running gear of golden oak, nickel-plated seat springs, and iron parts hand-forged from Swedish iron. For the more sedate, the Works also produced a carriage with large plate-glass windows, black-walnut corner posts, trim leather seats, and a cab lining of brown satin shagreen.

Most of the wagons built by Studebaker and their hundreds of competitors used steel springs and steel or wrought-iron tires. The phaetons, carriages and Victorias purchased by prosperous merchants, bankers, livery-stable proprietors, and, of course, "joy house" madams were trimmed with nickel steel, German silver, and colored leathers. They became as symbolic of the aristocrat and "sport" during the 1880s as electric broughams, Reos and Marmon Racers were during the first decades of the twentieth century. The buggy, buckboard, democrat-wagon and surrey—all with steel, leather and seasoned hardwood parts—became status symbols for the middle-class urbanite, traveling salesmen, ranch bosses and farmers. (The foreman of a cattle drive in the West and Southwest gained the nickname "wagon boss" because he usually rode the trail in a buggy or buckboard, drawn by a team of mustangs or painted ponies. The word *hoodlum* was introduced to the American language as the cowboy nickname for the youngster who drove the ramshackle box wagon assigned to forage firewood for the cook and water for the trail crew. Germans from the Dallas–Fort Worth area of Texas are assumed to have been responsible for the etymology, because *Hodalump* is a German word meaning "young tough guy." The word *chuckwagon* is similiarly indebted to the French word *chouque*, meaning "block or stump"; butchers first used *chuck* to denote the tough, but succulent, stew-meat in the block-like neck of a beef carcass.[7])

Two other words that have become common Americana are semantic echoes of the horse-powered traffic in city streets during the 1870s and 1880s. The Anglo-Saxon meaning of *hack* was to "chop at" or "whack." Horses drawing the coaches and carriages available for hire outside railroad stations, hotels and horsecar

terminals were beaten so routinely by drivers that the vehicles
took the nickname "hack" and the drivers were called "hacks" or
"hackmen."[8]

The Latin word *omnibus*, meaning "for all," was used as a term
for the box-like wagons that competed with the horsecar lines as
public vehicles.[9] An omnibus contained wooden benches running
the length of its windowed cabin. The driver's seat was suspended
out from the front, just as it was on a Victorian carriage. The vehicles would pick up or discharge passengers anywhere in a city
block. The passengers climbed aboard through a rear door, then
handed the five-cent fare up to the driver through a hole in the
front end of the roof. The American fetish for clipping words
reduced *omnibus* to *bus*. And thus it is still used.

The hack, as an ancestor of the taxicab, usually carried only one
"fare" on a trip, and was cleaner than an omnibus or a horsecar.
But the fee averaged a dollar for a one- or two-mile jog. This ex-
travagance, plus the "eternally wagging tongue" of the driver,
caused seasoned travelers to shun the hacks.

Horsecar lines continued to expand, too. In 1870, New York City
had twelve lines in operation. By 1880, every American city of
more than fifty thousand population had at least one horse-powered
street railway. Construction of a new line came to be a favorite
prelude for realtors in exploiting new suburban developments. A
plot of land was purchased. A horsecar line was built out to it.
While the rails and stone blocks of the line were being laid, a few
model homes were built on the plot. Then the realtors advertised
"Free rides every Sunday to the beautiful new community of
Clover Park." Within a year or two, most of the Clover Parks had
enough homes and shops to incorporate as villages.[10] The 1870–80
horsecars held seats for twenty passengers but could cram in
thirty-five or forty during the 7 A.M. and 6 to 8 P.M. rush hours.
Each car was pulled by one horse. It traveled at an average speed
of five miles an hour, with the conductor driving from the open
front platform. Fares varied from five cents in New York, Boston
and Chicago to seven cents in Philadelphia.

New breeds of horse status symbols began to pace the avenues
during the 1870s. More than 100,000 of the 200,000 "purebred"
horses imported to America between 1870 and 1900 were breeds
of carriage and coach haulers that had become fashionable in London, Paris or Berlin. Here, as their forebears had in the Old World,
they cantered landaus, barouches, broughams and Victorias of
wealthy commuters and their families along city avenues and suburbia's gravel roads. Usually their tails were atrociously bobbed
and crimped, and their heads were held unnaturally high by checkreins. (The late Stanley Walker satirized the era and its horse-
snobbery in the title of his excellent book *Mrs. Astor's Horse*.)
French and German breeds of coach horses, and the English Hackney and Cleveland Bay became the best-known of these imports.

"The general appearance of a coach horse in good condition,"
Professor Charles S. Plumb of Ohio State University wrote in
1906, "shows smooth, graceful body lines with a general fullness in
all the parts. The height should be about 16 hands and the weight
from 1100 to 1250 pounds for geldings or mares. . . . In quality the
coachers should be superior, showing the best of bone, feet and
hair. Action of the very best, high and strong at both knee and
hock, is important, while graceful carriage is equally essential. In
general appearance the best type of coach horse shows a long
arching neck, round full body, long level croup, high carriage of
tail and what is known as a 'coachy' or 'trappy' action. . . .

"Action in the coach horse is an absolute requirement. People
vary in the degree to which they desire this. The lover of the
Hackney desires a rather high, bold knee action of a flashy sort,
with a notable elevation of the foot at its highest point. The hind
legs have a powerful movement, the hocks are strongly bent or
flexed and the legs are carried well up under the body. This is what
is known as a 'trappy gait' and such a horse is a 'high stepper'. The
coach horse possessing such a movement is in great demand, and
brings the highest price. . . . Such a gait is not consistent with the
best speed, and wise lovers of the horse prefer less high action and
more reach and power. Further, with high knee action, comes a

greater concussion to limbs and feet, and consequently greater punishment and more rapid wearing out of the horse than would otherwise be the case. Especially is this true on the city pavement.

"Trueness of action is essential, whether a high stepper or not, the legs being carried forward in the same general line and the feet moved neither in nor out. The hocks should be firm and not show weakness, as springing wide apart in action, and the feet should be held true, neither turning in nor out at the toes. When either at walk or trot the horse should pass from or come toward the judge on the same true line, without sidewise gait, dragging feet, paddling, clicking, etc. Straight and regular movement should be sought for. Ordinarily a coach horse is expected to have a speed of about eight or ten miles an hour."[11]

The coachers were national or regional hybrids of the Great Horse matings with Celtic ponies, Arabs, Barbs, etc., which had been perfected through selective breeding. They lacked the nervousness of the saddle racer "Breds" and the nuzzling friendliness of the Morgans. The bobbed tails, haughty head stance and piston precision of their "goose step" contrived a comic-opera effect that harmonized with Strauss waltzes, marble-top sideboards, mansard roofs, red velvet draperies and ostrich-plume hats. So the coacher was ideal for hauling dowagers to the opera or a Fifth Avenue "viewing," and for delivering executives to their offices on Wall, Broad or State Streets precisely at 8:59 A.M.

The Hackney obtained its name from the early Norman word *haquenee*, meaning "horse." The breed was also nicknamed "nag" in northeastern England, a condensation of the Anglo-Saxon *knegan*, meaning "neigh." Hackneys were noted for a long-stepped pace, short legs, and a proud high lift of feet. Some of the famous sires, in Suffolk, Norfolk and York, are reputed to have trotted or paced twenty-four miles in one hour. The first American stud of Hackneys was established at Philadelphia in 1883 by A. J. Cassatt; the Cassatt mares averaged fifteen and a half hands in height and weighed between twelve and thirteen hundred pounds each.

The Cleveland Bay received its name from the Cleveland Hills

of Yorkshire where, folklore said, medieval landlords ordered
Celtic ponies and Norman horses crossed to develop a wiry breed
that could be used, like the Chickasaw ponies of our Southeast,
on pack trains over the primitive trails. Centuries later, crosses
with the Great Horse, and a few Barbs or Arabs brought home from
the Crusades, developed the breed as the favorite coach horse of
seventeenth-century London. Outbreeding between Clevelands
and "Breds" during the eighteenth and nineteenth centuries produced spirited foals that the British gentry considered superior as
hunters for their cross-country gallops with the hounds.

Initial American efforts to popularize the Clevelands for the
carriage trade were made by Illinois sales barns during the 1880s.
The imported purebreds averaged sixteen and a half hands and
weighed 1,350 pounds. Their normal color was bay, with black legs
and a white star on the forehead. But the breed failed to win many
admirers. The 762 stallions and 192 mares listed in its American
stud book in 1905 were used for crossing with other breeds. Colonel
William F. ("Buffalo Bill") Cody used a few Cleveland stallions
on his North Platte, Nebraska, ranch.[12]

The homeland of the Great Horse was the breed-up area for the
French and German coach types. The French coacher favored in
America came out of Normandy, where it was known as the *demi-
sang* ("half-breed"). It originated from matings between English
"Bred" stallions and Norman mares during the late eighteenth or
early nineteenth century. The average height was sixteen hands;
the weight of mares varied between twelve and thirteen hundred
pounds. The German coachers, also promoted as the Hanoverian
and Oldenburg breeds, originated in the lowlands of northeastern
Germany during the sixteenth and seventeenth centuries. Their
reputed ancestry included the Great Horse, the Celtic pony, Arabs
and Turkish horses captured during the frequent Balkan wars.
German coachers were distinguished by long, arched necks, large
bodies, long legs and predominantly brown or black coloration.
They, too, had been developed to an average height of sixteen

hands, but the mares often weighed fourteen to fifteen hundred pounds.

By 1900, American registrations of the Hackney, Cleveland Bay, and French and German coach purebreds totaled between forty-five hundred and five thousand, mostly stallions. Each breed had an American trade association, with routine promotion and advertising campaigns. The Hackney and Cleveland Bay associations concentrated their efforts on the suburbanites of New York City's Westchester, Long Island and Connecticut, on Boston's North Shore and South Shore, and on Philadelphia's Main Line and Bucks County.

The German, Hanoverian and Oldenburg Coach Horse Association of America established headquarters at Lafayette, Indiana. The French Coach Horse Society of America shared the offices of the American Percheron Horse Breeders Association near the horse-auction center in Chicago's Union Stockyards. Consequently, German and French coachers were more numerous than Hackneys or Cleveland Bays in the carriage lines waiting for the "Millionaires' Special" commuter trains each dusk at the rococo suburban stations ringing Chicago, Cincinnati, St. Louis, Milwaukee, Kansas City and Denver.

As expensive fads, coachers also helped to raise health and welfare standards for the other breeds. Coacher fanciers endowed semi-weekly clinics for ailing horses and household pets at the veterinary colleges in Philadelphia, Boston, New York City and Chicago. Their political influence persuaded cities to construct drinking fountains for animals at the curbs of major intersections and in market squares. These iron and marble troughs usually had two levels: a high one for horses and mules, and a low one for dogs and cats.

The growth of the woman-suffrage movement also influenced humanitarian progress for the family of *Equus*. The Territory of Wyoming granted suffrage to its women in 1869. Agitation for "equal rights" became stylishly smart. Development of the society

page by newspapers, the increase in colleges for women, coeduca-
tion at the state and privately endowed universities all encouraged
wives and mothers of the 1870–1900 era to voice public and intra-
family opinions about community affairs.

Since the family's horses were not only essential for transportation but were status symbols as well, agitation for better care and
grooming of the animals became another "social obligation" for
daughters, wives and grandmothers. Societies "for the prevention
of cruelty to animals" evolved in scores of cities. By 1900, more
than ten thousand college-trained veterinarians prescribed for livestock and family pets; our twenty veterinary colleges graduated
five hundred B.V.M.'s and D.V.M.'s a year.

The currycomb, the body brush, the hoof pick became standard
equipment on the shelves beside the horsestalls in family carriage
houses. A salt block, held parallel to the wall by metal clips, was
installed near the feedbox at the head of each stall. A clean water
pail hung on a nearby hook. Flour manufacturers, worried about
the hulls and oil-rich wheat and corn germs they sluiced into
rivers, seized on the notion of transforming these white-flour
wastes into "protein rich" horse and livestock feeds that could be
sold in fifty- and hundred-pound bags—and for extravagant retail
prices, if labeled with pseudo-scientific jargon.

Grandsires began to carry sugar cubes, or an apple or two, to
feed to the most wistful horses they encountered in their daily
strolls downtown. Each new mare or gelding received a name—
Susie, Hannibal, General, Hero—during an obstreperous family
council in which the three-year-old could shrill as freely as "big
sister" or "Gramma." Druggists bottled hundreds of formulas,
usually compiled from coal tar, alcohol, and a few drops of catnip
or vanilla, that were supposed to relieve muscular aches, destroy
worms in the intestinal tract, and generally tone up the "vital organs." Inevitably, these liniments and nostrums were labeled "Fit
for Man or Beast." Most carriage houses displayed half a dozen
bottles on the horsestall shelves.

Also, for sportsmen and breeders, the coachers added new categories to the horse show. The horse show grew out of displays of purebred animals, weight-pulling contests, and riding-skill exhibits that had been popularized since the 1830s by the annual state and county fairs. During the 1880s, breed associations invented a new promotional technique by sponsoring regional horse shows. At these exhibitions, horse fanciers with wealth or society-page status competed in a series of meticulously-judged events designed to demonstrate both horse and rider skills. The coacher events provided opportunities to judge driver skills and team perfection as a chaise or coach was paced, trotted or high-stepped around a dirt track. After 1910 the horse shows were as style-conscious and as important a news source for society-page editors as the regional saddle race and trotting meets.

Meanwhile the Percheron, Clydesdale, Suffolk, Belgian and other European hybrids of the Great Horse wrought change in farm and freight horses. The crossbreeding by purebreds, half-bloods and quarter-bloods was so effective that, after 1900, experts were forced to catalogue work horses by job classes. "Drafters run in the trade from 1,600 pounds upwards," reported J. H. S. Johnstone, the horse specialist of *Breeder's Gazette*. "The larger they are, the fatter and the more quality they possess, the better they sell. Loggers are inferior but big drafters. Wagon horses are a numerous delegation. They come in all sizes from 1,250 pounds to 1,450 pounds, and in all shapes from the classy one almost a coacher in conformation and used to draw the delivery wagon of a dry goods house, to the roughest sort of a team fit only to pull dirt out of an excavation. The Boston wagon horse weighs around 1,400 pounds, is preferably rather light in bone, of build almost typically Percheron and always very smooth. The eastern wagon horse, taken mostly for New York trade, is coachlike in conformation and quality, smaller than the Boston article and handsome. The Pittsburg [*sic*] wagon horse is a ruggeder proposition altogether and in weight around 1,450 pounds. This shows how futile it would be to try to describe wagon horses as a general classification. . . .

"Farm workers are anything and everything. If a horse in late winter and early spring will not class anywhere else, he goes as a farm worker. . . . Expressers may briefly be described as overgrown, low-quality coachers. They must have a bit of draft blood about them to give them size, but it must not show in preponderance. They must be able to get out and trot quickly and nervily with a big load behind them. They range in weight from 1,250 to 1,500 pounds—high-headed, smoothly turned, good acting horses with considerable style. . . .

"Horses for the fire, patrol wagon and mounted police service come from the ranks of the expressers, being selected, the first two on acount of strength and speed on the run, the latter for more or less excellence of saddle conformation, substance to carry weight and a bit of good looks as well. . . . The cavalry horse mostly purchased by Uncle Sam comes from the ranks of the business or pleasure horses and is mostly of trotting blood. No uniformity of type is insisted on. They come in all shapes, these troop horses. Officers' chargers are preferably of the conformation of the Kentucky saddle horse. Artillery horses are light expressers, weighing around 1,250 pounds and, like the fire and patrol horses, able to run."[13]

The get of these crosses performed much of the homesteader labor in the West as well as the multitude of freighting and delivery tasks in the cities and suburbs. "Buffalo Bill" Cody used Clydesdale, Percheron and Cleveland Bay stallions at his North Platte, Nebraska, ranch during the 1880s to breed up the "horses of the western range" he displayed during the European tours of his Wild West Show.[14] Several of Cody's personal mounts had "Kentucky blood." Cody's technique was typical of most of the "Wild Horse" West of the 1880s and 1890s.

In 1900, the National French Draft Horse Association, with headquarters at Fairfield, Iowa, listed 10,630 purebreds in its registry; the American Clydesdale Association, at Janesville, Wisconsin, carried 10,100 in its registry. Both associations were as strict as the Jockey Club compilers of the *American Stud Book* in limiting registry to "purebreds" and demanding proof of pedigree through four or five generations. So were the American Shire Horse Breeders Association of Wenona, Illinois, with 5,924 registrations, and the American Association of Importers and Breeders of Belgian Draft Horses, then preparing its first stud book at Wabash, Indiana, headquarters.

The presence of between twenty-six and twenty-seven thousand purebred descendants of the Great Horse in the United States constituted the largest array of one-type breeding stock in the country. The *American Stud Book* of the evolving Thoroughbred listed twenty-six thousand horses in its registry that year. The American Trotting Registry Association claimed "about eighteen thousand registrations"; the American Morgan Register, at Middlebury, Vermont, admitted "about five thousand".[15]

This diffusion of draft-horse blood across the continent,[16] the pompous cadence of the coachers, the continuing breed-up of the Thoroughbred and the saga-years of trail drives and the homesteader conquest of high-plain and mountain combine to make 1865–1900 the Golden Age for the horse in America. Then Dobbin became a family pet. The hayrides, sleighing parties, buggy rides, sulky races, circus parades, cavalry drills and Fourth of July celebrations all shaped to nostalgic folklore. Our folk music swelled with the hoof-cadenced trail songs of the cowboy and the "jingle bells" and "Old Dobbin" farm tunes. Our literature gained proud stature from the wagon-mood poetry of Whittier, Lowell and Whitman, and the equestrian prose of Sam Clemens, Owen Wister, Francis Parkman, Edward Westcott and Theodore Roosevelt. Horse moods and poses captured in the paintings of Winslow Homer, Thomas Eakins, Frederic Remington and Charles Russell became world famous. The terms "horse sense," "dark horse," "playing horse," "man on a horse," "Hold your horses!" all became standard Americana.

"We didn't use to mind bumps in the road," my father once confided to me. "Why, in my courting days, you'd go looking for the best ones in the township. Then you'd drive your young lady home that route from a church sociable or Epworth League meeting. The trick was, about fifty yards from a real thumper, to cluck the horse up to a jog. The buggy'd hit the top of the hillock with a crash, and sway like a perambulator. That skidded the young lady down the seat toward you. If she stayed there, warm and inviting, the courting could begin. That's why we called those bumps 'Thank you, ma'ams' and considered them important. Your mother and I began our courting on thank-you-ma'am roads. I guess, maybe, you might be considered sort of a product of 'm."

"GIT A HOSS!"

CHAPTER TWENTY

BETWEEN 1900 AND 1910, the human population of the United States increased by 21 per cent, from seventy-six million to ninety-two million. Through the same decade, our horse population increased 70 per cent, from thirteen million to twenty-three million.[1] This tremendous upsurge in horse power was solely due to defects in our technology.

In 1875, America's steelmakers produced 436,000 tons of the metal. By 1909, they were pouring almost twenty-seven million tons a year.[2] This wealth of moderately priced steel made possible the production of more intricate farm machines and the construction of taller buildings, larger factories, and hundreds of railroad lines. But the old, basic problem of transportation power remained partially unsolved.

Like the railroads, the new electric trolley cars could not plow a field, or haul steel girders and bricks to a construction site, or even deliver fresh mackerel from a fishing boat to the retail markets. Nor could automobiles sputtering and honking over the macadam paving on city streets navigate the quagmires, ruts and rocky lanes that served as public highways across most of our countryside. Thus, during the first three decades of the twentieth century, until automobile designers "caught up to the times," horses and mules were forced to provide much of the transportation and industrial power of our Machine Age.

The 1900–10 horse-power increase was used to develop huge

215

corn, wheat and sugar-beet crops in the West. Iowa became the leading horse state, with more than 1,400,000 in use on its farms and highways. During 1910, Illinois, Texas, Kansas, Missouri, and Nebraska, in that order, each worked more than a million horses. Minnesota, the two Dakotas, and Oklahoma, struggling against drought, pests and brutal winters, each used from 700,000 to 900,000 horses in wheat farming. Larger tillage machines, combines and steam-powered threshing machines became factors in the demand for horse power.

The struggle by the homesteader to wrest a living from the high-plain and mountain soils was the area's third major revolution in which the horse served as a key figure. The first began at Santa Fe in 1680 with the mount-up of the Apache-Navajo. Despite the American traffic to Oregon, Utah and California after 1840, red horsemen dominated most of the trans-Mississippi West until the end of the Civil War.

The second came with construction of the Union Pacific–Central Pacific transcontinental railroad between 1863 and 1869, setting off the rush of cattlemen, homesteaders, miners and lumbermen, and the ensuing battles with the Indian horsemen.

Revolution Three was the steel pattern laid on the land alongside each new glimmer of railroad tracks: first the sheet-metal and sod-block homes and stores; a few months or years later the threads of barbed wire across the hillsides. Then ripples of brown loam hissed up from the plow-blades, the planters clacked their ratchet teeth, the harvesters spun beater-blades into the wheat's tawny gold, and steam engines and threshers rumbled up the farm lanes behind ten-horse teams. This steel pattern pressed hard on the cattlemen's trail drives, ended his open range, and doomed the red horsemen to federal rations and tuberculosis on reservations too dry or too rocky to farm.

In 1866, American farmers planted 15,424,000 acres to wheat, and harvested an average yield of 9.9 bushels per acre. By 1900, the nation's wheat acreage totaled 42,495,000, and the average yield was up to 12.3 bushels. Minnesota grew 4,905,000 acres of wheat in 1900,

Kansas grew 4,660,000; California, the two Dakotas and Nebraska planted more than two million acres each. Pennsylvania, Texas, Tennessee, Ohio, Michigan, Indiana, Illinois, Iowa, Missouri, Washington and Oregon each exceeded one million acres of the crop.[3]

The wheat fever accelerated across the West during the first two decades of the twentieth century. A winter-wheat belt developed from the hardy "Turkey Red" strain smuggled from Russia to Halstead, Kansas, during the 1880s by a colony of Mennonite refugees. By 1915 Kansas was planting 8,475,000 acres to winter wheat, Oklahoma and Nebraska plowed another three million acres each for it, and the Dakotas and Minnesota gambled seed and fertilizer in more than seventeen million acres.

Meanwhile, the persistence of the Mormons in conserving home finances led to the manufacture of "sweetening" and livestock food from the roots of the Franco-German sugar beet. This new farm industry expanded from 175,083 acres in 1901 to 624,000 acres in 1915 and 978,000 acres in 1920. The bulk of the crop ripped ancient grass and brush covers from Colorado, Utah, Idaho, Montana, Wyoming, California, Nebraska and Michigan.[4]

The practice of fattening beef cattle and hogs on dried corn—a technique imposed by Chicago meat packers because of their failure to promote grass-fed beef and mast-and-root-fed pork to housewives—transformed the Midwest's prairie to a summer expanse of jade-green squares and oblongs rustling from Ohio to Idaho and as far south as the cactus desert of west Texas. Our national corn acreage expanded from 34,306,000 in 1866 to 83,320,000 in 1900 and 104,035,000 in 1910. Iowa, still a dirt-road and slab-hut frontier when the transcontinental railroad began its "Hell on Wheels" epic, horse-powered 8,048,000 acres of its hillsides and bottomland into cornland before 1900, then ripped open another two million acres before 1910. In 1910, Illinois, Iowa, Kansas, Nebraska, Missouri, Oklahoma and Texas planted 52,600,000 acres in corn; that was 53.5 per cent of the total for the entire United States.[5]

These transformations of virgin soil to wheat, sugar-beet and corn belts, each from five hundred to two thousand miles wide, could be achieved only with massive use of horse power. Most of the grain farms covered at least three hundred acres; some contained ten thousand acres. Oxen were too slow for the seasonal tasks on such large "spreads." And regional bias limited the use of mules. (From central Illinois southwest through Missouri, Arkansas and Oklahoma to Texas, the "Old South" traditions were strong. Between 1900 and 1915 the mule population in Texas, Missouri and Oklahoma trebled to a total of 1,315,000. But on the Northern plains the majority of homesteaders came from North Europe. They preferred the horse rather than the mule for field work and wagon tasks. Thus, between 1900 and 1915, the mule populations of Nebraska, North Dakota, South Dakota, Utah and Iowa increased by only about 80 per cent, to a 1915 total of 161,000. The heritage influence was most obvious in a comparison of Oklahoma and Utah: during the fifteen years, Oklahomans increased their mule population from 9,584 to 269,000; but Utah's farmers and freighters reported ownership of 1,615 mules in 1900 and only 2,000 in 1915!)

Not more than 25 per cent of the homesteader horses were cayuse, mustang, cow pony or the other types exalted in the "Wild West" books and stories by Ned Buntline, Prentiss Ingraham, Emerson Hough, Owen Wister, *et al.* Most of the feral horses were too small, and too fractious, for the plodding four-miles-an-hour task of plowing, planting, tilling, harvesting and processing a grain or sugar-beet crop. Available data indicate that horses normally used for the great "sod bust" of 1870–1920 were the get of range mares mated with stallions who carried from 10 to 50 per cent of one of the Great Horse blood lines.

An excellent analysis of the situation was presented during 1914 by the *Breeder's Gazette* authority J. H. S. Johnstone. "Individuality and speed superior to that possessed by the cayuse were required when the herds of range cattle began to take on extended proportions," Johnstone reported. "Each cattle baron strove to breed a line of cow ponies that would serve him well under any and all circumstances. The necessity of the situation developed a strain of hardy, fleet ponies, capable of sustaining great effort and hardship on scanty rations—the cow pony, of no particular breeding as a mass, yet possessing stamina next to none.

"Running at will on the open range, the production of these ponies was governed by the inexorable law of natural selection in so far as their environment was concerned. All sorts of stallions were turned loose on the range, picked up their bands of mares and got them with foal. The progeny fended for itself, survived or dropped out as the case might be, leaving only the best to reach maturity. In time the holdings of the range breeders became very great and prices of both the broken and unbroken were very low compared to what native-bred horses brought farther east. The supply was limitless, the use practically limited to cowpunching.

"Desultory improvement, attempted with pure-bred stallions of the meanest sort, proved that it was no great trick to ingraft the individuality of almost any pure-bred sire on the ranger. But the price to be obtained for the unbroken progeny was so low that most of the rangemen bought only stallions for which they had to pay trivial prices. It would not pay, they said, to put much money into stallions to turn out on the range. A few breeders followed a saner policy and these have succeeded in making much money.

"Then just about the time some impression was being made on the ranger by the use of pure-bred stallions, the depression of the early nineties hit the business so hard that it was impossible to get any sort of a remunerative price for a range-bred horse. . . . Then an enterprising genius established a cannery in Oregon and thousands of horses were slaughtered and made up into salt meat for export. From $1 to $2.50 was paid per head and the owners thought themselves lucky to get so much. . . .

"Range horses received no attention at all until Great Britain went to work to crush the Boer rebellion in South Africa. Her Brittanic Majesty's agents scoured the range country from the Rio Grande to the Yellowstone, paying what seemed enormous prices for everything able to carry a soldier. . . . Owners rounded up their bands and sold them off as closely as they could. It was a good riddance of bad rubbish.[6] Times improved. Horses became scarce in the East and prices began to climb skyward. Then it was . . . that the few breeders who had kept at the work of improvement came into their own. Offerings of draft-bred range horses were eagerly snapped up by the carload. . . . A better class of draft and other stallions was purchased and more sensible methods of breeding adopted. . . .

"Breeders who had piled two, three or four crosses of pure draft blood on either a native or a range foundation received prices not previously dreamed of. It was found that pure-breds could be produced on the range and perpetuate their characteristics with great prepotency. Free grazing was constricted. It became a choice of fewer and better or get out of the business. The net result today is that all draft-bred range horses are bringing unprecedented prices, as high as $161 having been paid per head for four-year-old geldings and mares by the carload of twenty head, unbroken, but weighing in grass flesh from 1,350 to 1,500 pounds. . . .

"The extraordinary development of the western .country—railroad, irrigation, lumbering and urban construction work—has absorbed every available horse of size on the northwestern range, prices increasing according to the weight offered. . . . High-class carriage and driving horses, too, are being produced on the range and the cow pony flourishes and brings prices double and treble those he brought in the good old days. . . . It does not seem that the cornbelt can soon produce a supply of drafters sufficient to its own and the needs of the East. It will be a long time before the Pacific Coast states can breed a sufficiency. The outlook is surely rosy enough to warrant the range breeders in making use of much better stallions than they have hitherto purchased."[7]

Johnstone's analysis was written in the *Breeder's Gazette* offices, only a few hundred feet from the nation's largest horse auction market at Chicago's Union Stockyards. He wrote as a professional horseman and market analyst. Thus he was not conditioned by the contemporary New York City and Boston and Philadelphia editors searching for "another lively Wild West story for our Christmas issue." Consequently, Johnstone's views of the "worthless range horse" of the 1880s and 1890s disagree with the "matchless mustang" stories being featured by popular magazine and book publishers in the East.

The infusion of Percheron, Clydesdale, Suffolk and other "purebred drafter" blood in the foals of range mares continued the hybridization of Western horses that began when Mormons, Texans and Californians imported blooded animals from Vermont, Kentucky, Tennessee, Virginia and Illinois to improve their native herds. It seems probable that Western horses of the 1860s differed as markedly from Western horses of 1680–1800 as the "range pony" of the 1880s did from the homesteader and freighter hybrids of the 1900–20 period. In view of the red man's passion for stealing horses, from white men as casually as from enemy tribes, similar changes must have occurred in his horse herds, too.

It is at least possible—and the contemporary correspondence and memoirs suggest that it was probable—that a few explorers, such as Lewis and Clark and Zebulon Pike, and the forerunners of the Mountain Men were the only Americans to see free-bred descendants of the so-called Andalusian horses. The introduction of Norman and Basque breeds by the Canadian French began at Detroit, Kaskaskia, Ste. Genevieve and New Orleans between 1700 and 1750. Records also indicate that hybrids from New York, Pennsylvania and the Cherokee-Chickasaw pastures of Tennessee and Mississippi were introduced to the high-plains between 1700 and the 1770s. These Easterners free-bred with the feral descendants of the Andalusians. The extent of the mating is, of course, impossible to determine. But this did occur in every region of the West. The two to three million "wild ones" alleged to have roamed the high-plains and mountains by the end of the Civil War could have carried as much Kentucky-Vermont-Virginia-Tennessee heritage as they did of the vaunted Andalusian blood.

The more substantial evidence, in the adaptability of *Equus* during the 1680–1910 return to his native West, is as impressive a saga as our traditional assumption that Andalusians, alone, dominated the trans-Mississippi West from Cortes and Coronado to Buffalo Bill and Teddy Roosevelt. The amazing "Wild West" truth is that *Equus* promptly and repeatedly adapted to each economic need.

The horses captured in New Mexico and Old Mexico between 1680 and 1750, plus any supplied by the New France *coureurs de bois* and the Cherokee-Chickasaw breeders, promptly adapted to the red man's needs, as well as to his crude economy. (By 1870 few Indian ponies stood more than fourteen hands high or weighed more than eight hundred pounds.) But mares and stallions from the feral and Indian herds mated with the Eastern imports of the Texans, Mormons, Californians and Oregonians to produce the essential cow pony, railroad work horse, and wagon teams of the 1865–1900 frontier. Again, when the westward march of the homesteaders, miners, lumbermen and merchants made the range ponies "worthless," matings with draft stallions produced foals heavy enough and patient enough to achieve the plow-up, the irrigation ditches, the oil-well drills, the first transcontinental highways, the telephone lines, plus the excavation drudgeries required to transform Omaha, Kansas City, Denver, Cheyenne, Laramie and Great Falls from muddy chaos to queen cities.

The range horse of the 1770s was suitable for the red man, but not for the cattleman or the homesteader. The range horse of the 1870s was ideal for the cattleman, but "rubbish" to the homesteader and industrialist. The range horse of 1900–30 completed the task of conquering and "civilizing" (or despoiling) the West, but earned the scorn of cowpunchers and Indians alike. Still, all three of these power-source revolutions focused on types of *Equus*, promptly adapting to human and technologic demands. That is the saga of the American West.[8]

Three colorful traditions emerged from the draft-horse-and-steel transformation of the West: the threshers' meal became a national symbol of abundant and superb "vittles"; the cowboy contest developed into the national sport now called "rodeo"; the hobo enjoyed both of them.

Harvest time on a wheat farm meant a week-long procession of tools, wagons, neighbors, hoboes and cumbersome engines up the lane. First came the harvester-binder machine, hauled by a team of half-bred or quarter-bred drafters. Close behind, a relief team clattered in with the wagonload of binder twine, burlap bags, feed sacks, water buckets and other equipment essential to the task of processing a burnished-gold field of ripe wheat into thousands of compact bundles ready for the thresher.

The neighbors and their sons arrived before sun-up on the morning the harvesting began. They were barely in the field when the "wimmenfolk" of the neighborhood drove up to the kitchen door and began unloading deep-dish ground-cherry, shoo-fly and blackberry pies; loaves of rye, wholewheat and buttermilk bread; bowls of potato and bean salads; baked hams; arm-long skins of sausage; smoked hocks; loaves of headcheese; sundry jars and crocks of dill pickles, sass, chow-chow, corn relish, chili sauce; blocks of dandelion-yellow cheddar cheese; and baskets of cookies. All of these vanished into the pantry or spring house except for the hundred pounds or so—smoking hot or spring-water cold, as custom dictated—arranged on red-checkered tablecloths for the field gang's mid-morning breakfast.

The pies, with "just a dab" of red-eye gravy to bring out their flavor, were in mid-sigh when a series of bellows and the clang of steel crunching gravel echoed across the kitchen. The threshing machine and its crew of hoboes had arrived. The first Gargantua in this procession was a ten-horse string panting against traces to roll the threshing machine's steam engine uphill to the barnyard. The engine looked like an 1840 railroad locomotive, even to its six-foot smokestack, barrel-like boiler and brass valves. It was mounted on steel-rimmed wagon wheels. Immediately behind rumbled the array of wheels, gears, vibrators, blowers and screens that, powered by a belt connecting it to the steam engine's flywheel, would separate the wheat kernels and chaff from the straw, then shimmy and puff all three into separate piles.

Wheat harvesting roared on, sun-up to dark, until the crop was "in the bag." Throughout, the kitchen brigade produced three mammoth meals a day, plus "snacks" at any hour and relays of lemonade, root beer, water, crullers and cookies to the scenes of man-labor by the prettiest unmarried daughters. Logically, "threshers' meal" became an American phrase as meaningful and sigh-inducing as the words *Delmonico, clambake* and *barbecue.*

Most of the dust-caked figures feeding wheat bundles into the thresher's hopper, filling the bags of kernels, stacking the straw into prim taffy-gold mounds were members of a profession spawned by this horse-machine age. Individually, they were adolescent idealists, Populists, Socialists, alcoholics, storekeepers who "lost their shirts" in the 1890 depression, ex-bullwhackers or wanderers born two generations too late to be Mountain Men or wagon-train scouts. Collectively, they hitched rides on freight trains and baggage cars out of Chicago, St. Louis or Memphis every July to sign on as thresher crewmen for the wheat harvests, toppers and loaders during the sugar-beet harvests, pickers and packers on the Los Angeles-to-Puget Sound progression of the Pacific Coast fruit harvests. During October they returned to Chicago's "Skid Row," New York's Bowery, or a job at a Florida hotel. They gave themselves the profession-name "hobo," presumably because of the fraternal greeting of "Ho, beau!" used at the trackside camps where they caroused, cooked slumgullion stew, and occasionally bathed or deloused.[9] The hobo was as significant a figure in the West's third revolution as the cowboy had been in the second, and the explorers, Mountain Men and scouts during the first. Like the horse, man adjusted to the onrush of steel and machines.

The third major contribution to our folkways that became popular during the plow-up of Revolution Three was the sequence of skill exhibitions inherited from the bull worshippers of prehistoric Crete, the centaur-horsemen of Macedon and Thessaly, the Hyksos charioteers, and those Hebrew slaves who invented, as herdsmen for the landlords of Egypt, most of the rope, branding-iron and cow-handling techniques we now associate with the "Wild West cowboy." These skill exhibitions developed from the "horseplay"—and the contemporary meaning of the word pertly illustrates its origin! —that followed a trail drive or a roundup. The Crackers held similar frolics during the 1750s. So did the ranchers and *vaqueros* of Alta California. It is probable that the Irish and Scotch cowboys of John Pynchon's trail crew "whooped it up" with demonstrations of horsemanship, calf roping and a few harum-scarum races a few hours after the 1655 drive of stall-fattened cattle reached Boston.

The skill demonstrations favored by the Crackers, the Californians, and the Texas cattlemen were also favorites of horsemen and herdsmen in the Mediterranean basin of 3000 and 2000 B.C.

The *bull-ride*, and even the *bull-dogging* act perfected by the great Negro cowboy-showman Bill Pickett between 1904 and 1911, never surpassed the bull-dance that climaxed religious ceremonies on Crete about 3000 B.C.[10] A few centuries later, the "bronze-clad" horsemen who invaded Greece via Macedonia and Thessaly, and thus created the legend of the Centaur, perfected the trick of bull-dogging cattle "by driving them around the arena—and then jumping on them and seizing their horns."[11] Like the Hyksos, these horsemen relished free-for-all chariot races and turned their bronco-busting into public spectacles.

In Egypt, herdsmen perfected the branding iron, rope throwing, and the bundle tie before 2000 B.C. Paintings on the walls of the tomb of Huy, chief herdsman for the young Pharaoh Tutankhamen, show his assistants branding cattle with the Pharaoh's mark.[12] Other tomb paintings from the Fifth and Sixth Dynasties depict livestock with one front leg and both hind legs tied "in the bundle," just as modern cattlemen do it.

Competitions between cowboys competent in these ancient horseback, cattle, and rope techniques became standard entertainment in Abilene, Dodge City and other Kansas "cowtowns" during the 1860s and 1870s. In the 1880s, cowboy contests were featured events at county fairs across Colorado, Wyoming and Montana. The directors of the Denver Exposition announced during September 1887 that a tournament by "genuine and experienced cowboys" would feature the October 13–14 "wonders" of their fair.[13] Prizes of fifty dollars each were posted for "the best time in catching, saddling and riding a wild bronco," and for "roping and hog-tying a wild steer." More than twelve thousand people attended the "tournament"; the secretary of the Colorado Humane Association threatened to bring suit against the Denver Chamber of Commerce for sponsoring such "cruelties." A year later, Prescott, Arizona, put on a larger, rowdier cowboy contest at its first Frontier Day celebration. The Pendleton Roundup, the Calgary Stampede, and Cheyenne's Frontier Days were all founded, with cowboy contests as stellar attractions, before 1900. Between 1900 and 1910, these contests began to use the name *"rodeo,"* the Spanish word for "roundup."

The rodeo fracased on to become one of the most popular spectacles in America. Its standard program of competitions—formally labeled "events" by the Rodeo Cowboy Association—remains as popular during the annual week or two at New York's Madison Square Garden, Boston's Winter Garden and Chicago's International Amphitheater as it does in Tucson, Cheyenne, Calgary and hundreds of county and state fairs.[14] Many of the roping, broncride, steer-wrestle and bull-ride contestants are college students, truck drivers, gas-station attendants, lawyers, farmers, or store clerks.

The "savage bronc" has similarly proved that a semi-feral environment on open range is not essential to a daily "declaration of independence." The most famous bucking horse of the 1930s was Midnight, a gentle black who was the pet of a schoolteacher in Alberta, Canada. Carrying the teacher home one dusk, Midnight shied at a tumbleweed frisked across the road by a prairie breeze. He bucked off the teacher and fled home. Thereafter, Midnight went into a studied rage whenever a rider attempted to "come aboard."

Another spectacular bucker, Tygh Valley, "went bad" when the boy he docilely carried to and from school decided to crack some nuts by mashing them with a rock against Tygh Valley's saddle.[15]

Farm horses with draft-horse blood, saddle mounts of Morgan,

Hambletonian and Chickasaw heritage, as well as milk-wagon plodders have, time after time, displayed middle-aged resentment to environment. Often these horses have become famous on the rodeo circuit.

Summer by summer while "threshers' meal," "hobo," and "rodeo" became symbols in our street language, the ratchety snarl of the automobile echoed farther into the countryside. The early models were merely expensive toys, limited to seasonal transportation on gravel or asphalt pavement. They became helplessly mired in the mud wallows, erosion gullies, and ruts that pocked the wagonways of the farm country and mountains. Their penchant for flat tires, broken springs, plugged fuel lines, burned-out spark plugs or helplessly spinning wheels caused some bright urchin—who probably became a $25,000-a-year slogan writer for an advertising agency!—to invent the jeering cry: "Git a hoss!" From the 1890s through the 1920s, the phrase was fashionable among rural and village youth.

Jim Carpenter of Atlantic City, Wyoming, told me how a homesteader named Boscovitch, sometime around 1911 or 1912, invented a saying that became standard banter in Atlantic City, South Pass City, and the other gold camps on the slopes of South Pass, Wyoming. Boscovitch ranched in the upper Sweetwater Valley, near the ruins of the Pony Express Station at Burned Ranch. One day a dusty automobile coughed into his yard. The driver asked for the best route to Oregon Buttes, then bragged that he intended to follow the "49ers" wagon ruts on through South Pass and across the desert to the Green River valley. Boscovitch advised against it, but gave the directions. A few hours later, the autoist walked back into the yard and offered Boscovitch five dollars to pull his car out of a gully a mile or two up the trail. Thereafter, Boscovitch told the story of the afternoon's work, with gestures and elaborate detail, whenever he came down to Atlantic City for supplies. He invariably ended with a mournful headshake and a fist bang on the counter, as he exclaimed, "Pye golly, I vouldn't know!! Dot feller say he got fifty-four horsepower in dot automobile but I pull him oudt mit two old skates!"

But better automobiles and better highways were as inevitable as canals and railroads had been a lifetime before. In addition to hauling Reos, Hupmobiles, Franklins, Stanley Steamers and Stutz Bearcats out of ruts and bogholes, draft horses performed two titanic tasks critical to the realization of the "Auto Age." They hauled machinery, tools and pipe into, and petroleum out of, the oil fields. They powered the machines that widened and water-proofed our inter-city highways.

The search for oil in the West began during the 1870s, and by 1905 had located great pools beneath California, Texas, Oklahoma, Wyoming and southern Illinois. Horses and mules supplied the initial power. Most of the test wells were bored in areas fifty to a hundred miles from a railroad. Drills, cables, girders, pumps and steam engines all had to be wagoned in, most of them over terrain crossed only by cattle and sheep trails. If the drillings brought in a "gusher," the petroleum had to be hauled out to a railroad siding. The freighters copied the railroad's train idea by hitching seven or eight ponderous wagons in tandem behind a twenty-five- or thirty-horse-and-mule "string." The hauls to some of the Texas and Wyoming fields were so long that these oil trains hitched on a sheep-wagon caboose, too, as the sleeping and cooking place for the crew.

Similar hitches of thirty, forty and even fifty horses were used in California and the Pacific Northwest between 1890 and 1920 when wheat ranchers invested in huge "combine" harvesting ma-chines to cut, thresh and bag the crop as they lurched across the fields.

Wheat combines, oil rigs, the abominable condition of highways, the continuing plow-up of virgin land, the expanding cities all influenced the steady increase of our horse and mule population. When World War I began in August 1914, Americans owned be-tween twenty-four and twenty-five million horses, and four and a half million mules. Thus more than half of all the horses on earth lived in Russia and the United States. Our horse population equaled the combined horse populations of Great Britain, Germany, the

Netherlands, France, Canada and Argentina. Iowa, with 1,600,000 horses—but only 58,000 mules—had more horses than all of Italy and Spain. Illinois, Texas and Kansas, with 3,700,000 horses, had almost as many as the Holy Roman Empire of Austria-Hungary and twice as many as the Empire of Japan. We had five times as many mules as Spain, the historic homeland of the mule.

We exported 355,000 horses and mules to Europe during 1915; this number represented less than 1 per cent of our supply, and market prices dropped 4.5 per cent during the year. Another 719,000 horses and 270,000 mules went overseas to the battlefields, supply lines and farms of the Allies between 1916 and 1919.

Horse and mule populations on our farms continued to increase. The federal government urged peak production of foodstuffs and land-grown supplies; newspapers and county agents harangued the theme that "Food will win the war." Farmers ripped open another forty million acres of virgin land, twenty-five million of it on the high-plains. The on-farm horse population reached an all-time high of 21,555,000 head in 1918. More than half of these labored in the corn and wheat belts between Ohio and the Dakotas. The 1914–19 period would go into agricultural history books under the nickname of "the silk shirt years"; wheat prices rose to $2.15 a bushel, corn to $1.25 a bushel, and cotton to thirty-six cents a pound.

But operating costs rose faster and higher. Farm tax bills increased from $624 million in 1913 to $1,497 million in 1921. Freight, fertilizer and feed costs all doubled. The wages paid to "the hired man" soared from $700 million in 1914 to $1,600 million in 1921.[16] During the same years, more than 1,500,000 young people migrated to military service and factory jobs; few of them ever returned to the land to live.

Coincidentally, the Auto Age finally lumbered outside the cities and suburbs. The federal government expanded its Office of Road Enquiry, surveyed the nation's two million miles of highway, and learned that 92 per cent of them were unimproved wagon tracks and livestock trails. So, in 1916, Congress passed a Federal Highway Act appropriating an initial $75 million to be spent on interstate road improvements. This work began during the war years. Between 1917 and 1925, almost fifty thousand miles of gravel, macadam, concrete, brick, and "graded and drained earth roads" were built on a shared-cost basis by federal and local governments. In his 1925 annual report, Secretary of Agriculture Jardine could proudly report that "one of the most important projects recently completed is the Wendover cut-off across the Great Salt Lake Desert between Salt Lake City and the Nevada line. The completion of this road brings to a successful conclusion a five-year effort to bridge the obstacle to transcontinental travel which has always been presented by the salt desert."[17] The new highways enabled automobiles and trucks to take over the horse-and-mule task of farm and city transportation.

Simultaneous improvements to the tractor launched another revolution on the American farm. In 1858, a Californian named W. P. Miller had designed a steam locomotive, mounted on a mammoth moving belt, that crawled along farm roads at an average speed of three miles an hour. A few of these vehicles were operated in lumber camps, mines and on the huge wheat ranches, but they were too expensive and too cumbersome for the average farm. By 1912, only nine thousand tractors—each weighing ten or eleven tons and capable of developing sixty horsepower—were in use on large grain farms.

In 1917, Henry Ford began production of the Fordson Tractor, at "flivver prices." During 1918 more than 133,000 farm tractors were sold, with Ford, International Harvester and J. I. Case as the three sales leaders. Both the U.S. Department of Agriculture and the state universities, hence the county-agent system, promoted the "efficiencies of mechanization" and pointed to the soaring taxes, hired-man and feed costs, and the migration of farm youngsters to the city to validate their case. Meat packers and tractor manufacturers then began to point out that horses and mules consumed one fourth of all the grain and grass crops produced in the nation. Trends in human population, they argued, indicated that these resources would be desperately needed for the production of meat animals and cereal foodstuffs for human consumption. The campaign was successful. When the Great Depression finally reached Wall Street during the fall of 1929, more than a million tractors were in use on American farms.

The decrease in horse population paced in direct ratio. Through the 1920s, horses disappeared from the countryside at an average rate of 500,000 a year. Almost all of the animals were sold to meat packers and processed into dog food, bone meal, cordovan leather, felt and glue. When World War II began, there were 10,440,000 horses in the United States.

In 1965, the mighty family of *Equus* had only four to five million descendants in our fifty states. But fewer than a million of these were on farms and ranches. Like the farmers' sons and daughters, most of America's horses had migrated toward the big cities. There, just as they had been during the age of knighthood, they became status symbols.

THE HOBBY HORSE—AGAIN

CHAPTER TWENTY-ONE

The prompt adaptation of *Equus caballus* to current human need over the past four thousand to five thousand years is one of the most remarkable achievements in the history of civilization. No other animal responded so readily and so repeatedly to man's social and economic demands. The creation of the Morgan, Thoroughbred, Quarter Horse, Tennessee Walking Horse and American Saddle Horse breeds in America during the nineteenth and early twentieth centuries was, like the 1850–1900 production of our drafters, critical to the United States's growth to a world power.

Since 1900, another demand has been made on the horse by Americans. It came from the cities and suburbs. *Equus* is responding as nobly to this need for a hobby as he did to our eighteenth-century demands for pack ponies, pacers, Conestoga teams, Cracker ponies and cavalry mounts, and to our nineteenth-century demands for racers, coachers, range horses and drafters.

The word *hobby* comes from *hob*: the rocking place beside the hearth. The sedate Irish horse favored by the squires, clergymen and other travelers of seventeenth-century England took the name Hobby Horse because its broad back and gentle gait carried a rider almost as comfortably as a rocker on a hob. The pursuit of leisure-time activity called a "hobby" also comes from *hob*. But, until the early decades of the twentieth century, leisure-time hobbies could be pursued only by the wealthy and by grandparents. The average

American was too exhausted after a ten- or twelve-hour workday to do much more than read the evening newspaper, chat an hour or two, and go to bed.

Through the 1930s, 40s and 50s, technology and labor legislation reduced the work day to nine, eight and seven hours, and the work week to five or four and a half days. Thereupon, since the human being is an inherently restless organism, the search for agreeable and socially acceptable hobbies—the sociologists prefer to call them "leisure-time activities"—became one of America's gravest problems. This caused the horse to return to the urban environment. The automobile and truck had banished him from both city and countryside, but the leisure-time backlash of the Machine Age reintroduced his saddle, racer, polo, hunter and pony types as "hobby horses."

The trotters, pacers and saddle racers should be included on any list of the pioneer influences that created our suburbias. Race tracks were always built on the edge of town or a few miles out into the countryside. The day's outing to a race meet was an intrinsic part of the appeal of the commercial horse race, especially for those spectators—and bet makers—who lived in the tenements downtown. Moreover, sufficient land area was needed to build paddocks, stables, grandstands, exercise areas, a clubhouse and other adjuncts that became essential as the hobby flourished. Also, a dirt tract and broad area open to wind and weather became an important factor in the wagering. Some racers perform better than others on wet tracks; they take the nickname "mudders." A rainstorm changes the betting odds and jockey, or driver, techniques for every race in the day's "card."

Hence race-track suburbs developed within easy carriage or omnibus distances from the downtown sections of New York City, Charleston, Philadelphia, Boston and New Orleans. Villages grew around each track. Wealthy horse fanciers bought up nearby farmlands and transformed them into country estates or stud farms that specialized in blooded and purebred saddle racers, trotters or pacers.

As railroads developed during the 1840s and 1850s, new race-track communities were founded an hour's ride out from a city terminal and at summer resorts and spas. The Race Track Special grew into an excellent source of revenue for railroads. Saratoga Springs, the most fashionable mineral-springs resort in the East, opened its Horse Haven Track for harness races during the 1850s. In 1865, William R. Travers, Cornelius Vanderbilt, Leonard W. Jerome and other wealthy New Yorkers organized the Saratoga Association for the Improvement of the Breed of Horses, and financed construction of a saddle-race track in a landscaped forty-five-acre park. The "August racing season" at Saratoga developed into a hubbub of formal receptions, balls, style shows and yearling sales that dominated the society pages of metropolitan newspapers.

Kentucky breeders and sportsmen emulated Saratoga in 1875 by founding the Kentucky Derby. True to the decentralist pattern, the meet they developed around Derby Day was held on a new suburban track built on the stud farm of a family named Churchill a few miles outside Louisville. (A newspaper reporter bestowed its grandiloquent place-name of Churchill Downs, in imitation of Epsom Downs, locale for the English Derby.) Partly in deference to Saratoga's August season, but principally because of the spring auctions of yearlings, the Kentucky Derby's run was fixed as "the first Saturday in May." It was limited to three-year-old "Breds."

The hypnotic lure of quick fortune by gambling on the "win, place or show" and "daily double" of the saddle racers gave the few thousand "Breds" far more adulation than the sport deserved. Much of this publicity grew from the circulation struggle between intra-city dailies and the pauper-salaries paid to newspaper reporters. (Heywood Broun, the most vocal founding father of the American Newspaper Guild during the 1930s, nicknamed members of the working press "the ragged individualists.")

The battles for circulation led to the institution of "Racing Extras" by afternoon papers. These necessitated a direct wire between principal race tracks and each newspaper's editorial department. The "fudge box" technique was used to insert the results of each race into a prominent spot on page one. Another circulation booster came with the appointment of a sports-writer, called the "handi-capper," who published a daily list of saddle racers he believed the most likely to win races at the larger tracks. One natural sequel of this was that most newspapers had one or more "bookies" lurking near the racing desk to accept bets from reporters, "news hens," copy editors, rewrite men, printers and copy boys. Turning most of the week's pay envelope over to a bookie to pay off "on the cuff" bets was a common sight in City Rooms during the 1920s and 1930s. And memoirs indicate that the same "gee-gee fever" prevailed in them during the 1880s and 1890s.

This journalistic intensity for the saddle racers, plus the publicity given "the aristocracy" at Saratoga, the Kentucky Derby, Pimlico, et cetera by the society and Sunday-supplement editors, exalted the "Bred" and his environment and convinced most hobbyists that saddle racers were the finest specimens in all of the *Equus* family. Thus race-track promoters and "Bred" breeders, in England and America, were able to popularize the adjective *thoroughbred* into a proper noun, and limit its use to validated descendants of Matchem, Diomed and Eclipse.

"Though *thoroughbred* was certainly used freely to designate horses registered in the General Stud Book (i.e. British)," report the editors of the Merriam-Webster Dictionaries,[1] "no official defi-nition of *Thoroughbred* appears to have existed prior to 1911. About this period, or a little earlier, came the attempt to justify the arbitrary preemption of *Thoroughbred* on the basis that it was the literal translation of Arabic *kuhailan* (kehailen or kehilan in usual English spelling). In point of fact this word apparently de-rives from *k'uhl* (kohl) presumably with reference to the black skin of Arab horses of purest lineage and it is defined in J. Milton Cowan's translation of Hans Wehr's *A Dictionary of Modern Writ-ten Arabic* as 'horse of noblest breed.' This is obviously no more a

synonym of *thoroughbred* in the earlier broader sense than are
English *Thoroughbreds* of mixed ancestry equal to the Arabic
concept of *kuhailan.*

"Between 1911 and about 1930, there is abundant evidence of a
militant determination to revise and restrict the word without
regard to historic usage or to logic. Perhaps particularly pertinent
is a clipping . . . of an article by G. Chapin taken from a, probably
New York, newspaper sometime during World War I. Comment-
ing on a scolding of the Holstein-Friesian Association by the *Breeders' Gazette* for applying the adjective to cattle, he points out that
none of the 18th and early 19th century sporting dictionaries use
thoroughbred. On American usage he states,

> In this country the early stud books of Mason and Edgar and
> Wallace gave prominence to the terms *race horse, turf horse*
> and *blood horse* but none of them had such a word as *thorough-*
> *bred* on its title page. S. D. Bruce was the first to use it in his
> *American Stud Book Containing Full Pedigree of all Thor-*
> *oughbred Stallions and Mares,* etc. published in 1868. . . . The
> term thoroughbred-trotter is frequently heard among horse-
> men identified with harness racing. . . . While freely conceding
> that the English race horse was the first thoroughbred horse,
> by reason of having been the first whose breeding was pre-
> served and recorded in a stud book, they as stoutly deny that
> he is the only thoroughbred horse.

"To sum up: we have no evidence contradictory to the hypothesis
that *thoroughbred* was used broadly in respect to livestock long
before it was restricted to a particular breed of horses. On the
contrary all our positive evidence strongly supports the position
and indicates that the restrictive pressure was artificially generated
in the early years of this century."[2]

Soon after the Civil War, realty prices—plus the slick asphalt,
brick and cobble paving used on downtown streets—began to pressure carriage and saddle horses toward suburbia, too. Property

values downtown rose to ten dollars . . . twenty dollars . . . fifty dollars . . . one hundred dollars per square foot. Only millionaires could afford to maintain a mid-city horse barn, carriage house and exercise yard. The peril of skidding on wet or icy pavement was as urgent an argument against city driving. Hundreds of horses were shot, or otherwise destroyed, in downtown areas each year after they broke legs or tore ligaments in falls on ice or wet pavement.

Yet millions of horses were forced to endure the pavement hazard until the automobile took over the task of powering freight, home deliveries, fire engines, police vans, road repairs and construction jobs.[3] Veterinarians and manufacturers attempted to counteract the pavement hazard by designing and promoting types of horse-shoes coated with rubber. "In cities," warned Dr. Joseph Hughes, president of the Chicago Veterinary College, "the worn slippery granite blocks, the greasy asphalt and the slope of the street from center to curb make slips and falls of such frequent occurrence that the hand-wrought shoe has been to some extent supplanted by combinations of iron and rubber, more especially in shoeing the front feet. . . . Rubber pads with tips would in all probability be in more general use but for the fact that large users of draft horses consider the cost prohibitive. There is no device in shoeing that has anti-slipping merit equalling that of the rubber pad. In heavy hauling in cities horses having calks on their shoes, while swinging and backing, trample each other, inflicting injuries on their hoofheads which becoming infected end in serious losses. Shoeing with rubber pads would lessen, if not entirely do away with such dangers. During winters, too, when there is much snowfall, rubber pads are the only devices that will prevent snowballing and permit horses to do an average day's work. . . . The draft horse should be well shod. We owe it to him. The gruelling labor to which he is daily subjected deserves recognition, at least to the extent of giving his feet intelligent attention. The massive strength, the pillar-like setting of the limbs under the body, the preservation of perfect conformation of legs and feet, the suppleness and freedom of step, the

firmness of hold on the ground, the promptness and energy with
which he presses his weight against the collar, are largely sub-
ordinate to the treatment given him in the shoeing shop."[4]

The only dirt-path and grass refuges remaining for the city horse
by the 1880s were in public parks, such as New York City's Central,
Chicago's Lincoln and Jackson, and Washington's Rock Creek.
Here the political influence of horse fanciers caused carriage drives
and riding paths to be built through miniature forests and hedges
of shrubs interspersed with gardens of flowers that could survive
the sooty atmosphere, diuretic dogs and cats, and hungry rodents.

Livery stables, specialty clothing stores, and harness shops
flourished on streets near the parks. The stables, usually operated
by ex-coachmen of obvious Scottish or Irish heritage, rented saddle
horses, coachers and vehicles by the hour or day. The clothing
stores specialized in British-colonial jodhpurs, tweedy jackets,
bowler hats, calfskin boots, riding crops and other apparel prescribed by *Harper's Bazaar* or *Leslie's Illustrated Weekly* as "cor-
rect Continental mode" for the equestrian. These garments, too,
were available "by the hour or week." The harness shops, redolent
of oiled leather, brass polish and varnish, sold or rented Western
saddles, English saddles, bridles, ten- and twenty-blade jackknives,
leather hats, and Swedish or Swiss "riding manuals," and had side
lines of balsam pillows, rawhide wallets, purses "hand-beaded by
Western Indians," and chromo posters of Buffalo Bill on a white
horse or circus riders jumping Arabians through fiery hoops.

Both the bridle paths and the dependent shops became fashionable. They were trysting places as well as patrol routes for "party
girls," gigolos and homosexuals. But primarily they attracted the
city dwellers for whom horseback riding was a pleasant hobby.

City park and suburban persistence of the saddle devotee en-
couraged the founding of the National Saddle Horse Breeders
Association at Louisville during 1891. A new breed, named the
American Saddle Horse (or Saddler), was created with Denmark,
John Dillard, Tom Hal and seven other stallions selected as the
foundation sires.[5] In 1906, Charles S. Plumb described the ideal

Saddler as showing "much style in carriage of head and arch of neck and tail, while a round, well turned, neat body is desirable. . . . The shoulders and pasterns must be sloping and long, the pasterns in particular being long, strong and springy, thus favoring an easy gait."[6]

Urban and suburban equestrians welcomed the Saddler, paid from $500 to $1,000 for yearlings carrying the blood of the foundation sires. By the time of World War One they had established the breed as star of the fashionable horse shows.[7] The variety of intricate "gaits" that became standard competitions at these shows was masterfully described by W. R. Goodwin, Jr., Saddler authority for the *Breeder's Gazette*: "The three natural gaits of a horse are the walk, trot, and gallop or run. Artificially, that is by education, the gallop is made into a canter, which is a gait performed by the same movement of the legs, but slower, more restrained and easier to ride. We then have one kind of a saddle horse called the *walk-trot-canter* or *plain-gaited horse*. . . . Easier gaits are the *running walk* and the *rack*. The *running walk* is called a slow gait, and there are two other gaits allied to it—the *slow pace* and the *fox trot*. . . .

"The rack is a four-beat gait. Each foot hits the ground at a separate interval in a one-two-three-four beat. The rack can be distinguished by ear as far as footfalls of the horse may be heard; each foot rings clear its own note on the hard ground. In teaching the rack, the horse is forced forward by the spur and restrained by the curb. His diagnoal gait is thereby broken up and he flies into a four-beat gait. The rack is easy for the rider, hard for the horse. It is a showy gait and is performed at great speed sometimes. The trainer who has a fast racking horse will generally keep him on that gait when in the show ring, hoping to dazzle the judge by the flashiness of the performance. . . . This gait has been officially named The Rack by the American Saddle Horse Breeders' Association, and hence the name 'single foot' should not be used, as it merely leads to confusion among the uninformed.

"This five gaits recognized by that association are the walk, trot, canter, rack and the running walk, or slow pace, or fox trot. Any

one of these three slow gaits will answer. Some horses can go only
one of them, some can show them all. When a horse can show these
five gaits, he is called a *gaited horse*."[8]

Numerous efforts were made to popularize other types of riding
horses and win acclaim—and sales!—for them as distinct breeds.
By 1965, only nine types were widely accepted as distinct "breeds":
Albino, Appaloosa, Arabian, Morgan, Palomino, Pinto, Quarter
Horse, Saddler, and Tennessee Walking Horse. (The Jockey Club,
New York City, listed only sixteen thousand Thoroughbreds in
its 1964 registry.) Among these, the Saddler, Quarter Horse,
Tennessee Walking Horse and Morgan were the most popular
nationally. The showy Palomino, with silvery mane and tail and
golden coat, is essentially a product of California and the Southwest, just as the Appaloosa is "the pride of Idaho." The stud book
of the Tennessee Walking Horse was not established until 1935,
with a Kentucky foal, Black Tom, of Morgan and Hambletonian
heritage, declared the foundation sire.[9] The Quarter Horse, with
heredity reaching back to the Virginia, Kentucky and Illinois
quarter-mile racers brought into Texas during the 1820s, finally
achieved its registry and recognition as a breed in 1940.[10]

But the popularity of the saddle horse declined steadily between
1900 and the late 1940s. The automobile, lawn croquet, baseball,
radio, bridge, canasta and television successively captured public
attention as hobbies and leisure-time pursuits. During this half
century, the race horse became the principal representative of
Equus' family to merit the attention of the average urban or suburban American. Even this interest was obviously not due to humanitarian considerations or to recognition of the horse's merits as a
means to physical fitness and relaxation. Instead, the hobby of
"betting on the gee-gees" grew into an American folkway as expensive, and often as habit-forming, as narcotics and alcohol.

Throughout the eleven years of our Great Depression (1929–
40), an average of fourteen thousand saddle and harness races
were run each year on commercial tracks. In 1933—the year
of the nationwide bank closings and the National Industrial Re-

covery Act—the twelve states with legalized race-track gambling earned $4,465,135.98 as their 7.5 to 10 per cent share of the bets *legally* placed at the eighty-eight race tracks within their borders.[11] In 1937, the seventeen states with legal betting received revenues of $10,038,830.64 from wagers on horse races. In 1938, the Massachusetts Racing Commission estimated, a total of $48,991,865 was wagered at Massachusetts tracks—and 69 per cent of it was placed as "$2 bets."

By the end of World War II, state revenues from horse-race betting soared toward $100 million a year; by 1958, it was up to $222 million. During 1962, California's government collected $30,682,269 from Thoroughbred races, $4,217,472 from Quarter Horse and county-fair races, and $4,250,210 from harness racing. New York in the same year grossed $64 million from Thoroughbred races and $46 million from harness-race betting. The twenty-four states permitting pari-mutuel betting that year grossed revenues totaling $212 million from Thoroughbred races and $69 million from harness races out of a total pari-mutuel "turnover" of $3,550 million. The attendance records for horse races in these states totaled 48,400,000: 33,073,712 paid to see Thoroughbred races and 15,358,311 paid to see harness races.

That year the Jockey Club listed 14,350 animals in the Thoroughbred registry; 7,392 were listed in the registry of the United States Trotting Association; the race-horse population of the United States totaled approximately 125,000.[12]

Resurgence of the saddle horse began after World War II when industries led the sprawl from downtown to suburbia, incomes soared, and the work week shrank. The first step usually was, and is, to "get a pony for the children." Then parents discover that horseback riding and carriage driving is not only excellent exercise but an absorbing leisure-time activity.

The extent of this resurgence is, in 1965, difficult to measure. The U.S. Department of Agriculture canceled its annual estimate of our horse population in 1959.[13] But by 1964 the two largest farmer cooperatives in the East, Southern States Cooperative and Agway,

Inc., found such widespread evidence of increasing horse populations in their suburbias and farms that they created house-brands
of horse feed especially mixed for brood mares, colts or adults.

"More and more people are putting their money where their
love is—in horseflesh and horsemanship," said Kenneth Hinshaw
of Agway. "This is creating a great new hobby horse industry.
. . . Horse feed sales in many of our territories show heavy percentage gains."

W. M. Corwin, director of information services for Southern
States Cooperative, reported similar trends south of the Potomac.
"In our five states—Virginia, West Virginia, Maryland, Delaware
and Kentucky—we have seen a sizeable upsurge in the number
of horses, particularly in the last five or six years," he wrote. "They
are naturally riding horses of various breeds and varieties and
some show horses. The idea of 'owning a horse' is becoming popular again, and the number is increasing month by month."

A survey in New York State, conducted by Professor Harold A.
Willman of Cornell University during the fall of 1964, indicated an
increase in horses in New York State from 47,371 in 1959 to 125,200
in late 1964.[14]

"Obviously," Dr. Willman concluded in announcing the preliminary report of his survey during February 1965, "[New York]
is in the midst of a horse boom and there are many reasons for this.
The horse has become a status symbol for young and old and for
entire families. . . . More and more race tracks, more leisure time,
the need for recreation and a means for relaxation from the pressures of daily work, and a greater emphasis on physical fitness have
stimulated an interest in riding and horse production. Down
through the ages the horse has given man friendship and pleasure
and his compatability undoubtedly will continue to keep him popular so long as people love the outdoors and sports. Horses have become an integral part of suburban life and important to rural re-
development programs. Horse ownership or riding and activities
associated with the horse business can bring enjoyment to many

adults and entire families and helps to curb delinquency and to otherwise keep many youth out of trouble."

Dr. Willman's survey, undertaken through the cooperation of 4-H Clubs, provided the most comprehensive data available in early 1965 on the resurgence of the horse in America.[15] The estimate of a 1965 horse population of three million by the U.S. Department of Agriculture was "educated guessing," but meaningless. The 166 per cent increase of horses in New York State between 1959 and 1964, as indicated by the Willman survey, obviously came from a surge of devotion to horsemanship in the suburbias of the state. Comparable enthusiasm was evident in many of our fifty states. Thus it seems probable that the horse population of the United States in the spring of 1965 was closer to five million.

So the horse and horsemanship assume still another role in the development of American civilization. The horse has become a means for Man to achieve mental therapy and maintain physical health in his technological environment. This situation is as beneficial to the horse as it is to Man, since medical science, balanced rations, sanitary housing, and—at long, long last—the devoted care of owners are combining to offer the horse the healthiest, happiest environment of all his fifty-five million years in North America.[16]

69. Chinese laborers and one-horse dumpcarts performed the Herculean task of building the Central Pacific's right-of-way across the Sierra Nevada between 1863 and 1868. This photograph of the bank and cut at Sailor's Spur is believed to have been taken in 1867. *Courtesy of the Southern Pacific Railroad.*

70. A drawing of Louis Napoleon made in 1878. *Courtesy of the Milner Library, Illinois State University.*

71. Percherons on the exercise track outside one of the Dillon Brothers' barns during the 1870s. *Courtesy of the Milner Library, Illinois State University.*

72. Levi Dillon's Percheron farm as an artist saw it in 1872. The railroad in the foreground is the main line of the Chicago, Alton & St. Louis. The building with tower in the left background is the first administration building of the Illinois State Normal School. *Courtesy of the Milner Library, Illinois State University.*

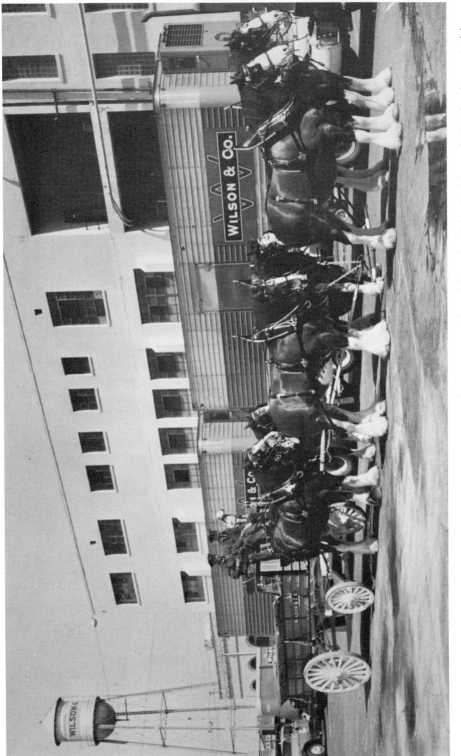

73. This show-team of Wilson & Company Clydesdales perpetuates the memory of the mighty role of the draft horse in the development of America's technology after 1865. *Courtesy of Wilson & Company, Chicago.*

74. The drafter-ranger hybrids developed during the last decades of the nineteenth century powered the excavations for the vast furnace and mill array of United States Steel on the Lake Michigan shore at Gary, Indiana. *Courtesy of the United States Steel Corporation.*

75. Mud wallows in spring and snowdrifts in winter made most rural roads impassable for six months of every year. *Courtesy of the Library of Congress.*

76. Surveys revealed that 92 per cent of all U.S. highways in 1900 had springtime mud wallows like this one in South Dakota. *Courtesy of the Bureau of Public Roads.*

77. Leather and silk Victoria carriages, drawn by teams of Thoroughbreds, Morgans or Arabians, were the equipage of millionaires, Presidents and brothel madams between 1870 and 1910. *Courtesy of the Library of Congress.*

78. Genteel saddle horses carried the veteran messengers who delivered messages and documents between the national Capitol and the White House during the closing decades of the nineteenth century. *Courtesy of the Library of Congress.*

79. Eight-wheel logging truck employed by Cady Lumber Corporation, Flagstaff, Arizona. Courtesy of F. Hal Higgins Agricultural Engineering Research Collection, University of California Library at Davis.

80. Five combine harvesters at work in a wheat field in Palouse County, Washington, during the 1890s. The machines are powered by 165 horses and mules. *Courtesy of the U.S. Department of Agriculture.*

81. A "Maude Muller" of the mechanizing West. *Courtesy of the Western History Research Center, University of Wyoming.*

82. Threshing-time in Nebraska's North Platte Valley about 1920. *Courtesy of the Western History Research Center, University of Wyoming.*

83. A thirty-eight horse team hauls a giant header-combine through a wheat field near Walla Walla, Washington, in 1902. *Courtesy of the U.S. Department of Agriculture.*

84. South Water Street, Chicago, 1900 to 1910. Courtesy of the Chicago Historical Society.

85. Photo of the twenty-two horse rig, with three drivers, hauling the seventy-ton girder used in the construction of the Charles A. Stevens Store, 1914. *Courtesy of the Chicago Historical Society.*

86. Waiting to unload potatoes at Atlanta, Texas, June 1904. *Courtesy of the U.S. Department of Agriculture.*

87. A Homburg hat was part of what the well-dressed milkman wore in New York City around 1900. *Courtesy of the Ravenswood–Lake View Historical Association.*

88. This 1914 painting of a popular racer named Peter Volo hangs in the gallery of the New York State Historical Association at Fenimore House, Cooperstown. *Courtesy of the New York State Historical Association, Cooperstown.*

89. "Whyncha git a hoss?" *Courtesy of the Bureau of Public Roads.*

CHRONOLOGY

Early Eocene Epoch (Approximately 55,000,000 B.C.)	The dawn horse, *Eohippus* (i.e. *Hyracotherium*), browsed in tropical jungles that covered the Laramie Plain and other basins of the American West.
Late Miocene Epoch (Approximately 30,000,000 B.C.)	*Merychippus* genus of Equidae evolved tooth, jaw, leg and other adaptations essential for grazing on the new grasslands of the Rocky Mountains highplain.
Late Pliocene Epoch (Approximately 3,000,000 B.C.)	*Equus caballus*, founder of the true-horse family, is believed to have evolved in Eurasia.
Pleistocene Epoch (Approximately 2,000,000 to 50,000 B.C.)	*Equus caballus* became one of the most numerous animal families in both North and South America.
9000 B.C.	*Equus caballus* still ranged in the American West, hence was contemporary of early red man.
9000–5000 B.C.	The horse family vanished from North and South America.
6000–5000 B.C.	A great natural catastrophe, perhaps the Deluge reported in Bible, Koran, etc., destroyed the Alaska-Siberia isthmus, created Bering Strait, and halted all land-animal migrations between Eurasia and the New World.
3000 B.C.	Broncbusters on steppes between the Black and Caspian seas succeeded in first domestication of the horse. Their plunder raids into Greece created the myth of the Centaur.
2180 B.C.	Ur was sacked by "barbarians" from mountains bordering the Russian steppes.
2000 B.C.	Tribes in the Danube Valley had domesticated horses.

245

1720 B.C.	The Hyksos introduced the horse-powered two-wheeled chariot to warfare and conquered Egypt.
1425 B.C.	Crete was conquered by Mycenaeans.
1194–84 B.C.	Grecian allies besieged Troy and finally conquered it by presenting to the Trojans a huge wooden horse in which Greek warriors were concealed.
1000 B.C.	Chinese perfected the first light cavalry, armed with bows and arrows.
500–449 B.C.	Darius the Great and his son, Xerxes, are credited as inventors of heavy cavalry tactics developed during the Persian Wars against the Athenian states.
58–51 B.C.	Julius Caesar's use of cavalry regiments during the Gallic Wars is believed to have initiated the breed-up of the Forest Horse into the Great War Horse.
A.D. 50–100	The first horseshoe, a leather boot with bronze sole, was invented to protect the hoofs of mail-carriers' mounts on the stone-surfaced vias of Rome.
100–400	Farmers in the North Sea Lowlands developed the "stripper" for harvesting grain.
620–32	The precepts of Mohammed unified Arabia and began the conquests by "the horsemen of Islam." Both the Barb and the Arabian breeds of horse are products of this warfare.
732	The Franks riding Great War Horses defeated the Moors near Tours, France. This was the "high tide" of the Islamic invasion of Europe. Since the stirrup was invented by the Franks, Tours may have been the first major battle in which stirrups were used.
1000	The term "cowboy" was being used in Ireland.
1000	The padded horse-collar was invented for drafter use in France or Germany.
1066	The Great War Horse cavalry of William of Normandy easily defeated the Saxon infantry at the Battle of Hastings.

1100	The Great War Horses used by knights of the First Crusade routed Islamic horsemen and contributed critically to the conquest of the Holy Land.
1337–1453	The Hundred Years' War between England and France influenced the development of Royal Studs and intensive horse-breeding programs in both countries.
1493	The second expedition of Christopher Columbus returned the horse to the New World and, during January 1494, landed a herd on the coast of Haiti.
1521	Juan Ponce de León landed fifty horses, from Cuba or Puerto Rico, on the Gulf Coast of Florida, probably at Charlotte Harbor.
1539–41	The horseback expeditions of Hernando de Soto and Francisco Coronado crossed our Southeast and Southwest, and almost met near the Oklahoma-Kansas border.
1541	Jacques Cartier landed twenty horses at the site of Quebec.
1585	Walter Raleigh sent horses to his colony at Roanoke, on the North Carolina coast.
1598	Juan de Oñate led his colonists into the Rio Grande Valley and established the first domestic horse herds in the West.
1620	Daniel Gookin delivered "Irish mares and asses" to Jamestown, Virginia.
1630–50	The Puritans landed English, and probably Irish, horses at Salem. The Dutch brought Flemish Great Horses to Manhattan Island. The Swedes brought horses to their colony in New Jersey and to eastern Pennsylvania.
1648	The Puritans began exporting horses to the West Indies.
1655	John Pynchon and his cowboy crew trail-drove fat-cattle from Springfield to Boston, Massachusetts.
1650–1700	The Chickasaws, Choctaws and Cherokees of western Tennessee and Missis-

sippi must have learned horsemanship
and bred up the famous Chickasaw
horse.

1680   The Popé Revolt in New Mexico drove
the Spanish from the Santa Fe–Albuquerque region for a decade, and provided the Apache-Navaho with from
three thousand to five thousand horses.
This launched horseback warfare on the
high-plains and ushered in the seventy-
to one hundred-year introduction of
horsemanship to Indian tribes west of
the Mississippi.

1687   Baron de Lahontan reported that the
Seneca nation of the Iroquois Confed-
eracy, near the site of Rochester, New
York, owned "plenty of horses."

1690   Virginia sportsmen started selective
breeding about this time for quick-
starting ponies to compete on the quarter-mile race tracks at Malvern Hills
and Middle Plantation. Thus the Quarter Horse began his trans-America
career.

1720s   The cowboy Crackers out of Charleston,
Savannah, etc., began wild-horse and
wild-cattle roundups in the Georgia-
Carolina highlands and established
their cow-pen communities across the
Southeast's frontier.

1730s   Pennsylvania German farmers in the
vicinity of Lancaster invented the
Conestoga wagon, bred up America's
first drafter—the Conestoga Horse—and
built America's first bank-barns.

1730   Samuel Gist of Hanover, Virginia, is
reputed to have imported Bulle-Rock, a
stallion descendant of the Darley Arabian. Records about the get of this first
of the English "Breds" in America are
vague and semi-mythical.

1740s   Cheyenne, Sioux and Crow warriors
were riding horses through the Rockies,
hence across the Laramie Plain. This
decade seems to mark the return of the
horse to his prehistoric homeland.

1750s	The practice of shoeing horses began in America. New England's jockey-ship horse trading to the West Indies and Central America was at its apex.
1750s	The Narragansett Pacer, a distinct and superior breed of saddle horse, had established Point Judith, Rhode Island, and adjacent grasslands as the Northeast's premier center for stud farming.
1755	More than 150 Conestoga horse teams established the first wagon route across the Alleghenies by hauling the supply train of the Braddock Expedition from the Potomac River valley to the scene of the French and Indian ambush and General Braddock's death, only seven miles from the site of Pittsburgh.
1760s	Benedict Arnold was one of the American "horse jockeys" who trail-drove Canadian horses through the wilderness from Quebec and Montreal to Rhode Island. (The intimate knowledge of the "north country" he gained on these trading trips was vital to the Americans during the Revolutionary War campaigns preceding the Burgoyne surrender at Saratoga in 1777.)
1761	Surveys revealed a total of thirty-eight carriages in Philadelphia.
1763	Benjamin Franklin and his daughter, Sally, drove from New York to Boston, allegedly in a one-horse shay, to determine the location of mileposts for the first inter-colony highway. The trip originated the Boston Post Road.
1767	A springless box wagon, hauled by four horses, inaugurated public transportation between New York and Philadelphia. The vehicle, called "The Flying Machine," made the ninety-mile journey in forty-eight hours.
1769	Fernando di Revera brought the California missions their first herd of horses and donkeys.
1780s	The Crackers began the drives of Virginia quarter-milers, Georgia Chicka-

saws and semi-feral ponies from their cow-pen communities across the Blue Ridge to the pasturelands of Kentucky.

1786   The South Carolina Jockey Club, America's first society for "gentlemen of the turf," was founded at Charleston.

1793   Figure, founding sire of the Morgans, was foaled at West Springfield, Massachusetts.

1796–97   George Washington's convictions about mules as the ideal work animals for the South led to the first large importation of mules and jacks from Spain.

1806   On February 15, Captain Meriwether Lewis of the Lewis and Clark Expedition wrote a description in his *Journal* about a Nez Percé breed of horses "pided with large spots of white irregularly scattered and intermixed with the black, brown, bey." Some authorities consider this to be evidence that the Nez Percé had already hybridized the Appaloosa as a distinct breed.

1820   The Conestoga wagon was redesigned into the smaller prairie schooner about this time. The change is presumed to have been the work of a village blacksmith in southern Ohio.

1823   On May 23, Old Top Gallant, a stallion, won the first professional trotting race in America. It was run over the Union Course on New York's Long Island.

1826–27   Downing and Abbot invented the Concord stagecoach.

1830–40   Heyday of the stagecoach on the Boston Post Road and the National Pike.

1833   The California missions reported ownership of sixty-two thousand five hundred horses, mules and donkeys.

1839   Edward Harris of Moorestown, New Jersey, imported the first Norman drafters (two mares and a stallion) to the United States.

1849–50	The Mormons imported Kentucky and Tennessee stallions and mares to Utah to improve their breeds of horse.
1849	Rysdyk's Hambletonian was born beneath a clump of oak trees on the Jonas Seeley farm, near Goshen, New York, during the night of May 4–5.
1855	Lexington established a four-mile saddle record of seven minutes nineteen and three-quarters seconds.
1861–65	Estimates indicate that between 1,200,-000 and 1,500,000 horses and mules died "in service" during the Civil War.
1865	The Saratoga Association for the Improvement of the Breed of Horses was founded.
1868	A Division of Veterinary Medicine, the first program offering degrees in veterinary medicine at an American university, was established at Cornell University.
1866–69	Blind Tom hauled rail up to spikers throughout the eleven hundred miles of construction for the Union Pacific Railway.
1867–69	Technologic need caused our horse population to increase by 37 per cent, and our mule population by 32 per cent, during the two years. This launched the program to develop competent draft horses by crossing native stocks with imported Great Horse breeds.
1875	The Kentucky Derby was inaugurated.
1880–1900	Heyday for the coach-horse breeds (Hackney, Cleveland Bay, Hanoverian and Oldenburg).
1891	The American Saddle Horse breed was established.
1900–10	Our national horse population increased by 70 per cent, from thirteen million to twenty-three million.
1919–20	The American horse population reached an all-time high, as a result of intensive farm programs during World War I.

1920–40	Introduction of the mobile tractor caused farmers to sell most of their horses to pet-food canneries.
1935	Studbook of Tennessee Walking Horse established.
1940	Studbook of the Quarter Horse established.
1965	Unofficial estimates indicate a total population of five million horses in the United States, with most of them used as family "hobbies" in suburbia.

HORSE SENSE

(A Glossary)

Albino: A registered breed of white saddle horse.

American Saddle Horse: A registered breed of saddle horse.

Appaloosa: A registered breed of saddle horse, noted for the dark brown or tawny patches of hair over his croup and buttock and the black and white stripes on his hooves. Tradition alleges that the American Appaloosa was bred up by the Nez Percé Indians in the Palouse River region of Idaho.

Baldface: A horse with prominent white markings on his face.

Barrel: The midriff.

Bay: A horse with a reddish-brown coat.

Belgian: A strong and gentle drafter, and the last of the European breeds of Great Horse to be introduced into the United States. The coats of Belgians are usually bay or chestnut-colored. The manes are often tan or off-white.

Bit: A metal bar, attached to the bridle, that fits into a horse's mouth and is attached to the reins by metal rings at each end.

Blaze: A large white hair patch on a horse's face.

Bog spavin: A swelling of the tissue in the hock joint.

Bone: A term used to indicate the strength of a horse's legs. It refers to the circumference of the cannon bone below the hock. A measurement of eight and a half to nine inches is considered good.

Bottom: The degree of stamina displayed by a horse. A horse with "plenty of bottom" is considered rugged and possessed of "staying power" in a race or on a ride.

Bridle: The harness used on a horse's head and attached to the reins.

Bronco: A feral, or semi-feral, horse in the West. Most Indian ponies and range horses were called broncos or "broncs." The word is Spanish and means "rough, rude, crabby."

Cannon: The leg bone between the hock, or knee, and the fetlock.

Canter: A riding gait, also called the "three beat." One forefoot strikes the ground on the first beat. The other forefoot and the opposite hind leg touch ground simultaneously on the second beat. On the third

253

beat, the other hind leg comes down. The cantering speed of modern horses averages ten to twelve miles an hour.

Cayuse: Historically, this was the nickname that cowboys from the Pacific Northwest gave the "broncs" they used on the 1870–80 trail drives through Montana to the new livestock markets along the eastern high-plains railroad lines. Never a distinctive breed, these tough, chunky ponies were named for the Cayuse tribe of red men.

Cleveland Bay: A breed of coach horse that originated in the Cleveland Hills of England. He is also used for hunting and riding.

Clydesdale: Scotland's picturesque breed of the Great Horse. He is usually a chestnut with a snow-white blaze from forehead to muzzle, and is noted for the "feather" of long fine hair that cascades from his hocks down across his hooves. The Clydesdale is the old favorite for hauling circus wagons or parade floats.

Cold-blood: A popular, and stupid, term for drafters and other horses that are not "purebreds." When English saddle-race promoters began their campaign to popularize the "Bred" during 1775–1800, they invented the phrase "hot-blood" to denote a "Bred" or a race horse of Arabian or Barb lineage. All other horses were grouped as "cold-bloods" but, most specifically, the Great Horse drafters. (See Chapter Eighteen and its Footnote 2 for a discussion of these terms and their probable origin.)

Colic: A dangerous ailment caused by constipation and resultant gas pressures against the heart. It can occur suddenly and, unless promptly relieved by medication, can be fatal.

Colt: A male horse under four years of age. The word is also used to indicate any young horse.

Croup: The rump.

Dam: This is a variant of *dame* which used to signify "Mrs." or "Mother." With horses, it still does.

Donkey: The domestic ass, *Equus asinus.* Male donkeys, called "jacks," are used to sire mules. The donkey is believed to have originated in Africa.

Drafter: A work horse, but specifically one of the national breeds of Great Horse. The word is also spelled *draughter.*

Dressage: An exhibition of intricate maneuvers and gait changes by a horse, during which his rider makes no perceptible use of hands or legs or the bridle.

Ear signals: Horses have unusually sharp hearing. The movements of their ears serve horsemen as "radar signals." When a horse points its ears forward quickly, it indicates that he has heard an unusual, or frightening, sound. An angry or disturbed horse lays his ears back against his poll. Horses often whinny (i.e. neigh) when they hear or smell other horses.

Feral horse: An untamed, undomesticated horse.

Fetlock: A tuft of hair on the back of a horse's leg, just above the hoof; also the leg joint beneath the hair tuft.

Filly: A young mare.

Foal: A baby horse, less than one year old.

Frog: The horny pad on the sole of a hoof. Its shape resembles the outline of a frog.

Gait: Any of the various foot movements of a horse, while walking or running. The five gaits of a saddle horse are: walk, trot, canter, rack, and slow gait.

Gaited horse: A horse that has been trained to display all five of the approved gaits in response to commands by his rider.

Gallop: The instinctive running style. It is a rapid series of leaps, with all feet leaving the ground simultaneously.

Gaskin: The upper part of the hind leg.

Gelding: A horse eunuch; a stallion whose testes have been removed.

Get: The offspring, or foals.

Girth: The strap—also called the "flank-strap"—attached to the bottom sides of a saddle. It buckles over the horse's belly and holds the saddle in position.

Glanders: A contagious disease contracted by horses, mules and other Equidae. It is characterized by swollen glands beneath the lower jaw, inflammation of the mucous membrane in the nostrils, and fever. Glanders was the most deadly horse and mule disease during the nineteenth century. It can be transmitted to human beings.

Grass-cutter: A race horse with a low fast stride; also known as a "daisy-cutter."

Great Horse: A condensation of Great War Horse, the ponderous "destrier" of the medieval knight. The term is used as a synonym for Belgian, Percheron, Shire or any of the regional breeds of European drafters.

Hackamore: A rope, or leather, bridle that controls a horse by exerting pressure on the nose. The hackamore was widely used in the West to break in colts or feral horses. The word is an Americanization of the Spanish *jáquima,* meaning "halter."

Hackney: Originally a coach horse, it is also bred to pony size. The Hackney makes an excellent saddler. The breed originated in England more than one thousand years ago.

Hand: The system of measurement used in determining the height of a horse. A *hand* is four inches, or the width of an adult man's hand, across the thumb. The term, and its use, are prehistoric.

Harness horse: Coachers are called "heavy harness horses," but the phrase usually applies to a Morgan, Standardbred or other type who paces or trots in a harness race.

Heaves: A lung disease, caused by the dilation of air cells in a lung. It is also called "broken wind."

Herring-gutted: A race-track term for a horse who is underdeveloped through the loins.

Hinny: The offspring of a male horse and a female donkey. The hinny is considered inferior to the mule (i.e. the offspring of a male donkey and a female horse) as a work animal. The word *hinny* is related to the Latin word for "whinny" or "neigh."

Horse: Any member of the genus *Equus caballus.* The word is ancient and is believed to derive from a phrase meaning "the leaper."

Horse boat: A ferryboat propelled by horses working on a treadmill.

Horse-drench: A dose of physic for a horse.

Horse power: The power exerted by a horse in pulling with a force that will raise 33,000 pounds a distance of one foot per minute. The word and definition are believed to have been originated by James Watt, inventor of the steam engine.

Hot-blood: A meaningless phrase now restricted to Thoroughbreds or purebreds with Barb or Arabian heritage. The phrase originated between 1775 and 1800 in England, and originally referred to the Arabian, Barb or "Bred" blood of a saddle racer. (See Chapter Eighteen and its Footnote 2 for a discussion of the phrase and its presumed origin.)

Inbreeding: Breeding two horses who are closely related, in an effort to improve certain characteristics. The technique rarely produces superior foals.

Jack: A male donkey, used to breed mules by mating with female horses.

Jenny: A female donkey.

Lameness: The most common ailment of a horse. A slight nodding of the head is an early indication. The area of the bruise or infection will become feverish.

Laminitis: A painful inflammation in the wall of a hoof.

Lipizzan: Beautiful white horses believed to be descended from Spanish and Moorish breeds. Unusually strong hindquarters enable them to make high jumps. They can learn to perform difficult feats of dressage. The most famous Lipizzans are those trained at the Spanish Riding School in Vienna, Austria.

Mare: A female horse.

Martingale: The forked strap of a draft horse's harness that connects the noseband to the girth between the forelegs. It prevents the horse from rearing or throwing back its head. Wagonmen used to decorate martingales with varicolored leather rosettes or with brass medallions that had been engraved with horseshoe, tulip, thistle or other "lucky" symbols.

Morgan: A registered descendant of Figure, the extraordinary stallion reared by the Vermont singing master and composer, Justin Morgan. The Morgan is one of the four most popular breeds for saddle or carriage use.

Morning-glory: A race-track term for a horse who performs admirably during morning workouts, but usually fails to "win, place or show" in the afternoon race.

Mule: The offspring of a male donkey (i.e. jack) and a female horse. Mules performed valiant services in the South and West between 1800 and the 1940s, thus became the subjects of much regional humor and folklore.

Mustang: The word is an Americanization of the Spanish *mesteño,* meaning "wild horse." The mustangs of the nineteenth century West were not a breed. The word was used to indicate any feral, or unbroken, horse.

Muzzle: The snout, including the mouth, nostrils and lower jaws.

Nicks: A technical stud term used to denote a system of breeding horses who seem to compensate each other in temperament and physical factors. The theory assumes that the stallion and dam will each provide certain qualities in the foal. The "nick" mating between Fair Play and Mahubah produced Man O' War.

Normand: A recently adopted name for the French coach horse.

Oldenburger: A regional breed of German coach horse.

Outbreeding: The usual stud system for breeding stallions and mares who are not closely related in blood lines.

Pace: The running gait in which the legs on each side move forward in unison. Pacing and trotting are the two accepted gaits for harness racing.

Paddling: A natural defect in a horse's gait, in which he tends to move his feet at an oblique angle, thus cutting down his speed.

Paint: A horse with contrasting spots, or streaks, of hair coloration. *Paint* and *pinto* are synonyms, since *pinto* is a Spanish word that means "spotted."

Pastern: The lower end of a horse's leg, between the hoof and the fetlock.

Percheron: The Great Horse originated in The Perche of Normandy and first imported to the United States in 1839.

Piebald: A horse whose black coat has white hair spots or streaks. He can also be called a *paint* or a *pinto.*

Points: A collective term for the legs, mane and tail, normally used in describing a horse's coloration. Thus a horse with white legs, mane and tail has "white points."

Poll: The top of the head or, more specifically, the area between the ears.

Polo: The most popular horseback game. It is played by two teams of four players each who, using long-handled mallets, attempt to drive a wooden ball through the opponent's goal. The word *polo* is Tibetan, but the game is supposed to have originated in Persia. James Gordon Bennett, the newspaper publisher, introduced it to the United States during 1876. Polo ponies must be light and fast and are preferably part, or all, Thoroughbred.

Pony: Technically, any horse not over fourteen hands in height. Historically, most ponies are regionally-bred descendants of the ancient Celtic pony. The most popular pony breeds in the United States are: Shetland, Welsh, Connemara, Hackney and Dartmoor.

Posting: A method of saddle riding, in which the rider adapts to the pace of the horse. By pushing down on the stirrups, the rider raises then lowers his body in unison with the hoofbeats.

Przewalski horse: The wild Mongolian horse domesticated by the Chinese before 2000 B.C. It is scientifically named *Equus caballus Ferus Pallas.* Less than a century ago a Russian geographer-explorer, Nikolai Mikhailovich Przewalski (1839–88), first scientifically identified living members of this Oriental branch of *Equus caballus.* (The name is also spelled Przhevalsky.)

Purebred: Dictionaries still classify this word as an adjective, although it is often used as a noun. Specifically, it means: belonging to a breed with recognized characteristics that have been maintained through several generations of unmixed descent.

Quarter Horse: A registered breed only since 1940, but with a heritage tracing to the quarter-path races run in Virginia before 1690. Noted for his stamina and speedy getaway, the Quarter Horse type was the favorite of range riders and trail crews during the 1865–1910 heyday of cattle ranching in the West. The Quarter Horse, in 1965, was one of the four most popular horse breeds in the United States.

Race horse: Any horse bred and trained for racing on a track. The most popular forms of horse racing in the United States are: saddle and harness. Professional saddle races are restricted to Thoroughbreds and Quarter Horses. Professional harness races are limited to two types of stride: the pace and the trot.

Rack: An acquired gait in which the horse is trained to lift each foot high, and individually, as he walks. It is also called the "single-foot."

Ringbone: An abnormal bony growth just above the hoof, on the pastern. It can be hereditary, or it can be caused by travel over macadam, concrete and other hard-surface roads. Ringbone inter-feres with the horse's stride and gives him a tendency to stumble.

Rodeo: The most ancient horseback exhibition. Most of its featured "events" originated in Greece and the Near East before 2000 B.C. Professionally, it is a competitive exhibition of cowboy skills in roping and riding bulls, calves and bucking horses. Professional rodeos in the United States each year have a total gate of twenty-five million spectators.

Shire: An English breed of Great Horse. It was developed in the mid-land counties, or shires, during the age of knighthood.

Skewbald: A horse with a coat spotted in any color *except* black. A Skewbald is also a *paint* and a *pinto.*

Slow gait: The four-beat gait, also known as the "running walk." The horse nods his head in time with the distinct hoofbeats. Tennessee Walking Horses excel in the slow gait.

Snip: A small white patch of hair near the muzzle.

Spavin: A disease of the hocks. *Bone spavin* is an abnormal enlarge-ment of the inner or lower part of the joint. *Bog spavin* is an enlarge-ment of the joint tissue.

Splint: A bony growth on the inside of the foreleg. It is common among horses in modern suburbias, since it is caused, usually, by travel over hard-surface roads.

Stallion: An adult male horse.

Stamp his get: A stallion who displays a marked ability to pass his characteristics along to his offspring is said to be able to "stamp his get."

Standardbred: Also called the American Trotting Horse; the approved breed for harness racing.

Star: A small white hairpatch on the forehead.

Stayer: A race-track term for a horse who can sustain his racing speed beyond a mile and a quarter.

Stifle: The kneelike joint above the hock in a hind leg.

Suffolk Punch: A light drafter developed in Suffolk, England. It is usually chestnut-brown in color. Until the 1930s it was a favorite for use on milk wagons and store delivery vans.

Tack: The harness of a saddle horse.

Tarpan: Believed to have been the first branch of *Equus caballus* to be domesticated, thus the mount of the Centaur and the drafter of the Hyksos' chariots. His scientific name is *Equus caballus Gmelini Antonius.*

Tennessee Walking Horse: A recent breed of saddler, and one of the most popular. It is noted for its high, proud slow-gait step.

Thoroughbred: The most popular American saddle racer. All Thoroughbreds are registered descendants of the English "Breds."

Thrush: An inflammation in the cleft of the hoof's frog, usually caused by unsanitary stable conditions.

Top line: The top contour of a horse from the ears back to the tail.

Touched-in-the-wind: Said of a horse who emits a whistling or wheezing noise during a gallop. It is commonly caused by overexertion.

Trot: One of the two running gaits permitted in professional harness races. The trotter lifts the front leg on one side of his body and the hind leg on the other side of his body simultaneously. Both feet must hit the ground at the same instant.

Using horse: An all-around good performer who can be used either as a saddler or in harness.

Walk: A show gait in which the horse lifts his feet one at a time and puts them down in the same order.

Windgalls: Small swellings above the fetlocks, but rarely a cause of lameness.

Withers: The area between the shoulder blades and the highest point of the back.

Yearling: A one-year-old horse.

NOTES

Chapter One

1. A monument honoring Wister, and built principally from agatized wood, stands opposite the Virginian Hotel in downtown Medicine Bow. Wister first visited Medicine Bow in 1885 and said of it in his journal:

   "This place is called a town. 'Town' will do very well until the language stretches itself, and takes in a new word that fits. Medicine Bow, Wyoming, consists of:

1	Depot house and baggage room
1	Coal shooter
1	Water tank
1	Store
2	Eating houses
1	Billiard room
6	Shanties
8	Gents and Ladies Walks
2	Tool houses
1	Feed stable
5	Too late for classification
29	Buildings in all."

2. Geologists and paleontologists divide pre-history into four gigantic eras, and each era into a series of epochs. The most recent era is the Cenozoic, during which modern life forms evolved. The time span of the Cenozoic is estimated at about seventy million years. Paleocene time and Eocene time were the earliest epochs in the Cenozoic era and are assumed to have lasted thirty million years. They were succeeded, respectively, by the Oligocene (fifteen million years), the Miocene (fourteen million years), the Pliocene (eleven million years) and the Pleistocene (one to two million years). Geologic and biologic changes since approximately 25,000 B.C. are cited as occurring in the Recent epoch.

3. George Gaylord Simpson, *Horses* (New York: Doubleday & Company, Natural History Library of Anchor Books, by arrangement with Oxford University Press, 1961), pp. 75–76. Also, interviews with Dr. Paul McGrew.

4. The name of Coney Island, the famous New York City amusement park, originated from the thousands of rabbits that lived there during Dutch and early English colonial periods (1630–1700). The word *cony* (of which *coney* is a variation) appears in the plural in the Bible; Psalm 104, verse 18 states "The high hills are a refuge for the wild goats; and the rocks for the conies."

5. This assumption is based on the paleontologists' discovery of primitive types of grass seed in rocks formed during late Oligocene and early Miocene time.

6. George Gaylord Simpson, *op. cit.*, pp. 173–81.

7. The time span of the Miocene epoch is estimated at fourteen million years, or 140,000 centuries. The so-called "dawn history" of civilization began in Ur, Egypt and Crete only fifty centuries ago. Our Christian era approaches its twenty-first century. During a time span comparable to Man's "recorded history," the ancestors of *Merychippus* may have evolved one new tooth ridge or one more infinitesimal layer of enamel.

8. Interviews with Dr. McGrew, 1962–65.

9. George Gaylord Simpson, *op. cit.*, pp. 197–200.

10. Both the mammoth skull and the *Equus caballus* fossils are in the collections of the Geology Museum at the University of Wyoming.

Chapter Two

1. Both tarpans and Przewalskis have been genetically rebred by zoologists. Early in the 1960s, they were on display at the Animal Park of Hellabrunn, near Munich. A few feral Przewalskis are believed to have survived in Outer Mongolia.

2. Frederick E. Zeuner, *A History of Domesticated Animals* (London: Hutchinson & Co., 1963), pp. 306–11.

3. Unpublished manuscript, "Man Mounts the Horse," from the Colonel Edward N. Wentworth Collection in the Western History Research Center, University of Wyoming, Laramie, Wyoming.

4. Herbert Wendt, *It Began in Babel* (Boston: Houghton Mifflin Company, 1962), p. 113.

5. Frederick E. Zeuner, *op. cit.*, pp. 317 and 337.

6. *Ibid.*, pp. 367–73.

7. Herodotus, *The Histories*, Book IV, in Jacquetta Hawkes (ed.), *The World of the Past* (New York: Alfred A. Knopf, 1963), p. 455.

8. Frederick E. Zeuner, *op. cit.*, p. 334.

9. Carleton S. Coon, *The Story of Man* (New York: Alfred A. Knopf, 1954), p. 272.

Chapter Three

1. Samuel Eliot Morison, *Admiral of the Ocean Sea,* Vol. II (New York: Time, Inc., 1962), p. 376.

2. James Westfall Thompson, *A History of Livestock Raising in the United States, 1607–1860,* Agricultural History Series No. 5 (Washington: U.S. Department of Agriculture, 1942), p. 10.

3. John Winthrop, *Winthrop's Journal "History of New England,"* edited by James Kendall Hosmer (New York: Charles Scribner's Sons, 1908).

4. An example of medical diagnosis, reported in 1684 by Baron de Lahontan, is typical of the age. Writing from "Monreal" on November 2 about the expedition of "Mr. de la Barre, the Governor-General, against the Iroquese," the Baron reported (page 71, Volume I, *New Voyages to North America*): "Towards the end of August Mr. de la Barre joyn'd us; but he was dangerously ill of a feaver, which rag'd in like manner among most of his militia. . . . This feaver was of the intermitting kind; and the convulsive Motions, Tremblings and frequency of the Pulse that attended the cold Fit, were so violent, that most of our sick men dy'd in the second or third Fit. . . . Mr. de la Barre's Physician, who in my opinion knew as little of the true causes of Feavers as Hippocrates or Galen, and a hundred thousand besides; this mighty Physician, I say, pretending to trace the cause of the Feaver I now speak of, imputed it to the unfavourable qualities of the Air and the Aliment. His plea was that the excessive heat of the season, put the Vapours or Exhalations into an over-rapid Motion; that the Air was so over-rarefy'd, that we did not suck in a sufficient quantity of it; that the small quantity we did receive was loaded with insects and impure Corpusculum's, which the fatal necessity of Respiration oblig'd us to swallow; and that by this means nature was put into disorder: He added that the use of Brandy and salt Meat sowered the Blood, that this sowerness occasion'd a sort of coagulation of the Chyle and Blood, that the Coagulation hindered it to circulate thro' the Heart with a due degree of Celerity; and that thereupon there insued an extraordinary Fermentation, which is nothing else but a Feaver."

5. J. Markham, G. Jeffries and Discreet Indians (*sic*), *The Citizen and Countryman's Experienced Ferrier* (Baltimore, 1797).

6. *Gentleman's Magazine,* Vol. XX, (London, 1751), p. 487.

7. J. F. Smithcors, *The American Veterinary Profession* (Ames: Iowa State University Press, 1963), p. 37.

8. *Ibid.,* pp. 32 and 51.

9. Alvar Nuñez Cabeza de Vaca and three companions were the only survivors of the Narváez expedition. Cabeza de Vaca's story of their

1528-36 journey from Texas to Mexico began the legend of the Golden Cities of Cibola and determined the goals of both the De Soto and Coronado expeditions.

10. Frere Isidore, *Elevage du Cheval* (La Trappe, P.Q.: Les Manuels d'Oka, 1940), p. 18.

11. Fairfax Harrison, *"The Equine F.F.V.'s" Virginia Magazine of History and Biography* (October 1927), Vol. XXXV, No. 4, p. 365.

12. Baron de Lahontan, *New Voyages to North America* (Chicago: A. C. McClurg & Co., 1905), Vol. I, p. 45.

13. James Westfall Thompson, *op. cit.*, p. 64.

14. James Adair, *History of the American Indians* (London, 1775), pp. 230–31.

15. Dr. David Ramsay, *History of South Carolina* (Charleston, 1809), p. 403.

16. Stevenson W. Fletcher, *Pennsylvania Agriculture and Country Life, 1640–1840* (Harrisburg: Pennsylvania Historical and Museum Commission, 1950), p. 42.

17. Baron de Lahontan, *op cit.,* p. 131.

Chapter Four

1. Deane Phillips, *Horse Raising in Colonial New England*, Memoir 54 (Ithaca: Cornell University Agricultural Experiment Station, 1922), p. 892.

2. Robert West Howard, *Two Billion Acre Farm: An Informal History of American Agriculture* (New York: Doubleday, Doran and Co., 1945), p. 19. Also various publications of the American Meat Institute, Chicago, Illinois.

3. The importance of the horse in medieval warfare caused most of Europe's rulers to ban horsemeat from the diet of their subjects. These laws were not enforced on the European mainland after the gun and cannon ended the knight's dominance over warfare. Crop failures and wars between 1400 and 1870 reintroduced horsemeat to the European diet. The splendid *Larousse Gastronomique* by Prosper Montagne (New York: Crown Publishers, 1961) details the gastronomic history of horseflesh with particular reference to its reintroduction in Paris in 1865. Montagne edicts that "a variety of recipes in the BEEF section can be used for horsemeat." But the prejudice against horseflesh persisted among the English. They brought it to America, and their heirs rigidly enforced it. The word *horsemeat* in America became a derogatory simile for "inferior meat." Typically, during the early spring of 1965, a grand jury in New York City investigated what newspapers headlined as a "horse-

meat scandal." The alleged crime was the "adulteration" of sausage, bologna and frankfurters by the addition of horsemeat.

4. Deane Phillips, *op. cit.*, p. 898.

5. My authority is Kathleen Hoagland, editor-author of *1,000 Years of Irish Poetry* (New York: Devin Adair, 1950). Mrs. Hoagland gallantly assisted my research when, as an editor of *Farm Journal*, then as Roving Editor for the American Meat Institute, I became intrigued about the Atlantic Seaboard origins of our cattle and horse industries. The word *cow* is Old Norse; *boy* is Middle English and East Frisian. The popular presumption that *cowboy* was first used in America to identify the pro-British guerrillas in the lower Hudson Valley during the Revolution is a product of haphazard research, plus, apparently, some wishful thinking by a few residents of northern Westchester and Putnam counties, New York. The epithet "cowboy" was given to these Tories by American leaders because it was already in general usage, from Maine to Georgia, as a derogatory nickname for the illiterate "roughnecks" herding cattle in the backcountry. The Revolutionary War usage gave the word such an unpleasant intimation that cattle herdsmen in the East adopted the English term "drover" as their profession name. But "cowboy" reappeared in Texas between 1830 and 1840 and was initially used to identify cattle rustlers and gunmen. Despite its popularity with "Wild West" authors and movie scriptwriters, "cowboy" still holds derogatory implications among professional cattlemen, east and west.

6. Deane Phillips, *op. cit.*, pp. 894–95.

7. James Westfall Thompson, *A History of Livestock Raising in the United States, 1607–1860*, Agricultural History Series No. 5 (Washington: U.S. Department of Agriculture, 1942), p. 54.

8. Wayne Andrews and Thomas C. Cochran (eds.), *Concise Dictionary of American History* (New York: Charles Scribner's Sons, 1962), p. 808.

9. During 1940, Colonel Edward N. Wentworth, then director of the Livestock Bureau of Armour & Company, first called my attention to the Pynchons and their pioneer fat-cattle drives. He later reported the 1655 drive on page 308 of *Cattle and Men* (with Charles W. Towne; Norman: University of Oklahoma Press, 1955). When I became Roving Editor of the American Meat Institute in 1954, I resolved to undertake more extensive research of the Pynchons and their pioneering in both meat packing and cattle marketing. The report given here is a condensation of data graciously made available to me by the Connecticut Valley Historical Society's staff at the William Pynchon Memorial in Springfield. The John Pynchon record books preserved there contain a wealth of data on commerce and agriculture in Massachusetts between 1652 and 1703.

10. The site mentioned here is now Windsor Locks, Connecticut. Warehouse Point, on the east shore of the Connecticut River, opposite Windsor Locks, is the site of Pynchon's meat-packing plant and warehouses. John Pynchon's stall-feeding and roundup took place at, or near, Warehouse Point.

11. Deane Phillips, *op. cit.*, p. 899.

12. John Winthrop, *Winthrop's Journal "History of New England,"* edited by James Kendall Hosmer (New York: Charles Scribner's Sons, 1908). Winthrop reported a ship "lying before Charleston with 80 horses on board bound for Barbadoes." (Vol. II, p. 327.)

13. Deane Phillips, *op. cit.*, p. 904.

14. Alice Marie Earle, "The Narragansett Pacers," *The New England Magazine* (January 1890), Vol. III, p. 39.

15. *Ibid.*, p. 40.

16. Deane Phillips, *op. cit.*, p. 924.

17. *The Edinburgh Encyclopedia*, Vol. I (Philadelphia, 1832), pp. 332–41.

18. James Fenimore Cooper, *The Last of the Mohicans*, Household Edition (Boston, 1890), p. 14.

19. Wilkins Updike, *History of the Episcopal Church in Narragansett, Rhode Island* (New York, 1847), p. 515.

20. Frances M. Caulkins, *History of New London* (New London, 1895), pp. 254–55.

21. *Ibid.*, p. 345.

Chapter Five

1. George E. Hyde, *Indians of the High Plains* (Norman: University of Oklahoma Press, 1959), pp. 4–5.

2. Duane Burner, "Dig They Need Not, But Dig They Do," *The New York Times* (January 24, 1965), Section X, pp. 1 and 26.

3. Oliver La Farge, *The American Indian* (New York: Crown Publishers, Inc., 1956), pp. 138–41.

4. George E. Hyde, *op. cit.*, pp. 18–19; Frank Gilbert Roe, *The Indian and the Horse* (Norman: University of Oklahoma Press, 1955), pp. 74–75; The Smithsonian Series, Vol. IV, *North American Indians* (New York: Smithsonian Institution Series, Inc., 1944), pp. 144–50.

5. George E. Hyde, *op. cit.*, p. 21.

6. Cleve Hallenbeck, *Land of the Conquistadores* (Caldwell, Idaho: The Caxton Printers, 1950), pp. 159–60; and L. Bradford Prince, *Spanish Mission Churches of New Mexico* (Cedar Rapids: The Torch Press, 1915), p. 55.

7. George E. Hyde, *op. cit.*, p. 18.

8. Francis Parkman, *LaSalle and the Discovery of the Great West.* (New York: New American Library, Signet, 1963), pp. 298–99.

9. La Salle established Fort Crevecoeur at the site of Peoria, Illinois, during January 1680, and early in 1682 supervised construction of a fort at Starved Rock, near present La Salle, Illinois, on the Illinois River.

10. Cleve Hallenbeck, *op. cit.*, p. 179.

11. *Ibid.*, p. 94.

12. George E. Hyde, *op. cit.*, p. 57.

13. Francis Parkman, *op. cit.*, p. 79.

14. *Ibid.*, p. 321.

15. Robert Leslie Jones, "The Old French-Canadian Horse: Its History in Canada and the United States," *Canadian Historical Review,* 1917, p. 135.

16. William A. Hunter, *Forts on the Pennsylvania Frontier* (Harrisburg: Pennsylvania Historical and Museum Commission, 1960), p. 77.

17. This was the initial *coureur de bois* trail between Montreal and the West. Canada's Transcontinental Highway No. 17 now parallels it from Montreal to North Bay, Ontario.

18. Oliver La Farge, *op. cit.*, p. 143.

19. George E. Hyde, *op. cit.*, p. 79.

20. Floyd C. Shoemaker (ed.), *Missouri Day by Day* (Jefferson City: State Historical Society of Missouri, 1942), p. 401.

Chapter Six

1. James Westfall Thompson, *A History of Livestock Raising in the United States, 1607–1860,* Agricultural History Series No. 5 (Washington: U.S. Department of Agriculture, 1942), p. 54; and Fairfax Harrison, "The Equine F.F.V.'s," *Virginia Magazine of History and Biography* (October 1927), Vol. XXXV, No. 4, pp. 329 ff.

2. Philip Alexander Bruce, *Economic History of Virginia in the Seventeenth Century,* Vol. I (New York and London: Macmillan and Company, 1895), p. 249.

3. James Westfall Thompson, *op. cit.*, p. 55.

4. Philip Alexander Bruce, *op. cit.*, p. 312.

5. James Westfall Thompson, *op. cit.*, p. 45.

6. *Tacky* was an Old South name for the wild ponies of the coastal areas. The word then meant "dowdy, shabby."

7. Denzil Batchelor, *The Turf of Old* (London: H. F. & G. Witherby, Ltd., 1951), p. 13.

8. Fairfax Harrison, *op. cit.*, p. 367.

9. *Ibid.*, p. 331.

10. *Ibid.*, p. 331.

11. Johann David Schopf, *Travels in the Confederation, 1783–1784* (Philadelphia: W. J. Campbell, 1911), Vol. II, p. 64.

12. Fairfax Harrison, *op. cit.*, p. 367.

13. John H. Logan, *A History of the Upper Country of South Carolina*, (Charleston: S. G. Courtenay & Co., 1859), p. 149.

14. James Westfall Thompson, *op. cit.*, p. 62.

15. *Ibid.*

16. Lewis Cecil Gray, *History of Agriculture in the Southern United States to 1860* (Washington: Carnegie Institution Publication No. 430, 1933).

17. James Westfall Thompson, *op. cit.*, p. 66.

18. Experiments conducted during 1958 measured the speed of a black-snake whip's "popper" and revealed that it emits a rifle-like report at instant of impact because it breaks the sound barrier. Robert West Howard, "The Crackers," *This Is the South* (Chicago: Rand McNally & Co., 1959), p. 51.

19. Johann David Schopf, *op. cit.*, p. 223.

Chapter Seven

1. James Westfall Thompson, *A History of Livestock Raising in the United States, 1607–1860*, Agricultural History Series No. 5 (Washington: U.S. Department of Agriculture, 1942), p. 48.

2. Stevenson W. Fletcher, *Pennsylvania Agriculture and Country Life, 1640–1840* (Harrisburg: Pennsylvania Historical and Museum Commission, 1950), pp. 47–48.

3. *Ibid.*, p. 50.

4. James Westfall Thompson, *op. cit.*, p. 49.

5. Stevenson W. Fletcher, *op. cit.*, p. 83.

6. *Ibid.*, p. 82.

7. *Ibid.*, p. 247.

8. Lewis Evans, "A Brief Account of Pennsylvania," 1753. Files of the Philadelphia Society for Promoting Agriculture.

9. John Strohm, "The Conestoga Horse," in *Report of the Commissioner of Agriculture for the Year 1863* (Washington: U.S. Department of Agriculture, 1863), pp. 175–80.

10. Stevenson W. Fletcher, *op. cit.*, pp. 259–60.

11. William Douglass, *A Summary, Historical and Political, of the First Planting, Progressive Improvements, and Present State of the British Settlements in North-America* (London: R. and J. Dodsley, 1760), Vol. II, p. 333.

12. Stevenson W. Fletcher, *op. cit.*, p. 262.

13. John and Alan Lomax, *Best Loved American Folk Songs* (New York: Grosset & Dunlap, 1947), pp. 38 and 60–61.

Chapter Eight

1. Stevenson W. Fletcher, *Pennsylvania Agriculture and Country Life, 1640–1840* (Harrisburg: Pennsylvania Historical and Museum Commission, 1950), p. 249.

2. *Ibid.*, p. 245.

3. Joseph Doddridge, *Notes on the Early Settlement . . . of the Western Parts of Virginia and Pennsylvania, 1763–1783* (Philadelphia, 1824), p. 146.

4. Stevenson W. Fletcher, *op. cit.*, p. 467.

5. Stewart H. Holbrook, *The Old Post Road* (New York: McGraw-Hill Book Co., 1963), p. 7; and Joseph B. Stephens, "Connecticut's Famous L and M's," *Yankee Magazine* (June 1964), Vol. XXVIII, No. 6, pp. 86–87.

6. Coaches are mentioned in Samuel Pepys' *Diary* (I, 64 and I, 116). The use of the word *coach* to denote a "tutor" or "trainer," such as a "football coach," was a seventeenth-century play on words, and implied that the student or trainee would "get on fast."

7. Kenneth Roberts, *March to Quebec* and *Rabble in Arms* (New York: Doubleday and Company, 1940 and 1947) are far and away the best sources for authentic detail about Benedict Arnold's 1775–77 services to the American cause.

8. C. L. Flint, *The Horses of New England* (Patent Office Report for 1861, Senate Executive Document, 37th Congress, Second Session, 1861–62), pp. 388, 393, 396.

9. Fairfax Harrison, "The Equine F.F.V.'s," *Virginia Magazine of History and Biography* (October 1927), Vol. XXXV, No. 4, pp. 338–39.

10. *Ibid.*, pp. 335–36.

11. Stevenson W. Fletcher, *op. cit.*, pp. 251–53.

Chapter Nine

1. Oliver La Farge, *The American Indian* (New York: Crown Publishers, Inc., 1956), pp. 148–60.

2. Eusebio Francisco Kino was born at Segno in the Austrian Tyrol c. 1644. The area was famous for its cattle production.

3. Thomas Cochran and Wayne Andrews (eds.), *Concise Dictionary of American History* (New York: Charles Scribner's Sons, 1962), p. 466.

4. George E. Hyde, *Indians of the High Plains* (Norman: University of Oklahoma Press, 1959), pp. 81–82; and Francis Butler Simkins, *A History of the South* (New York: Alfred A. Knopf, 1956), p. 36. Colonial plantation owners preferred Negro to Indian slaves because the Negroes showed greater resistance to measles, chicken pox, typhoid and other "white-man diseases" and were better field workers.

5. Francis Butler Simkins, *op. cit.*, p. 36.

6. There are numerous references to enslavement and cannibal feasts by the Iroquois in New York history. Explanations of the origins of Indian slavery and of official approval of the Indian slave trade by Quebec officials in 1709 are presented in Baron de Lahontan, *Voyages to North America* (Chicago: A. C. McClurg Company, 1905), pp. 169, 504–5, etc.

7. Oliver La Farge, *op. cit.*, p. 148.

8. George E. Hyde, *op. cit.*, pp. 186–98.

9. Zebulon M. Pike, "The Journey to Pike's Peak," in *The Great West*, edited by Charles Neider (New York: Coward-McCann, Inc., 1958), p. 80.

10. Robert Moorman Denhardt, *The Horse of the Americas* (Norman: University of Oklahoma Press, 1947), p. 249.

11. *Ibid.*, pp. 245–48. Reproduced by special permission of the publisher.

12. Robert H. Lowie, *Indians of the Plains* (Garden City: The Natural History Press, American Museum Science Books, 1963), p. 45.

13. Oliver La Farge, *op. cit.*, p. 156.

14. Robert H. Lowie, *op. cit.*, pp. 119–21.

Chapter Ten

1. Frederick E. Zeuner, *A History of Domesticated Animals* (London: Hutchinson & Co., 1963), pp. 381–83.

2. Chapter 36, verse 24 of Genesis in the King James version states that Anah "found the mules in the wilderness, as he fed the asses of Zibeon his father."

3. Frederick E. Zeuner, *op. cit.*, p. 383.

4. Samuel Eliot Morison, *Admiral of the Ocean Sea* (New York: Time, Inc., 1962). Vol. II, p. 647.

5. James Westfall Thompson, *A History of Livestock Raising in the United States, 1607–1860*, Agricultural History Series No. 5 (Washington: U.S. Department of Agriculture, 1942), p. 113.

6. Charles W. Towne and Edward N. Wentworth, *Cattle and Men* (Norman: University of Oklahoma Press, 1955), p. 122.

7. Johann David Schopf, *Travels in the Confederation, 1783–1784* (Philadelphia: W. J. Campbell, 1911), Vol. II, p. 48.

8. Quoted in J. F. Smithcors, *The American Veterinary Profession* (Ames: Iowa State University Press, 1963), p. 75.

9. Frazier and Robert Hunt, *Horses and Heroes* (New York: Charles Scribner's Sons, 1949), p. 42.

10. Frederick Law Olmsted, *A Journey in the Seaboard Slave States* (New York: Dix & Edwards, 1856), p. 47.

11. J. T. Warder, "Mule Raising," in *Report of the Commissioner of Agriculture for the Year 1863* (Washington: U.S. Department of Agriculture, 1863), p. 184.

12. James Westfall Thompson, *op. cit.*, p. 75.

13. J. T. Warder, *op. cit.*, pp. 184–85.

Chapter Eleven

1. Stevenson W. Fletcher, *Pennsylvania Agriculture and Country Life, 1640–1840* (Harrisburg: Pennsylvania Historical and Museum Commission, 1950), pp. 154–5.

2. Captain George (Gilbert) Imlay, *A Topographical Description of the Western Territory of North America* (London: Printed for J. Debrett, 1793), pp. 150–51.

3. James Westfall Thompson, *A History of Livestock Raising in the United States, 1607–1860*, Agricultural History Series No. 5 (Washington: U.S. Department of Agriculture, 1942), p. 89.

4. Fairfax Harrison, "The Equine F.F.V.'s," *Virginia Magazine of History and Biography* (October 1927), Vol. XXXV, No. 4, p. 337.

5. *Kentucky: A Guide to the Bluegrass State*, American Guide Series, Federal Writers' Project, Works Projects Administration (New York: Harcourt, Brace & Co., 1939), p. 179.

6. *Ibid.*, p. 95.

7. Bradley Smith, *The Horse and the Blue Grass Country* (New York: Doubleday & Company, 1955), p. 29.

8. *Ibid.*, p. 48.

9. William A. Hunter, *Forts on the Pennsylvania Frontier, 1753–1758* (Harrisburg: Pennsylvania Historical and Museum Commission, 1960), pp. 65, 67, 73, 77, 81.

10. Carl F. Klinck (ed.), *Tecumseh* (Englewood Cliffs: Prentice-Hall, 1961), p. 23.

11. Now a section of U.S. Highway 41, the Henderson-Madisonville Road is still known locally as "Harpe's Head Road."

12. Otto A. Rothert, *The Outlaws of Cave-in-Rock* (Cleveland: Arthur H. Clark Co., 1924).

13. Richard Dillon, *Meriwether Lewis* (New York: Coward-McCann, 1965), p. 348.

14. Waldemar Kaempffert, *A Popular History of American Invention* (New York: Charles Scribner's Sons, 1924), Vol. I, p. 78.

15. *The New England Magazine*, 1831, Vol. I, p. 177.

16. Roger Mortimer, *The Jockey Club* (London: Cassell & Company, 1958), p. 10.

17. Charles E. Trevathan, *The American Thoroughbred* (New York: The Macmillan Company, 1905), pp. 19–27.

18. Quoted in Bradley Smith, *op. cit.*, p. 30.

19. J. T. Warder, "Mule Raising," in *Report of the Commissioner of Agriculture for the Year 1863* (Washington: U.S. Department of Agriculture, 1863), p. 189.

Chapter Twelve

1. Frazier and Robert Hunt, *Horses and Heroes* (New York: Charles Scribner's Sons, 1949), p. 49.

2. Jeanne Mellin, *The Morgan Horse* (Brattleboro: The Stephen Greene Press, 1961), p. 46.

3. Mitford M. Mathews (ed.), *A Dictionary of Americanisms* (Chicago: University of Chicago Press, 1951), p. 1080.

4. D. C. Linsley, *The Morgan Horses* (New York: C. M. Saxton and Company, 1857).

5. The name "Morgan" is ancient Welsh. Dictionaries define its origin as the Welsh word for "sea dweller." Thus the name of King Arthur's sorceress sister, Morgan le Fey, literally translates as "the sea-dweller fairy."

6. Junius Spencer Morgan, a cousin of Justin Morgan, was born at West Springfield, Massachusetts, in 1813. Starting as a dry-goods clerk, he prospered rapidly and in 1854 went to London to become a partner of the financier George Peabody. In 1864, he founded the New York City banking firm that became—under his son's direction—J. P. Morgan & Company.

7. Charles H. Barrows, *The History of Springfield in Massachusetts* (Springfield: Connecticut Valley Historical Society, 1911), p. 101.

8. Louise E. Koier, "Man Overshadowed by a Horse," *News and Notes of the Vermont Historical Society* (July 1955), Vol. VI, No. 11.

9. *Ibid.* The *Fantasy* was recorded by the Eastman Rochester Symphony Orchestra and marketed as a Mercury imprint.

10. D. C. Linsley, *op. cit.*

11. Jeanne Mellin, *op. cit.*, p. 186.

12. Elmer N. Wentworth, "A Tribute to the Morgan Horse," an address delivered at the Iowa State Fair in August 1897. From the Edward N. Wentworth Collection, Western History Research Center, University of Wyoming, Laramie, Wyoming.

Chapter Thirteen

1. Stevenson W. Fletcher, *Pennsylvania Agriculture and Country Life, 1640–1840* (Harrisburg: Pennsylvania Historical and Museum Commission, 1950), p. 467.

2. Johann D. Schopf, *Travels in the Confederation, 1783–1784* (Philadelphia: W. J. Campbell, 1911), Vol. I, p. 42.

3. Stewart H. Holbrook, *The Old Post Road* (New York: McGraw-Hill Book Co., 1962), pp. 43–44.

4. Edith I. Coombs (ed.), *America Visited* (New York: The Book League of America, n.d.), p. 20.

5. Stevenson W. Fletcher, *op. cit.*, p. 473.

6. *Ibid.*, p. 475.

7. *Ibid.*

8. Elmer M. Hunt, "Abbot-Downing and the Concord Coach," *Historical New Hampshire* (November 1945), Vol. I.

9. Stewart H. Holbrook, *op. cit.*, p. 45.

10. Elmer M. Hunt, *op. cit.*

11. Lillian Frances Newton, "The Concord Coach," *Old Time New England* (January 1943), Vol. XXXIII, No. 3.

12. Ill-feeling between Lewis Downing and J. S. Abbot caused the partners to dissolve Downing & Abbot in 1847. Abbot formed his

own carriage factory and became Downing's greatest rival for the carriage and Western-stagecoach trade. After the Civil War both firms were absorbed by Wells-Fargo and reorganized as Abbot & Downing. Their large factory at Concord continued to manufacture coaches, broughams, democrat-wagons, gigs, etc. until 1928.

13. W. J. McKnight, *A Pioneer Outline History of Northwestern Pennsylvania* (Philadelphia: 1905), pp. 379–80.

14. Thomas B. Searight, *The Old Pike: A History of the National Road* (Uniontown, Pennsylvania: 1894), pp. 147–48.

15. Stewart H. Holbrook, *op. cit.*, pp. 55–63.

16. James W. Spring, *Boston and the Parker House* (Boston: J. R. Whipple Corporation, 1927), pp. 140–44.

Chapter Fourteen

1. Deane Phillips, *Horse Raising in Colonial New England*, Memoir 54 (Ithaca: Cornell University Agricultural Experiment Station, 1922), p. 891.

2. William Pynchon, *The Diary of William Pynchon of Salem*, edited by F. E. Oliver (Boston, 1890).

3. Deane Phillips, *op. cit.*, p. 924.

4. Stevenson W. Fletcher, *Pennsylvania Agriculture and Country Life, 1640–1840* (Harrisburg: Pennsylvania Historical and Museum Commission, 1950), p. 201.

5. In contrast to modern "slanguage" use, the word *square* indicated "superiority" during the nineteenth century. The terms "square-gaited," "square-pacer," and "square-trotter" were in common use, and all meant "superior" or "instinctive." Thus Mitford M. Mathews in his mighty *Dictionary of Americanisms* (Chicago: University of Chicago Press, 1951) cites usage as early as 1832 that states, "The horse is . . . valuable according to his performance as a square, or natural, trotter, a pacer or a racker. . . . When a pacer is got to a square trot, he is kept at it by the nicest kind of handling" (p. 1624).

6. George Barnard in *Spirit of the Times*, XII (1842–43), 10; as quoted by Robert Leslie Jones, "The Old French-Canadian Horse: Its History in Canada and the United States," in *Canadian Historical Review*, 1917, pp. 134–35.

Chapter Fifteen

1. Donald Jackson, *Letters of the Lewis and Clark Expedition and Related Documents, 1783–1854* (Urbana: University of Illinois Press, 1962).

2. Frank Gilbert Roe, *The Indian and the Horse* (Norman: University of Oklahoma Press, 1955), p. 261.

3. William E. Connelley (ed.), *Collections of the Kansas State Historical Society* (Topeka: Kansas State Printing Plant, 1925), Vol. XVI, p. 263.

4. *Maximilian, Prince of Wied, Travels in the Interior of North America* (London, 1843).

5. Francis Haines, *Appaloosa: The Spotted Horse in Art and History* (Fort Worth: Amon Carter Museum of Western Art, 1963), pp. 77–78.

6. Donald Jackson, *op. cit.*, Vol. I, pp. 258–59.

7. Clark Wissler, "The Influence of the Horse in the Development of Plains Culture," *The American Anthropologist*, Vol. XVI (1914), pp. 1–25.

8. Timothy Flint, *The History and Geography of the Mississippi Valley* (Cincinnati: E. H. Flint and L. R. Lincoln, 1832), pp. 103–4.

9. James Westfall Thompson, *A History of Livestock Raising in the United States, 1607–1860*, Agricultural History Series No. 5 (Washington: U.S. Department of Agriculture, 1942), p. 103.

10. *Ibid.*

11. *Ibid.*

12. J. Frank Dobie, *The Mustangs* (Boston: Little, Brown, 1952, and New York: Bantam Books, 1958), p. 163.

13. Frazier and Robert Hunt, *Horses and Heroes* (New York: Charles Scribner's Sons, 1949), p. 236.

14. *Utah: A Guide to the State*, Federal Writers' Project of the Works Progress Administration (New York: Hastings House, 1941), p. 229.

15. Frank C. Robertson, "Expressly About Ponies," in *Hoofbeats of Destiny: The Story of the Pony Express*, by Robert West Howard, *et al.* (New York: New American Library, Signet, 1960), p. 149.

16. Correspondence with the author, 1964.

17. Hubert Howe Bancroft, *History of Utah* (San Francisco: The History Co., 1889), p. 297.

18. Josiah Gregg, in *Commerce of the Prairies* (Philadelphia: J. W. Moore, 1850), Vol. I, p. 307, agrees.

19. W. S. Campbell, the gracious late professor at the University of Oklahoma who wrote under the *nom de plume* "Stanley Vestal," reported in his authoritative book *The Old Santa Fe Trail* (page 17 of the Bantam Frontier Classic edition) that many Conestoga wagons with "blue beds and bright red wheels" were used in the Santa Fe trade, and that they were powered by teams of Eastern horses. This

introduces the potential, before 1840, of Conestoga horses for the East-West breed-up at both Missouri and New Mexico studs.

20. James Westfall Thompson, *op. cit.*, p. 116.

Chapter Sixteen

1. James Westfall Thompson, *A History of Livestock Raising in the United States, 1607–1860*, Agricultural History Series No. 5 (Washington: U.S. Department of Agriculture, 1942), p. 135.

2. Waldemar Kaempffert, *A Popular History of American Invention* (New York: Charles Scribner's Sons, 1924), Vol. II, pp. 251–52.

3. Edward B. Williams, "The Present Condition of the Farmer," *The New England Magazine* (1890–91), Vol. III, p. 12.

4. James Finlay Weir Johnston, *Notes on North America, Agricultural, Economic and Social* (Edinburgh and London: W. Blackwood & Sons, 1851), Vol. I, p. 165.

5. Waldemar Kaempffert, *op. cit.*, Vol. I, p. 113.

6. Blake McKelvey, *The Urbanization of America, 1860–1915* (New Brunswick: Rutgers University Press, 1963), p. 76.

7. John Strohm, "The Conestoga Horse," in *Report of the Commissioner of Agriculture for the Year 1863* (Washington: U.S. Department of Agriculture, 1863), pp. 175–80.

8. James Westfall Thompson, *op. cit.*, p. 70.

9. Quoted in Robert Leslie Jones, "The Old French-Canadian Horse: Its History in Canada and the United States," in *Canadian Historical Review*, 1917, p. 130.

10. Quoted in Robert Leslie Jones, *op. cit.*, p. 130.

11. Robert Leslie Jones, *op. cit.*, pp. 139–41.

12. *Ibid.*

13. Jessie M. Dillon, "Normal and the Horse Industry," *Journal of the Illinois State Historical Society*, January 1937.

14. *Ibid.*

15. James Westfall Thompson, *op. cit.*, p. 136.

16. Correspondence with G. B. Thorne, vice president of Wilson & Company, during August 1964.

Chapter Seventeen

1. John Lawrence, *A Philosophical and Practical Treatise on Horses and on the Moral Duties of Man towards the Brute Creation.* (Lon-

don: H. D. Symonds, Paternoster-Row, 1802), second edition, Vol. II, pp. 185–91.

2. Dr. J. F. Smithcors, author of the excellent history *The American Veterinary Profession* (Ames: Iowa State University Press, 1963), provided the following scientific explanation of the terms "hot blooded" and "cold blooded," in correspondence with the author, September 28, 1964.

"These terms undoubtedly go back to the concept of the four humors as the basis for temperament; disturbances in these constituted the basis for humoral pathology. Your observation that most everyone knows—but not why—is well taken; the most recent[!] explanation I was able to find occurs in Lawrence's *Philosophical and Practical Treatise on Horses* (1796), and even this presupposes some acquaintance with the concept of the four humors—blood, phlegm, black bile and yellow bile. An individual with a warm, active temperament was considered to have an excess of blood (literally, and not in the abstract sense) and thus to be *sanguine*; but this usage has been confounded by extension of 'blooded' to mean purebred in some instances and hot blooded in others—*consanguineous*, for example, referring to common ancestry. Conversely, an individual with a stolid temperament was thought to have an excess of phlegm, hence cold or phlegmatic.

"With the importation of Arabian horses into England during the 18th century, these terms found ready application to equine temperament. Thus, by comparison with the heavy, phlegmatic and, therefore, 'cold blooded' European horse, the fiery Arab (also Barb the Turk) was sanguine or 'hot blooded.' Then with the infusion of Arab blood into English stock to produce the Thoroughbred, the term 'hot blood' was extended to include the pride of the British and, later, to the Standardbred. A 'blood horse,' however (especially by breeders of Thoroughbreds), is commonly considered to be only a Thoroughbred; thus *The Blood Horse* is published by the Thoroughbred Owners and Breeders Assn. And 'cold blooded' often means not being a Thoroughbred or having at least some Thoroughbred 'blood.' "

3. Roger Mortimer, *The Jockey Club* (London: Cassell & Company, 1958), pp. 20–21.

4. *Ibid.*, p. 3.

5. Charles S. Plumb, *Types and Breeds of Farm Animals* (Boston: Ginn and Company, 1906), p. 10.

6. Quoted in J. F. Smithcors, *op. cit.*, p. 51.

7. Charles S. Plumb, *op. cit.*, p. 21.

8. M. W. Kay, G. & C. Merriam Company, publishers of Merriam-Webster dictionaries, Springfield, Massachusetts; in a letter to the author, May 1, 1964.

9. Charles E. Trevathan, *The American Thoroughbred* (New York: The Macmillan Company, 1905), pp. 1–2.

10. *Ibid.*, pp. 223–24.

11. Sir Winston Churchill's maternal grandfather was Leonard W. Jerome, born at Pompey Hill in upstate New York. "My mother, the second of Leonard Jerome's daughters, was born in Rochester in the year 1854," Sir Winston recalled in the Preface of his auto-biographical *My Early Life: A Roving Commission* (New York: Charles Scribner's Sons, 1930). "[Grandfather] was a magnificent looking man with long flowing moustachies, a rather aquiline nose, and very bright eyes. All these I remember. He was accustomed to drive about New York on important occasions in a coach with a team of six horses of which he was an expert Whip. He has good claims to be regarded as the father of the American Turf, and Jerome Park, the old race-course now built over, was named for him. He formed the Jockey Club and was long its Vice-President. He owned the famous racehorse, *Kentucky*, who never knew defeat. He was one of the original founders of the Academy of Music in New York, helped to start opera, befriended Jenny Lind and Patti, and educated Miss Minnie Hauk, the creator of the role of Carmen."

Chapter Eighteen

1. Wayne Andrews and Thomas C. Cochrane (eds.), *The Concise Dictionary of American History* (New York: Charles Scribner's Sons, 1962), p. 192.

2. Jeanne Mellin, *The Morgan Horse* (Brattleboro: The Stephen Greene Press, 1961), p. 186.

3. "We have investigated the disease of Glanders in horses and men," a veterinarian wrote the editors of *Prairie Farmer* in 1865. "And after much experience, we have settled down on the grand panacea. It is one powder and one blue pill. Take one tablespoonful of Du-Pont's best rifle powder, and put it in the mouth of a good musket, and ram down the paper on top of it, then take one blue pill of lead of an ounce or less in weight, and ram home on top of that, and then go to the patient *in the stable*, and go through the military manual of firing; but be sure to kill the horse, and burn him and the stable, bridles and everything that has come in contact with him." Cited in J. F. Smithcors, *The American Veterinary Profession* (Ames: Iowa State University Press, 1963), p. 262.

4. J. F. Smithcors, *op. cit.*, pp. 667–68.

5. Frazier and Robert Hunt, *Horses and Heroes* (New York: Charles Scribner's Sons, 1949), p. 129.

6. General Lee's description of Traveller to an artist, as quoted in Fairfax Harrison, "The Equine F.F.V.'s," *Virginia Magazine of History and Biography* (October 1927), Vol. XXXV, No. 4, p. 370.

7. Frazier and Robert Hunt, *op. cit.*, pp. 136–37.

8. An advertisement in San Francisco newspapers during February 1860. Cited in Robert West Howard, *et al*, *Hoofbeats of Destiny: The Story of the Pony Express* (New York: New American Library, Signet, 1960), p. 58.

9. The horsemanship and humanitarianism of the Pony Express are further detailed in Robert West Howard, *op. cit.*

10. An attempted Indian ambush of General Dodge and a patrol of U.S. cavalry in the mountains seventy-five miles north of Denver on September 22, 1865, actually determined the sites of Cheyenne and Laramie. The routes taken by General Dodge's rescuers and by the fleeing Crow warriors revealed Lone Pine Pass across the mountains, then—and still—known locally as the "Black Hills."

11. Quoted in J. F. Smithcors, *op. cit.*, p. 644.

Chapter Nineteen

1. Horace Capron, "Report of the Commissioner," in *Report of the Commissioner of Agriculture for the Year 1869* (Washington: U.S. Department of Agriculture, 1870), p. 13.

2. Quoted in J. F. Smithcors, *The American Veterinary Profession* (Ames: Iowa State University Press, 1963), p. 88.

3. J. R. Dodge, "Report of the Editor: Agricultural Patents of the Year," in *Report of the Commissioner of Agriculture for the Year 1869* (Washington: U.S. Department of Agriculture, 1870), p. 315.

4. "Report of the Statistician" in *Report of the Commissioner of Agriculture for the Year 1867* (Washington: U.S. Department of Agriculture, 1868), p. 43, and "Report of the Statistician" in *Report of the Commissioner of Agriculture for the Year 1869* (Washington: U.S. Department of Agriculture, 1870), p. 47.

5. The sons were Henry, Clement, John Mohler, Peter and Jacob. Stephen Longstreet, *A Century on Wheels: The Story of Studebaker* (New York: Henry Holt and Company, 1952).

6. *Ibid.*, pp. 43–45.

7. Ramon F. Adams, *Western Words* (Norman: University of Oklahoma Press, 1945).

8. This usage preceded the introduction, during the 1870s, of the Hackney breed of horse. However, *hackney*, too, took a secondary meaning of "drudge" and "hired out."

9. Mitford M. Mathews, *The Dictionary of Americanisms* (Chicago: University of Chicago Press, 1951), p. 1160.

10. Blake McKelvey, *The Urbanization of America, 1860–1915* (New Brunswick: Rutgers University Press, 1963), pp. 76–85.

11. Charles S. Plumb, *Types and Breeds of Farm Animals* (Boston: Ginn and Company, 1906), p. 59.

12. Agnes Wright Spring, *Buffalo Bill and His Horses* (Fort Collins: B. & M. Printing Company, 1953), p. 9.

13. J. H. S. Johnstone, *The Horse Book* (Chicago: The Breeder's Gazette, 1914), pp. 113-15.

14. Agnes Wright Spring, *op. cit.*, p. 20.

15. *Yearbook of the United States Department of Agriculture, 1900* (Washington: Government Printing Office, 1901), p. 647.

16. During 1964, I heard two veteran horsemen—in Massachusetts and Wyoming—testify to family dependence on drafters during the 1890s. Alfred Allen, a lecturer-guide at the unique Old Sturbridge Village museum in central Massachusetts, grew up on a Massachusetts farm and spent most of his adult years as an executive with farmer organizations. When I asked him whether his father owned "carriage horses," he gave a derisive snort. "We were plain farm folks," he rumbled, "and never had the money to buy any of those fancy coachers. We used drafters, mostly Percherons, for field work, and drafter geldings for wagon hauls and buggy trips to town. They made good time and looked smart." Two months later I explored the eastern slopes of Wyoming's South Pass with James Carpenter as my guide and host. Mr. Carpenter, then seventy-seven, migrated into the gold camp of Atlantic City, Wyoming, when he was three years old. I asked him what breed of horses his father and brothers drove during the family's journey across the deserts from Nebraska in 1890. "They had a lot of Percheron blood in them," he replied. "Those big fellows worked out better on the trail, and up here. You need a lot of heft and stamina in your horses when you go homesteading."

Chapter Twenty

1. According to U.S. Census figures, the population of the United States was 75,994,000 in 1900, and 91,972,000 in 1910. Statistical reports in the Yearbooks of the U.S. Department of Agriculture for the same decade report a horse population of 13,537,000 on January 1, 1900, and of 23,021,000 on January 1, 1910.

2. Douglas A. Fisher, *The Epic of Steel* (New York: Harper & Row, 1963), p. 304.

3. *Report of the Commissioner of Agriculture for the Year 1866* (Washington: U.S. Department of Agriculture, 1867) and *Yearbook of the United States Department of Agriculture, 1900* (Washington: U.S. Department of Agriculture, 1901).

4. These figures are available in the Yearbooks of the U.S. Department of Agriculture for the years 1901, 1915, and 1920.

5. Yearbooks of the U.S. Department of Agriculture for the years 1900 and 1910.

6. The British search was not so rewarding as Johnstone's report implies. The Yearbooks of the U.S. Department of Agriculture report that our total horse exports rose from 45,778 head in 1899 to 103,020 head in 1902, then slumped back to 34,007 head in 1903. Her Majesty's buyers seem to have been more favorably impressed by American mules, because our mule exports jumped from 6,755 head in 1899 to 43,369 head in 1900, 34,405 head in 1901, 27,586 head in 1902, then dwindled to 4,294 head in 1903. All told, it appears that approximately 150,000 range horses and 100,000 mules sailed to South Africa to campaign for the "Widow of Windsor."

7. J. H. S. Johnstone, *The Horse Book* (Chicago: The Breeder's Gazette, 1914), pp. 235–37.

8. By far the best detailed research on the so-called wild horses of the West is in *The Wild Horse of the West*, by Walker D. Wyman (Caldwell, Idaho: The Caxton Printers, 1945, and Lincoln: University of Nebraska Press Bison Book 144), and in *The Mustangs*, by J. Frank Dobie (Boston: Little, Brown, 1952, and New York: Bantam Books, 1958).

9. Nels Anderson, *The Hobo: The Sociology of the Homeless Man* (Chicago: University of Chicago Press, Phoenix edition, 1961).

10. Sir Arthur Evans, *The Palace of Minos* (London: Macmillan and Company, 1921).

11. *Ibid.*

12. Charles W. Towne and Edward N. Wentworth, *Cattle and Men* (Norman: University of Oklahoma Press, 1955), p. 34.

13. Robert West Howard and Oren Arnold, *Rodeo: Last Frontier of the Old West* (New York: New American Library, Signet, 1961), p. 34.

14. The standard events of a modern rodeo, all more ancient skill contests than the Spaniards' bull fight or Asia's cock fight, are: bareback bronc riding, saddle bronc riding, calf roping, single steer tying, team tying, dally-team roping, steer wrestling, the bull ride, the spectacularly dangerous clown acts and "fracases" that can include wild-cow milking, a wild-horse race, a barrel, a chuckwagon race, jousting tournaments, or a "potato race." Usually a rodeo also includes "contract events" featuring trick riders, trained pigs and/or a cowboy movie star riding a Palomino through a dressage routine while he plays on a neon-lit guitar and "nasals" "Home on the Range."

15. Robert West Howard and Oren Arnold, *op. cit.*, p. 48.

16. Robert West Howard, *Two Billion Acre Farm: An Informal History of American Agriculture* (New York: Doubleday, Doran and Company, 1945), p. 179.

17. *Yearbook of the United States Department of Agriculture, 1925* (Washington: Government Printing Office, 1926), p. 37.

Chapter Twenty-one

1. M. W. Kay, G. & C. Merriam Company, publishers of Merriam-Webster Dictionaries, Springfield, Mass.; corespondence with the author, May 1, 1964.

2. Use of *Thoroughbred* as a proper noun did not appear in standard American dictionaries until the 1930s.

3. Most American cities used horse teams on fire-fighting equipment until the 1920s. Rochester, New York, reputed to have America's only public memorial to the fire horse, retired its last team on February 16, 1927.

4. Joseph Hughes, "The Foot of the Draft Horse and His Shoeing," *Breeder's Gazette*, Christmas, 1912.

5. The name was changed, in 1889, to The American Saddle Horse Breeders' Association.

6. Charles S. Plumb, *Types and Breeds of Farm Animals* (Boston: Ginn and Company, 1906), p. 27.

7. Sales prices of $500 to $1,000 for "superior saddle horses are not uncommon," Plumb reported, adding that "Major David Castleman of Kentucky is reported to have sold the stallion, *The Moor 1907* . . . for $7,500." Charles S. Plumb, *op. cit.*, p. 32.

8. An editorial, *Breeder's Gazette*, June 10, 1903.

9. During the first week of September, Shelbyville, Tennessee, observes a Tennessee Walking Horse National Celebration. The breed's registry listed 66,000 animals in the late fall of 1964.

10. The American Quarter Horse Association, with headquarters in Amarillo, Texas, did not open its registry until 1940. It has become a popular "family horse" in suburbia and is a favorite mount on the hundreds of "dude ranches" operating both in the East and in the West; it is an excellent saddle racer. During the mid-1960s, the association admitted an average of 35,000 horses a year to its registry.

11. The Reverend John Richard O'Hare, *The Socioeconomics of Horse Racing* (Washington: Catholic University of America Press, 1945), p. 39.

12. As reported in the *Breeder's Gazette* on January 1, 1963.

13. Farm publications agreed with the decision. On January 27, 1957, the *Drovers' Journal* of Chicago carried the following editorial, under the pert title of "Swan Song for a Farm Era":
    "The swan song, if any were needed, of the horse and mule on the American farm would seem to have been sung with the recent an-

nouncement by government census takers that farm tractors now outnumber those historic beasts of burden.

"By 1954, they point out, the horse and mule population had shrunk to about 4 million head, or only about one-sixth of the peak total of 25,200,000 reached in 1920. During the same 34-year period, the number of tractors rose from 246,000 to nearly 4,700,000—about 700,000 more tractors than horses and mules.

"The 1954 nose count showed there were fewer horses and mules than when the first census was taken back in 1840. There were 4,300,000 head on farms then. The new tabulation showed that more than half of all horses and mules left on farms was in the 16 states of the South, where 1,100,000 farms averaged two each.

"Texas had the greatest number of horses in 1954—244,000 head. North Carolina had the largest mule population—179,000. The famed Missouri mule was down to a mere 22,000, compared with the Missouri peak of 389,000 in 1920.

"If the superior number of the mechanical monsters isn't swan song enough, then perhaps the recent action of the army in giving up the last of its mules would qualify. Both represent historic landmarks, to be sure.

"At any rate, a fine, noble era of farm work animals has passed, except for a remnant here and there. It is an era loaded with nostalgia for most farmers to recall today, but it won't be long until horse and mule farming will exist only in the history books. Many an old horse and mule man will probably be more than happy to be long gone before that time comes."

14. H. A. Willman, *New York Equine Survey*, Animal Husbandry Series 2 (Ithaca: Cornell University, 1965).

15. Current neglect of concise data about the horse by government agencies was vividly illustrated during December 1964 in the author's correspondence with William A. Burchardt, editor of *Oklahoma Today* magazine. Oklahoma, as the former "Indian Territory" and scene of some of the most storied horse episodes in the history of the American West, has the Trail of Tears, the Chisholm Trail, Will Rogers' career, and the Miller Brothers' great Wild West Show in its heritage. It is the home of the unique Indian Museum and folk center at Anadarko, as well as the Western Heritage Center and National Cowboy Hall of Fame near Oklahoma City. But Bill Burchardt wrote on December 15, 1964, that no horse count had been made in the state since 1960 when the state's horse and mule population had decreased to 91,000. "The U.S.D.A. office here estimates the count would now run around 80,000," he said. "These totals have never been broken down as to breeds, but (the guess is) there would be about 2,000 mules and 'very few' draft horses. Most of our horses are working cow horses; we have a big range cattle industry. . . . Some of us have been trying to get the U.S. D. A. to bring these figures up to date, but no luck so far."

16. Farmers' Bulletin No. 2127, titled *Light Horses* and revised by U.S. Department of Agriculture writers in November 1962 provides an excellent overview of modern American "hobby" horses. The text was prepared by W. E. Ensminger, a distinguished Animal Science authority at Washington State University. The publication should prove a valuable investment for any horse hobbyist. It is available from the Superintendent of Documents, U.S. Government Printing Office, Washington 25, D.C., for twenty cents. The "light horse" breeds described and photographed in the text include: American Albino, American Saddle Horse, Appaloosa, Arabian, Cleveland Bay, Connemara pony, Gotland Horse, Hackney, Missouri Fox Trotting Horse, Morgan, Morocco Spotted Horse, Palomino, Pinto, Pony of the Americas, Quarter Horse, Shetland pony, Standardbred, Tennessee Walking Horse, Thoroughbred, and Welsh pony.

ACKNOWLEDGMENTS

The environmental research on this book began at South Addison, New York, during the spring of 1908. I was born there that April. My father was pastor of the Methodist Episcopal "charge." In accord with Methodist tradition, my mother was the church organist and choir director. Thanks for critical assistance in gaining casual awareness of the mighty role of the horse in America's social, economic and religious life must be extended first of all, then, to the late Reverend C. J. and Clara Jane West Howard, and to the numerous geldings, stallions and mares who served our family—and Methodism—in New York and New Jersey until the first Ford snarled into our parsonage barn during 1922.

Thanks for the horse-awarenesses that stimulated the 1962–65 research on this manuscript are similarly deserved by my Grandpa Jim, and by M. Glen Kirkpatrick of Asheville, North Carolina, Wheeler McMillen of Moorestown, New Jersey, and Wesley Hardenbergh of Lake Zurich, Illinois.

The late James C. ("Grandpa Jim") Howard was our family's most imaginative storyteller and had worked as a coachman in New York City, Chicago, London and San Francisco. He knew horse history and horse habits and, at times, seemed to derive more pleasure from talking with (not "to" but "with") his chestnut gelding and gray mare than he gained from the side-porch and parlor audiences with his "kin." I must have humored him, because I was privileged to share—with the horses—the wedges of Herkimer "rat cheese," soda crackers, filched blueberry pie and horse-lore during furtive sessions "away from those women," in the harness room of his barn at East Herkimer, New York.

Several decades later, as my senior editors at *Farm Journal*, "Kirk" Kirkpatrick and "Chief" McMillen guided my serendipities as the magazine's Roving Editor. They were responsible, thus, for friendships that developed with Wayne Dinsmore of the American Horse & Mule Association, DeWitt Wing of *Breeder's Gazette* and the U.S.D.A.'s Office of Information, John Pickett of *Pacific Rural Press*, Professor Robert ("Mr. Bob") Ashby of the University of

Illinois, Colonel Edward N. Wentworth, then director of the Livestock Bureau at Armour & Company, and scores of other rural wisemen who knew the breadth of the Equidae contributions to the "American Way."

Wesley Hardenbergh, as president of the American Meat Institute, encouraged my fascination with the socio-economic aspects of our livestock history during my years as Roving Editor at A.M.I.

Special thanks are due, too, to Paul McGrew, professor of paleontology at the University of Wyoming, to Gene Gressley, director of the Western History Research Center, University of Wyoming, to Alfred Stefferud, the beloved scholar and 1945-65 editor of the U.S.D.A. *Yearbook*, to F. Hal Higgins, director of the Agricultural History Center on the Davis campus of the University of California, and to J. F. Smithcors, generous author of *The American Veterinary Profession* and Technical Editor of *Modern Veterinary Practice*.

The cooperation of the following individuals and organizations contributed to the manuscript and the illustrations:

CANADA: Pierre Brunet of the Public Archives of Canada, and the librarians of the Canada Department of Agriculture, Ottawa.

CONNECTICUT: Joseph B. Stephens, author and photographer for *Yankee* magazine.

ILLINOIS: Paul Angle, director of the Chicago Historical Society; Robert Hertel, director of libraries, Illinois State Normal University, Normal; Alvin L. Krieg, district director of public relations, United States Steel Corporation; Franklin J. Meine, author and editor; Gerald B. Thorne, vice president, Wilson & Company; Paul Zillman, livestock specialist, the American Meat Institute.

MASSACHUSETTS: Alfred Allen of West Brookfield; the late Paul Deland, onetime blacksmith's apprentice and the astute "Headmaster" of the *Christian Science Monitor*; Dean A. Fales, Jr., director of Essex Institute, Salem; M. W. Kay, editor at G. & C. Merriam, Springfield; James Keeney, director of public relations, Old Sturbridge Village; Katharine L. McIntire, West Springfield Public Library; Mrs. Davis G. Maraspin, assistant to the curator, Old State House, Boston; Mrs. Glenwood J. Sherrard, president, the Parker House, Boston; Mr. and Mrs. Edward C. Williams, Jr., of Wellesley Hills.

NEBRASKA: Miss Mildred Goosman, associate curator, the Joslyn

Art Museum, Omaha; George E. Hyde, the great scholar of Indian prehistory, and his urbane sister, Mrs. Mabel I. Reed, both of Omaha; Mr. and Mrs. Walter G. Zimmermann, Omaha.

NEW HAMPSHIRE: Paul E. Estaber, editor of *New Hampshire Profiles*, Portsmouth; Judson Hale, managing editor of *Yankee*, Dublin; Stephen T. Whitney, photographer at East Concord; Mrs. Russell B. Tobey, librarian, the New Hampshire Historical Society, Concord.

NEW JERSEY: Clayton and Kathleen Hoagland, Rutherford.

NEW YORK: Donald C. Anthony, associate librarian, the New York State Library, Albany; Miss Frances Long, associate editor, Follett Publishing Company, New York City; Kenneth Hinshaw, editor, *The Agway Cooperator*, Syracuse; Blake McKelvey, author of city historian, Rochester; Warren A. Ranney, director of public relations, Agway, Inc., Syracuse; Fred L. Rath, Jr., vice director, New York State Historical Association, Cooperstown; H. A. Willman, professor emeritus in Animal Husbandry, New York State College of Agriculture, Cornell University, Ithaca.

OKLAHOMA: Savoie Lottinville, director, University of Oklahoma Press, Norman; William Burchardt, editor, *Oklahoma Today*, Oklahoma City.

SOUTH CAROLINA: J. B. Douthit, Clemson.

UTAH: Mrs. June Stewart, assistant to the state archivist, State Archives, Salt Lake City; George E. Stewart, attorney, Roosevelt.

VERMONT: Avah Buckman, Woodstock; Lawrence Van Benthuysen, University of Vermont; Richard G. Wood, director, Vermont Historical Society, Montpelier.

VIRGINIA: W. M. Corwin, Director of Information, Southern States Cooperative, Richmond.

WYOMING: James Carpenter, Atlantic City; Harold Del Monte, Hotel Noble, Lander.

Extraordinary Thank You's must be expressed to the three people who shared every moment of the 1962–65 research and painstakingly studied every word, comma, numeral and photo: Louis Zara, my editor at Follett; Malcolm Reiss, my agent at Paul R. Reynolds & Son; and my amazing wife, Elizabeth Zimmermann Howard.

ROBERT WEST HOWARD
Rochester, New York
March 22, 1965

INDEX

ABOUT THE AUTHOR

A long and varied career in agricultural journalism, sociological reporting and research in Americana preceded Robert West Howard's decision to undertake the four years of coast-to-coast research that yielded the data for this book.

Mr. Howard has been an associate editor on the *Farm Journal,* the editor-in-chief of *Pathfinder,* a vice-president for public relations at Antioch College, the coordinator of publications for the Adult Education Association of the U.S.A., and the roving editor for the American Meat Institute. He is the author of *Two Billion Acre Farm; Real Book about Farms; The Great Iron Trail; The Wagonmen; The Race West: Boomtown to Ghost Town; The Boatmen;* and *The Flag of the Dreadful Bear,* as well as a co-author of *Educational Planning by Communities* (with Paul Essert) and *Rodeo: Last Frontier of the Old West* (with Oren Arnold). He is also editor and co-author of *This Is the West; This Is the South; Hoofbeats of Destiny;* and *The Bench Mark.* In 1957 he received the Maggie Award and in 1958 the Spur Award of the Western Writers of America, both for *This Is the West.*

Mr. Howard is a member of the Chicago Corral of The Westerners, the Western History Association, Western Writers of America, the National Press Club, the Chicago Historical Society, the Utah Historical Society, the New York State Historical Association, and the Authors Guild. His home is in Rochester, New York.